SUPERBOOK

THE WORLD OF SUPERHERO MOVIES ACCORDING TO SMERSH POD

SUPERBOOK

THE WORLD OF SUPERHERO MOVIES ACCORDING TO SMERSH POD

JOHN RAIN

POLARIS
PUBLISHING

First published in 2023 by

POLARIS PUBLISHING LTD
c/o Aberdein Considine
2nd Floor, Elder House
Multrees Walk
Edinburgh
EH1 3DX

www.polarispublishing.com

ISBN: 9781915359131
eBook ISBN: 9781915359148

British Library Cataloguing-in-Publication Data
A catalogue record for this book is available on request from the British Library.

Designed and typeset by Polaris Publishing, Edinburgh
Printed in Great Britain by MBM Print, East Kilbride

For Alex, James, and Christopher Reeve

With special thanks to Hannah Winser, Clive Mantle, Peter Burns, Polaris, Alison Rae, Paul Litchfield, Dan Thomas, Dean Burnett, Stephen Graham, Neil Brooke, Tim Colman, Tom Neenan, Tom Crowley,B Mum, Dad, Chris, and the rest of my classic family. I couldn't have done all this without you.

CONTENTS

INTRODUCTION

THIS IS NO FANTASY, NO CARELESS PRODUCT OF WILD IMAGINATION

There are pyjamas, then there are *pyjamas*. Mine were the latter. It was 1982 (although it could have been '81). I was five years old, with not a care in the world, as problems hadn't been invented back then. Although my memories of childhood are extraordinarily hazy, I remember those pyjamas. A winsome work of pale blue, red-ringed collar, magical 'S' on the chest and, as a finishing garnish, buttons on the shoulder, ready for that deep red cape to be affixed.

As a child I was obsessed with the Christopher Reeve *Superman* films. I'd seen a house fly, I'd seen a dragonfly, but I'd never seen a man fly – until I was at Steven Savage's birthday party. His dad worked for a toy company, and therefore he had all the *Star Wars* toys in a big box, even the rarest ones, which obviously caused chaos. To calm the storm, his parents put on *Superman II*, and the room fell silent. I distinctly remember stopping like a rabbit in headlights, hypnotised by the sight of Christopher Reeve ascending the Eiffel Tower and rescuing Lois. Soon afterwards, I got my magic pyjamas and spent most of my spare time around the house with that cape flapping around my shoulders, belting out the theme and feeling like I could sail out of the window and brush a ceiling of clouds in the night sky.

While – like every other kid at the time – I still had a very healthy interest in *Star Wars* action figures, my bedroom walls were a shrine to my love of the last son of Krypton. They were covered in Superman wallpaper, and above my bed was a poster I had taken from *Look-in* magazine of Clark transforming in the midst of a red and blue blur in an alley.

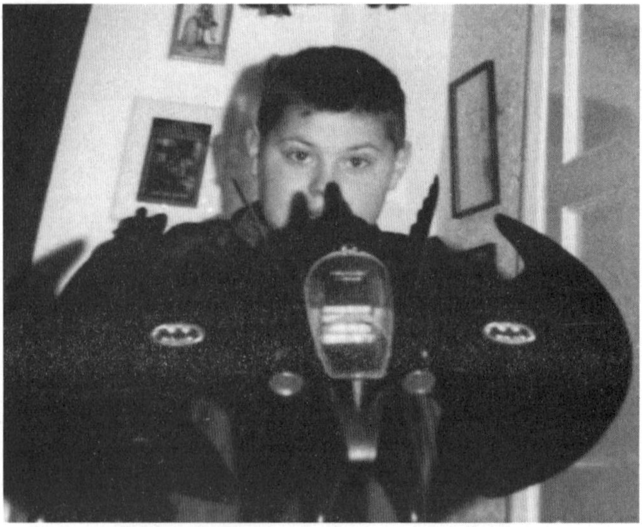

Jump forward to 1989, and a similar phenomenon had gripped me: 'Batfever'. I had the toys, the Prince album, the Elfman album, the comic book of the film and all the T-shirts I could eat. The very idea of a serious Batman film just seemed like the most exciting and vital thing for a twelve-year-old who'd read the comics but was raised on repeats of the daft sixties TV show and movie. *Batman* really was everything I'd imagined and more. Its success opened the doors to more and more heroes and heroics, packing out cinemas. Sadly, the triumph was short-lived. The first big superhero boom that began with such a bang in 1978 died a poignant and painful death in 1997, but it was a life well lived, with many fun adventures along the way despite doddering vital signs.

So, come with me now, as we break through the bonds of earthly confinement and travel through time and space in the six known dimensions. We need to pick up twenty videos from Blockbusters to see if they stand up against the modern might of the superhero genre, or if they simply fall into ruin and disarray, like Superman being exposed to kryptonite – forever locked in the shadow of the bomb that is 21st-century Marvel.

ONE

SUPERMAN: THE MOVIE

1978

YOU'LL BELIEVE A MAN CAN FLY!

In 1974 Alexander Salkind, Ilya Salkind and Pierre Spengler (European uber-producers) bought the rights to Superman from DC comics. The Salkinds and Spengler's approach to making movies was very much like Real Madrid or Manchester City's approach to football: sign big names and the rest will fall into place. They started off by signing Mario Puzo (Oscar-winning writer of *The Godfather*) at a salary of $600,000 (which by today's standards is an absolute fortune) to write the film.

Next, they signed up Marlon Brando at a cool $3.75 million (and 11.75% of the box office) with a contract stipulation that he would only work for twelve days (and at that probably only half-arsed), and then they bagged Gene Hackman for a snip at $2 million. Soon afterwards, Puzo delivered his script for *Superman*: over 500 pages long, in two parts and probably weighing ninety tonnes. Though the Salkinds were very happy with it, they were worried it was slightly too long (a bit of an understatement), so they hired husband-and-wife team David and Leslie Newman for rewrites. Their script came back leaner but with a camp tone that included a cameo appearance by Telly Savalas as Kojak, presumably waving his lollipop at the Son of Jor-El as he soared over his bald head.

Guy Hamilton, director of Bond films such as *Live and Let Die*, *Diamonds Are Forever* and *Goldfinger*, was hired to direct. At the time, Hamilton was living in Italy as a canny tax exile. Many British celebrities and high earners were living abroad during this time as tax in the UK was cripplingly high (as much as 75%). From his studio in Rome, Hamilton had shot test footage, and sets were being built at a combined cost of over $2 million. Production was racing ahead at the rate of a speeding bullet.

Meanwhile, countless actors were approached to play the Man of Steel himself. Robert Redford, Paul Newman, Burt Reynolds, Patrick Wayne, James Caan, James Brolin, Christopher Walken, Nick Nolte, Kurt Russell, Jeff Bridges and David Soul all turned it down. How could you begin filming *Superman* without Superman? The producers were keen to start filming as soon as possible, otherwise they could risk losing Brando and Hackman, both of whom were in high demand.

So, in 1976 production moved to England, but Hamilton couldn't come back to the UK without being hit with a huge tax bill, so he disappeared into the Phantom Zone and the director's chair fell empty.

Things looked to be stalling once again until the producers happened to see the 1976 horror classic *The Omen*, directed by Richard Donner, and they loved what they saw. Donner was immediately hired for $1 million. Donner's first directorial decision was to start from scratch and abandon all the previous work on the project. 'They had prepared the picture for a year and not one bit was useful to me,' he said later. Dissatisfied with the goofy script and irreverence to the subject matter's comic-book origins, Donner brought on board the one man he knew who could improve on the length and tone of the script and give it real class: legendary screenwriter and script doctor Tom Mankiewicz (who had most recently worked on *Diamonds Are Forever*, *The Man with the Golden Gun* and *The Spy Who Loved Me*).

When Donner called in 1976, Mankiewicz jumped at the chance to work on *Superman*. According to Mankiewicz on the *Superman* DVD documentary, 'Not a word from the Puzo script was used. It was well-written, but still a ridiculous script. It was 550 pages. I said, "You can't shoot this screenplay because you'll be shooting for five years."' Mankiewicz went into creative overdrive, breaking down every aspect and rooting the script in reality as much as possible (even conceiving the idea of having each Kryptonian family wear a crest resembling a different letter, thus justifying the 'S' on Superman's costume). Donner agreed, giving the production of this movie a byword it had to live by: 'Verisimilitude'. It became the motto of the entire production, with Donner having a sign made of Superman saying as much in the production office. The audience had to believe a man could fly; without that the whole exercise was pointless.

Incidentally, the Writers Guild of America refused to credit Mankiewicz for his extensive rewrites, so Donner gave him a creative consultant credit, much to their annoyance.

As the curtains draw back, it's more akin to a rollercoaster chuntering to the top of the climb: grinding through the gears before teetering on adventure, ready to release you into the hard dopamine hit of the opening credits, a work of art designed by R/Greenberg Associates, with streaking luminous crystal letters zooming through space from the depths of the cosmos.

Krypton, a vast branch of Iceland, is tucked away in the freezing depths of the universe. A trial is taking place. General Zod (Terence Stamp), Ursa (Sarah Douglas) and Non (Jack O'Halloran) are in the dock, and it seems to be sponsored by Hula-Hoops. Jor-El (Marlon Brando) submits his evidence to the jury of retired old British actors, who don't seem to need much in the way of convincing. The trio are found guilty of treason and sedition, and their punishment is to be placed inside a flying mirror and fired into space for all eternity, which doesn't sound too bad, given what's happening on Earth at the moment.

In 1988 Terence Stamp appeared on a chat show (*One to One*) with British broadcaster Michael Parkinson. He was asked about his experience of working with his hero, Marlon Brando. 'He really doesn't learn the lines,' revealed Stamp. 'He has them written up big behind the lights. In the scene I did with him, I was waiting to do the scene, and I saw him. He had a little bit of paper. What he was trying to do, he was trying to learn the first line so that as he turned towards me, he could be speaking before he had it written down. He was trying to learn this one line, so it looked natural. I couldn't believe it. So, I went up to him and I said, "Marlon?! What are you doing? How are you going to play Lear and Macbeth if you can't learn a line?" He said, "I've learned them already."'

Jor-El then heads to see the Krypton elders to tell them that it's not really normal to have a giant sun slowly nudging its way towards your planet, but he's told that it's all fine; it's merely their world pining for the fjords. He's to say no more about it, or attempt to leave, as the last thing Krypton needs is to panic about what a giant sun is doing getting closer and closer with each waking day. If anyone asks why, just tell them it's resting. Jor-El promises that he won't attempt to leave or cause panic, and heads back to his flat to see his wife Lara (Susannah York), where they immediately set about sending their son Kal-El to Earth in a spaceship made of crystals that looks like something out of *Footballers' Wives*. He tells her that they're firing Kal-El into space as he'll be better than everyone on Earth in every conceivable way and this will give him an advantage, which sort of speaks volumes about nepo babies in general.

As Krypton begins to crack, rattle and shake, Kal-El's tiny spaceship rises and smashes through the first of his many earned glass ceilings. Jor-El and Lara attempt to flee, and you can be sure as shit he's heading to the council chamber to show his arse and shout, 'I told you! Eat this motherfuckers!' But, sadly, before he can reach the room, the planet explodes.

Through the endless gulf of space, Kal-El hurtles in his spaceship, but he's not alone. Luckily, his dad has packed a crystal with thousands of years' worth of dictations for him to listen to, with stories of the history of Krypton, segments of Shakespeare, Einstein and his theory of relativity, and how Anna Ford has become the first female newsreader. Which all goes to show that despite their obvious scientific greatness, Krypton was seriously lacking on the culture front. Combined with their climate change denial and refusal to do anything about saving the environment, that makes Krypton pretty much a big fat Tory planet.

Down on Earth, farmer Jonathan Kent (Glenn Ford) and his wife Martha (Phyllis Thaxter) are out on a drive when they witness something crash-land in a field. When they go to investigate, they find Kal-El standing in the crater, completely billy bollocks naked. While they're changing a blown tyre on their truck and discussing whether they should keep a naked-ass baby from space that they found in a field, the jack on the truck slips, sending it down on Jonathan's legs – but it's stopped just in time, held up by little Kal-El.

Richard Donner refers to Smallville as the Norman Rockwell section of the movie. Peppering it with an Americana of dirt roads, picket fences, long corn and shafts of glorious sunlight, with sweeping crane shots almost holding a microscope to the wide-open spaces of the Midwest of past picture postcards, cinematographer Geoffrey Unsworth (to whom the film is dedicated) uses beautiful soft tones and even softer lenses to bathe the vistas in a warm, glorious pastel glow.

Clark Kent (Jeff East, dubbed by Christoper Reeve) is racing home from a football practice where Brad, a horrible jock bully, has made his life harder. Clark isn't allowed to play football as he would probably kill someone, so he's a humble waterboy, forced to tidy jockstraps and helmets. He's more powerful than a locomotive, though, and easily outruns one on the way home – but if we're being honest, he clearly hasn't quite got his super legs yet. He runs as if he's being held up with wires and shot at half-speed.

Jeff East wasn't entirely over the moon about having his voice replaced in such a prestigious movie. The *Pumpkinhead* actor later told the Superman Homepage in 2004: 'I wasn't happy about it because the producers never told me what they had in mind. It was done without my permission but it turned out to be OK. Chris did a good job, but it caused tension between us. We resolved our issues with each other years later.'

He poses smugly by a tractor as Brad passes, slightly freaked out that he's got there before him, but at the end of the day he won, and his dad is essentially God, so fuck you, Brad. As Brad's car speeds away, a watching Jonathan asks Clark if he's showing off a bit, at which point Clark tells him he would love to murder Brad, but, annoyingly, he has to hide his powers. Jonathan tells him he needs to wind his neck in as the government will take him away if they find out about him. He gives him a stirring speech about how he was sent to Earth for a reason, and that it wasn't to score touchdowns or murder jocks. This eases Clark's mind, and as he heads back home, Jonathan stops, grabs his wrist (something he said he heard a friend of his did when he had a heart attack) and utters his final words, 'Oh no,' before collapsing into the dirt. Glenn Ford is only in the film for minutes, but his performance has such heft that when Jonathan dies he leaves the audience mourning a great man that they felt they knew well.

Martha is laying out the breakfast Cheerios (some honest product placement) when she notices that Clark is already awake and standing at the end of the field amongst the corn. He tells her he has to go, as a green crystal has talked to him and told him to go north, all of which sounds like code for meth. But she understands. She's always known this moment would come, and as they embrace, John Williams' score paints the gorgeous canvas with beautiful strokes of red, white and blue.

Clark arrives at the northest of north, and throws the green crystal into the ice, whereupon it creates the Fortress of Solitude, and I would like to know what he was expecting to happen. It's a vast, crystal stately home, wrapped within fierce winds of snow and blankets of punishing ice, offering scenic views of polar bears and formless white. Home sweet home, I guess.

The late, great production designer John Barry (*Star Wars*, *A Clockwork Orange*) designed this colossus of a set, and it's truly a sight to behold. Taking over the vast 007 stage at Pinewood, it uses every inch of the epic hangar, and its piercing white beams and shimmering crystals provide yet another wonderful example of this film weaving iconic magic in every frame. Sadly, Barry would pass away in 1979 while making *The Empire Strikes Back*, at the stupidly young age of forty-four. A truly visionary designer and master of illusion taken way before his time.

After monkeying with some crystals, Clark's brought face to face with the giant fizzog of Marlon Brando's Jor-El, which I assume was to scale. He once again takes him through the history of his home world, and they spend at least twenty years hanging out, with the conversation probably being as dry as shit. Just how do you stay interesting for twenty years? Even Bowie struggled to do that.

But at the end, it's all worth it, as once the consultation period is over, we're presented with Christopher Reeve as Superman, standing high on a pedestal of ice, wrapped in a bundle of red, white and blue. A beautiful living statue of a man of steel, built and moulded by David Prowse over many days and hours at his gymnasium. As he receives his theme and takes off, flying right by the camera with grace and style, the audience truly believes that a man can fly. Reeve nailed the wire work in this film; one of his many hobbies included hang-gliding, so he was able to adjust his body with fluid balance while being arrowed through the air.

'I approached the role seriously,' Reeve said in his autobiography *Still Me*. 'I've always felt that an actor should never judge a character but should commit fully to the process of bringing him to life.

In this respect, *Superman* and Henry James and Chekhov and a French farce are no different from the actor's point of view. I always flatly refused any invitation to mock the Superman character or send him up.'

Metropolis. The Big Apricot. A bustling modern city filled with millions of people, fast cars running up and down the streets like hungry rats, and the tight air choking with fumes and smoke. It's a world away from the serene peace of Smallville, but it's here that Clark Kent now calls home. He gets a job immediately, of course (classic nepo baby), working for *The Daily Planet*, and its gruff editor Perry White (Jackie Cooper) lays down the law, underlining the great principles of reporting, before introducing Clark to the paper's top reporter, Lois Lane, and her spelling mistakes. Margot Kidder's Lois is an absolute joy: ruthless, streetwise and tough, forever chasing down stories and pinning them down expertly on her typewriter. She's just broken a dynamite exposé on drug and orgy parties in a senior citizens' home (a great gag), but her nose is slightly out of joint. Clark has been handed her city beat, due to the fact that although he seems like just a mild-mannered reporter, he treats his editor-in-chief with respect, has a snappy, punchy prose style and is the fastest typist seen in forty years. She's not particularly enamoured with Clark and his Midwest ways: the cliché of sending half his salary to his silver-haired mother, saying words like 'swell' as if it's 1939, and his genial demeanour.

'I based the character of Clark Kent on the young Cary Grant,' Reeve said in *Still Me*. 'There's a wonderful scene in *Bringing Up Baby* in which he plays a palaeontologist working on a dinosaur, and he's up a ladder that's rocking back and forth. He looks terribly awkward and afraid while Katherine Hepburn looks brash and fearless as she comes to his rescue. He has a shyness, vulnerability, and a certain goofiness that I thought would be perfect.'

As the two new colleagues walk out onto the street together, Clark is immediately met with the other side of Metropolis: not its wonderful areas of natural beauty, hot-dog stands or fresh fruit stalls, but a robbery at gunpoint. Clark suggests they do exactly what the man says as he has a gun in their face, but Lois has seen it all before and pulls the old 'drop the purse and kick the man' trick, much to Clark's abject terror, especially when a bullet fires and he sinks to the floor. The robber flees empty-handed, and Lois tends to her new friend, fearing the worst. Clark is OK, though, telling her in the most pathetic way possible that he must have passed out. As she rolls her eyes and walks away, Clark beams a beautiful smile, his eyes shining behind his glasses, opening his palm to reveal that he caught the offending bullet and saved her life.

Otis (Ned Beatty), a rotund, bumbling sack of a man nestled under a straw boater, makes his way to his secret hideout, blissfully unaware that he's being followed by police detectives trying to find out more about his mysterious boss. He meanders through the giant main station while under the playful spell of John Williams' 'March Of The Villains', and slaloms through the train tracks, heading home via a secret door to meet his boss, Lex Luthor (Gene Hackman).

As with Brando, when Gene Hackman was cast, the film gained another layer of authority and kudos. When Donner met with him for the first time, Hackman was sporting a fine seventies moustache. 'I showed up for the first day of make-up tests for *Superman* with a fine Lex Luthor moustache I'd grown for the role,' Hackman told the *Hollywood Reporter*. 'Dick [Donner], wearing his own handsome moustache, told me mine had to go. He bargained to lose his if I did mine. True to his word, he celebrated my last razor stroke by gleefully pulling off the fake whiskers he'd acquired for the occasion.' And from that moment on the two became dear friends for life. 'Dick made it fun, and that's why the films turned out that way, too.'

Otis bundles through the door only to be told he was followed (again), and poor Miss Teschmacher (Valerie Perrine) has to witness him murdering a police officer by forcing the poor man in front of an oncoming train with a moving wall.

Lex's home is an abandoned underground railway station converted to a state-of-the-art villain's lair, an eagle's nest of flashing machines, fascist portraits, ornate decorations and a beautiful swimming pool. Lex, a towering intellect, a criminal mastermind, is brewing the crime of the century, and clues his two numbskull assistants in on it: an upcoming twin-missile test will enable him to commit the greatest real estate swindle of all time. 'Son, stocks may rise and fall, utilities and transportation systems may collapse. People are no damn good, but they will always need land and they'll pay through the nose to get it! Remember, my father said . . . land.'

Lois Lane has had better evenings. She's all dressed up, clinging for dear life to a teetering helicopter, with nowhere to go. She was due to meet the President on *Air Force One*, but life is just something that happens while you're busy making other plans, and instead of taking off with no problems, the helicopter has got itself stuck on the side of the giant *Daily Planet* building, with death being the inevitable next destination. As she screams for help, and her grasp becomes looser by the second, it's not looking great.

Clark exits work for the evening and is immediately puzzled by the crowd of people outside looking up at the sky. He pauses to take a look before immediately turning on his heels and racing towards the screen, pulling open his shirt to reveal the 'S' logo and dashing into a set of revolving doors and emerging as Superman for the first time in the wild.

'Say, Jim, that's a bad outfit,' announces an observer, as Superman pushes himself up and away into the sky and soars to the roof to save the day. The news cameras can scarcely believe what they are seeing as they capture the image of a man in blue flying through the air. 'Don't worry, miss, I've got you,' Superman says with an air of perfect chivalry.

Reeve's Superman carried a weight of iconic universality perfectly – and immediately. Armed not only with incredible charm and charisma, but also the most wondrous hero theme in cinema history, the music and imagery work in unison to send pulses racing, hair standing and smiles beaming. As easy as it is to accept that this machine works perfectly, it's equally easy to imagine how it could all have gone horribly, instantly wrong, like a botched experiment in a petri dish. But there it is, purring away on the screen: sleek and beautiful, forever locked in amber. Perfect.

'You've got me? Who's got you?!' Lois retorts in panic, as he carries her back to the roof to safety.

'I certainly hope this little incident hasn't put you off flying, miss,' he replies, like a big boy scout with a beaming smile. 'Statistically speaking, of course, it's still the safest way to travel.' Lois asks who he is, and he tells her, 'A friend,' before flying off in an expertly delivered wire shot, leaving Lois to faint at the appropriate comic moment.

Superman's first night on the job is a perfect sequence, beginning at once with a piece of sublime camera trickery from Donner, with the camera and Superman upside down from one another, at muddled ends in the sky, before taking a few loops and righting in perfect harmony.

'As I was hoisted up, the crowd roared their approval,' Reeve said in *Still Me*. 'They didn't care about the crane or the wires; they were willing to look past all of it. There was Superman flying up the side of a building. That's when I knew the movie would work.'

With robberies foiled, cats rescued and *Air Force One* saved, Superman has made quite a name for himself on his first night, though he's probably still wondering what the story is with that woman who slapped her daughter for lying about seeing a flying man. The news is flooded with reports of his acts of daring rescue, and asks the question: is he real or the result of some sort of mass hypnosis? Like that effect when Barbra Streisand married Nelson Mandela.

Perry White wants an exclusive. Every other newspaper has pictures, stories and headlines, but he wants the *Daily Planet* to own this story – after all, it did basically fall in their lap. As he roars questions in an attempt to inspire his writers – who is this flying man? What makes him tick? What football team does he like? – Lois finds a note among her things requesting a meeting at her place that evening at eight o'clock, sent from 'a friend'. This is either from the new flying man who rescued her, or a Jehovah's Witness, so it's best to play it safe and not wear her special bra. Perry leaves the team with a final inspirational sentence: 'I tell ya, boys and girls, whichever one of you gets it out of him is gonna wind up with the single most important interview since God talked to Moses.'

On the balcony of Lois's frankly enormous apartment, she waits patiently for her new friend to arrive. She's dressed in a powder-blue, wafty chiffon evening gown and has a table set for two, along with a trusty packet of cigarettes and a bottle of fizz, just in case he's a proper lad. Just when she thinks he's not going to arrive, he swoops on to her terrace and announces himself. The interview begins, and it's more akin to Paula Yates and Michael Hutchence on the *Big Breakfast* bed than Frost/Nixon. She probes him for details, and he reveals some key facts:

1) He's from a planet called Krypton.
2) He never lies.
3) He eats, has sex, pisses and shits.
4) He can't see through lead.
5) He's single.
6) He doesn't feel pain.
7) He's never timed how fast he can fly.

All of which reads like your average, common or garden sociopathic male Tinder profile.

To answer Lois's question about flight, he asks her if she fancies a spin. She thinks he's joking, but he's not, and as she drops her notepad, he takes her into the sky for a graceful flight around the city, up into the clouds, to freedom and far from the cares of the world. A charming, delicate sequence, swaddled in love and affection, with the two leads holding hands as they drift through thick cloud and thin air. The altitude clearly gets to Lois at one point, as she begins to perform free-form poetry in her head that has sadly been picked up on her microphone. He brings her back with her head spinning and her heart racing. As he turns and says good night, floating away serenely, Lois utters, 'What a super man,' to herself, and after the clunking noise dissipates, the name is born. There's a knock on Lois's door, and it's Clark ready to take her out on a dinner date, but he finds her bewildered and lost in thought. As she wanders away to fetch a coat, Clark is pleased with his work, and briefly decides to tell her the truth, removing his glasses, earnestly adjusting his face, softening his stiff hunch and gaining a couple of inches in height in the process. In a world before CGI, Christopher Reeve was his own ILM. 'I remembered George Reeves on TV as Clark Kent in *Superman*. How could a thick pair of glasses substitute for a believable characterisation? Right away I saw great opportunity: I would attempt to create more of a contrast between the two characters. After all, Lois Lane shouldn't have to be blind or dim-witted.' As Lois returns, still dazed and confused, Clark has gone back to his bumbling self, and as he shows her out of the door, a huge smile shines across his face. The night had gone very well indeed.

There's special interest in the following day's edition of the *Daily Planet*. Lois's article is an endearing piece detailing a perfect evening with a special person who can go to the toilet, and fly, though not at the same time. It's all food for thought for Lex Luthor. He's on the cusp of the crime of the century and could do without this 'Superman' getting in the way of it. So, he sets another plan in motion: if Krypton exploded thirty years ago, there must be pieces of it floating out there that would be radioactive to Superman, possibly kill him, or at the very least give him horrible cancer. Within moments he's scoured his library and whipped a page out of a journal showing a green piece of meteor that recently crashed in Addis Ababa (before they won

Eurovision). With that secured, the 'Crime of the Century' can begin, with Lex also having programmed the twin rockets to fall on altered targets.

Clark arrives at work to find that Lois has gone off to report on a story about some maniac who's buying up worthless pieces of land for extortionate prices (it's got to be Trump) and young Jimmy Olsen (Marc McClure) has gone with her on his first assignment. White is pleased he has Clark on his own, as he wants to give him a pep talk about how he should be more aggressive and confident. White didn't get where he is today without that attitude, and he tells Clark that he'll need to up his game if he wants to succeed. But his words soon fall away from Clark's ears as an ultra-high-frequency message from Lex Luthor starts to play through the air. Lex tells Superman that he's going to drop a poison gas pellet containing a propane-lithium compound through the air ducts of the city within five minutes. So, while White blathers on, Clark jumps out of the nearest window, which must have been deeply distressing for his *Daily Planet* colleague to witness, and is somehow able to transform from his business suit into the Superman suit via a short blurring motion before flying down into the belly of the city and tracking down the frequency. Within minutes he's smashed down Lex's door and is asking for the location of the deadly gas pellet.

'Somewhere in the back of my mind, actually,' Lex jokes, admitting he made the whole thing up and just wanted to meet him face to face. A joke Superman doesn't particularly enjoy. There's a brilliant energy during this scene, with Hackman riding the devilish quality of Luthor and Reeve standing stoic, unimpressed with anything he has to say. 'Is that how a warped brain like yours gets its kicks? By planning the death of innocent people?' asks Superman with moral authority. 'No, by *causing* the death of innocent people,' Lex retorts. He's beginning to enjoy their duel, toying with him. He shows Superman a map of Southern California, in particular the San Andreas Fault, and explains that everything below the line is the most expensive real estate in the world and everything north of it is worthless desert, which just so happens to be owned by Lex Luthor Incorporated. It's a barren wasteland, yet somehow already has a branch of Costa Coffee. It also just so happens that if a rocket were to drop on the right area, Southern California would collapse into the sea, sending millions into a watery, rubble-filled grave and giving Roland Emmerich a massive erection. Lex then produces a piece of acetate, detailing his new West Coast post-blast, with such brilliant names as Marina Del Lex, Luthorville, Lex Springs, Lexington and Teschmacher Peaks.

And in a perfect act of comedy, scrawled in a corner, in thick black pen: Otisburg. A little place for Lex's assistant that Lex is very unhappy to accommodate. His girlfriend Miss Teschmacher seems to have a tit-themed place of her own, and presumably Lex has already secured the hookers and blackjack tables. Superman is unimpressed with the new utopia laid out before him, although he'll probably visit the peaks. He calls Lex a dreamer and tells him his plan will never work. It's a complicated operation, sure, and took a lot of work, but phase one is already complete. Miss Teschmacher updates the room on the progress and lets slip that its two missiles have launched, one to the Fault and one to Hackensack, New Jersey, which causes panic in the eyes of Superman, as there's a really good IKEA there.

Lex claims that he can stop all this in one swift act. He has a hidden detonator, but won't say where it is, so Superman gives the room a quick X-ray scan, looking in drawers, safes and cupboards, eventually concluding that it must be in the lead chest Lex is perched upon like a garden gnome.

Unfortunately, he's wrong. Inside the chest, on the end of a thick chain, is a big lump of glowing, deadly kryptonite. He recoils but is too weak to escape and too weak to stop Lex putting it on him like a lethal medal before pushing him into the swimming pool. With Superman out of the way, Lex goes off to watch the Crime of the Century come to pass, stopping briefly to deliver a sublime piece of physical comedy when Miss Teschmacher informs Lex that her mum lives in Hackensack. Without missing a beat, Lex looks at his watch, then back up at her, and shakes his head.

'Miss Teschmacher, please. You can't just stand there,' begs Superman, treading water in Lex's pool and imploring her to free him and help save the millions of lives that are directly in danger. She considers his pleas and makes him promise he'll save her mum first. If he promises to do that, she'll help him escape. He agrees, but before she removes the chain, she plants a kiss on his lips, declaring that he wouldn't have let her afterwards. Poor Miss Teschmacher always falls for the wrong men, though her relationship with Lex is definitely unclear and may well just be cover for when he goes full *Deliverance* on Otis.

The chain and kryptonite are thrown into a nearby drain, spilling down in a pleasing visual motion, and Superman launches himself through the ceiling (a stunt performed by Vic Armstrong that was done in reverse, essentially a headfirst plummet through a false floor) and away to stop the bombs. He catches up with the first one quickly, reaching into the flame and sending it upwards into space to harmlessly explode. However, the second hits the target, triggering a major earthquake. As devastation begins to hit everywhere, Superman charges around fixing what he can.

But amid the chaos, a red car is hit by a landslide, its door ripped off in one swift motion. The windshield is shattered, smoke billows from the engine, and inside lies Lois under piles of gravel, dirt and rocks. After all his conscientious work righting all the wrongs of the quake, fixing all the holes and blocking all the leaks, Superman missed Lois, and as he carefully removes her from the broken vehicle and places her on the ground, he considers what he can do next. The air is still, and only the sound of the wind can be heard. He gets to his feet in disbelief and, with a quick shake of the head, through a mist of mumbled words putting everything his father said about interfering with human history to one side, he roars into the sky to put things right once and for all.

Academics have opposing views on whether what follows is possible. Some say no, others say no, don't be stupid, but Superman knows best, and he decides that he will make the entire world spin backwards in order to turn back time. Although some say this would actually lead to major ocean currents switching from the Atlantic to the Pacific, changing the planet's climate drastically, in actual fact it works, so fuck you, science. Time does indeed go backwards, with dams rebuilding, fault lines repairing, babies going back up mothers and poo going back up bottoms, but most important of all, Lois is brought back to life.

He returns to the car to find her alive and well and moaning about how hard her day has been. He explains that he's been kind of busy saving millions of lives and, not to humblebrag, but also bringing her back to life. She apologies eventually, but, you know, it's all a bit ungrateful, and I'm sure he won't forget that in a hurry.

After delivering Lex and Otis to prison, Superman rises to Earth's orbit, smiling that smile, with that glint in his eye, reassuring the world below that he's keeping a watchful eye on us all, and although he made babies go back inside mothers and probably ruined an entire series of *You've Been Framed*, he'll always be there to fight for truth, justice and the American way.

Superman arrived in December 1978 and, thanks to Richard Donner, Tom Mankiewicz, John Williams, Christopher Reeve and their joint commitment to verisimilitude, it was a smash hit. We believed a man could fly, and it became the benchmark that all superhero films would follow from that day onwards. The son becomes the father, and the father, the son.

TWO

FLASH GORDON

1980

PATHETIC EARTHLINGS . . . WHO CAN SAVE YOU NOW?

In the wake of *Star Wars*' box-office Poseidon, there was a gold rush of space adventures attempting to cash in on the exploits of Luke Skywalker. Legendary Italian producer Dino De Laurentiis was no different and had been wanting to get *Flash Gordon* made since he acquired the rights in the sixties. If only someone like, oh, I don't know, George Lucas, had approached him about wanting to make it into a film? Imagine if that had happened and he was unable to get the rights from Dino De Laurentiis, so he made *Star Wars* instead? I'd imagine the person that held those *Gordon* rights would probably regret that . . . but what do I know?

Ming the Merciless (Max von Sydow) is bored. Proper bored. So bored he alerts General Klytus (Peter Wyngarde), a becloaked weirdo of unknown extraction who is wearing a gaudy gold mask like he's off to the Met Ball. Emperor Ming asks for a new plaything – and this would be a totally different story if Klytus had brought out Boggle. However, Klytus points him towards an obscure body in the S-K system called 'Earth', and they decide to use a weather computer to cause climate-related mayhem (very Tory). They send bad winds, stock footage of bad winds and HOT HAIL – which sounds like a disco porn film from 1978. They then laugh, and probably high five, and then definitely return to an awkward, pregnant silence where they're both wondering if they should go and make some Pot Noodles or have a wank.

Queen's 'Flash' theme blasts out over lovely old Flash images from the comic books. Their involvement really underlines the dichotomy of the production. Dino wanted an earnest space adventure with sumptuous production design and a serious tone. Whereas Mike Hodges, the director, wanted it to be a tongue-in-cheek spoof of sorts, with classically trained actors romping with flamboyance. According to Brian May (in an *Independent* interview in 2015), when Queen played the theme to the production team, Hodges was hopping on the spot applauding while De Laurentiis sat stony-faced, rooted in his chair. 'It's very good,' said De Laurentiis from behind a big cigar, 'but it is not for my movie.' He was, of course, very wrong, as there's never been a theme that captures the spirit of a movie quite like 'Flash' does. It tells you all you need to know – and more.

On Earth a plane is being readied by Robbie Coltrane. Flash Gordon (Sam J. Jones, a hulking, blond all-star football player and ex-Marine) boards along with travel agent Dale Arden (Melody Anderson), who is clearly scared of flying. Flash attempts to ease her nerves by telling her he has been watching her at the hotel and 'I couldn't believe a girl like you was alone', which isn't at all creepy and is sure to soothe her worried mind as they sit together among the stormy clouds.

Sam J. Jones constantly clashed with Dino De Laurentiis, and their relationship soured to the point that he refused to return for overdubs in post-production, so the decision was made to bring in actor Peter Marinker to replace most of his dialogue. Some of Sam still remains, and it's to Marinker's credit that the lines are so wonderfully blurred.

As Flash attempts to mansplain air pressure to Dale, the clouds turn bright red and Ming appears to grab the pilots, presumably just chucking them out into the sea or placing them in Klytus's horrible sex dungeon.

Meanwhile, over at his secret Hammer lab, Doctor Hans Zarkov (Topol) is trying to convince his assistant Munson (William Hootkins) to go up into space with him in his newly built rocket. *At gunpoint.* This sort of feels like an argument they have nightly, and it may well be a role-playing thing. I'm not one to kink-shame. Zarkov says that the scientific community has dismissed his theories and no one takes him seriously, which makes me wonder if David Icke has a rocket as well. Before they can really get into it, Flash's plane crashes on his house and Munson is killed in the impact. As Dale and Flash emerge from the wreckage, Zarkov tells them he has a phone in his rocket and, after a scuffle, they're launched into space – and unconsciousness. It's here that Queen introduce music that feels like it was written for a trippy sex orgy rocket ride – like someone pressed the wrong button. As our protagonists snuggle inside the rocket, they gently float through space, eventually dropping through a sensual black hole that looks like a yassified goatse.

They crash-land on the planet Mongo, which is basically a vast, barren wasteland with a grand luxury castle in the middle (think Center Parcs). A wonderful metaphor of class: the rich have it all, and the poor have nothing (again, think Center Parcs). They're greeted by Ming's gaudy-gold bastard-guards, who extend a giant golden handshake to Flash, but instead of a picture of a Spitfire or a carriage clock, he's given electric shocks.

Emperor Ming walks a steady adagio out onto the stage of his grand palace. He's warmly bathed in red and yellow, with a dirty synth theme burning its way out of the speakers as he reaches the summit. His subjects stand around in due reverence and hail him as their true leader. There's the Hawkmen from the levitating city and their king, Vultan (played by a wonderfully 1,000% Brian Blessed), Prince

Barin of Arboria (Timothy Dalton cosplaying as Errol Flynn) and Prince Thun of Ardentia (George Harris), to name just a few. They are there to present Ming with their tributes (not like that). Vultan of the Hawkmen offers a tribute of a giant ice jewel, presumably stolen from a giant G&T, but Prince Barin says it belongs to them. They're about to have a fight when Klytus stops them, essentially telling them that they can't fight here as it's the war room.

In the documentary *Life After Flash*, Blessed reveals that von Sydow had no idea how to approach the part of Ming and asked Blessed for his advice a mere twenty minutes before filming his entrance. Brian advised him that Ming is a 'magician. Very sexy, very erotic, and a master of sex.' This apparently did the trick for the Swedish great and, according to Brian, he went off happily and filmed the scene. Excuse me for a second while I liberally sprinkle a vast pinch of salt on that story.

Ardentia brings a tribute of loyalty, which is only a few steps away from bringing charcoal from the garage on Christmas Day or sponsoring a donkey in his name. Klytus questions the size of his loyalty, and Thun reassures him that it is massive, so no worries there. Ming asks him to throw himself on his own sword: consider this bluff called. Thun takes a moment, and after declaring that this deed will be an example to all, then tries to kill Ming, which, while brave, leads to Ming killing him anyway. So, as gestures go, it's as fruitless as a supermarket after Brexit (my name is Ben Elton, goodnight).

'This Ming's a psycho,' Flash whispers to Dale (in an example of an undubbed Sam J. Jones), but a floating, Ming-sympathising droid tells on him, and as the room shoots a glance at Flash, Princess Aura (Ornella Muti) steps out of the crowd and basically has a Diet Coke break. Fun fact: she has a small person for a pet, named Fellini (Deep Roy), after the legendary Italian film director who was once attached to make this film but dropped out.

'Pathetic Earthlings, hurling your bodies out into the void,' Ming says, chastising our heroes, intimating that this is a local planet for local people, and there's nothing for them here.

Ming points his ring at Dale (not like that) and shoots her with horny rays that make her dance around like she's Donna Summer on late-night German telly. 'Did you ever see such a response?' Ming asks Klytus. 'No, truly. She rivals even your own daughter.'

The spell wears off, and Dale regroups with her friends. 'What happened to me?' she asks Flash. 'I don't know, but it was pretty sensational,' he replies from behind his erection.

Ming also likes what he sees and wants Dale to be prepared for his pleasure (ribbed?). Flash, though, tells Ming to forget it, and takes on his entire army in a rudimentary game of football, sending them tumbling and rolling around the room. Dale breaks out her mildly embarrassing cheerleading game, looking for the whole world like a soccer mom who's just downed a full crate of beveraginos. However, the joy is fleeting as Flash is overpowered and sent for execution.

'Bring in the emperor's concubine,' Klytus drools from behind his mask as Flash hangs in chains in a dungeon. Dale runs in, distressed at Flash's beaten appearance, but looking absolutely resplendent in her red Danilo Donati costume.

Donati worked heavily in Italian cinema, and his influence throughout this film is titanic. Packed with lush colours and ornate magnificence, there are shades of Oz via Liberace, especially with Ming's palace. There's no doubt that without Donati (and Gilbert Taylor's lush cinematography) this film would simply be filed under 'just another space movie', and not the camp classic it has become. Fun fact: Carole Hersee also worked on the costumes for this film, and you will know her better as the original test card girl, who clocked up 70,000 hours of television time – more than any other person in history.

R.I.P. Flash. Gassed to death in a chamber while Brian May noodled, his body placed in a giant black coffin that reads 'Flash Gordon. Earthling. Executed by Ming', you have to love the attention to detail from the coffin designers here. They've both observed the I.P. of Flash by incorporating his logo while also making the text as METAL as possible. The box lies peacefully in a darkened room, cared for by cloaked goblins. Princess Aura enters with Dr Howard Hughes from *Ever Decreasing Circles* (Stanley Lebor), who is playing a doctor. They quickly set about bringing Flash back to life. 'I'm a fool for you, Aura,' the horny doctor says as he injects Flash with come-back-to-life serum. As he delivers the life-bringing juice, he asks Aura if they can meet up again the following weekend, which seems a bit tragic, seeing as he's just brought her new fancy man back to life. But you can't blame him for trying. Flash slowly awakes as Aura gropes him all over and announces that they need to move fast before the lizard people come to bury him, which must be the weirdest possible thing you can hear when you come back from the dead.

Zarkov's day isn't going much better. He's strapped to a table with a laser pointed at his head while Ming tells him that if he hadn't come snooping, he wouldn't have to destroy Earth, which just sums up humanity, doesn't it? 'I thought it might amuse you to know this before your mind is gone,' Ming says, with all the loaded threat of a Michael McIntyre gig. They are going to empty his mind, in 'the same way you empty your pockets' (in a tray at the airport?), and as the laser burns a blue line into his head, we witness lots of Zarkov's memories racing through the video monitor in fast motion, like Benny Hill's *This Is Your Life*. These even depict the death of his wife in a swimming pool, but it's played in such a way that suggests she died, came back to life and was then thrown in a swimming pool, which would definitely make me pause the process and ask what the fuck have I just watched. Klytus sees an image of Hitler and mentions that he showed promise, which makes one imagine a *Mongo's Got Talent* contest where Hitler arrives on the back of a V-2 rocket and plays the spoons with banjo accompaniment.

Aura and Flash are making their way across the tie-dye skies to Arboria. Her plan seems to be to just hide him there for a bit, maybe just sort of wait until it all blows over. She wraps herself around him and tells him all about her secret pleasure moon where she has galactic knee-tremblers. There can be no doubt she intends to ravage young Flash, and leave him less of a man and more the last balloon at a kids' party. In the midst of this extreme sexual tension, with Aura effectively lapping him up, Flash asks if he can use the telepathic communicator to call Dale and see if she's OK or needs anything from the shops, and you have to wonder if he's OK.

Dale receives his psychic call with great excitement, as she was sure he was dead. She's been given some Pan Galactic Gargle Blaster and is all set to marry Ming, which is obviously the last thing she wants (giving off huge Charles and Diana vibes). Flash tells her he will come and rescue her while Aura carries on trying to seduce him. 'THIS GIRL IS REALLY TURNING ME ON,' he blurts out apropos of nothing, and when Dale asks what he means, he says, 'It wasn't about you,' and you have to conclude that this bloke is a fucking idiot.

Dale is visited by Suzanne Danielle with more Mongo Night Nurse, which one can only assume Ming gives to all his prospective brides, and sort of doesn't bear thinking about. However, things will not go that way today. Dale is a New York broad, and she has moxy. She uses her street smarts to simply suggest that Suzanne drinks it herself, which she does and then passes out. Genius. Dale then runs off, murdering *four* Mongo Imperial Guards as she does so, who all disconcertingly squeal like pigs as they expire. Within moments Dale bumps into Zarkov, but not the Zarkov she knows. After his reprogramming he now talks in monotones and is devoid of personality, like he's been prepped for hosting a show on Open University. She gets him up to speed, telling him Flash is alive and heading for Arboria. Sadly, Klytus is listening in to their chat in the operations room, staffed solely by bald, middle aged men wearing swimming goggles, and he commands that an exit is given to them. After they push a button, Zarkov tells Dale that he knows a way they can escape.

After Aura announces she's going to drop her flaps, their ship lands on Arboria, and she is greeted gleefully by Prince Barin –

until he notices that she's brought the big lunk with her. Barin, a clearly classically educated, urbane man of distinction doesn't take too kindly to another rooster in the hen house. Especially one who looks like a *Rocky Horror* impersonator who sells Sex Wax in pub car parks. Talking of *Rocky Horror*, Fico (Richard O'Brien) watches on as Peter Duncan from *Blue Peter* is guided by playwright John Osborne to perform the Arborian test of manhood that involves sticking your hand in a hole in a tree stump to see if a fat crab will bite you. Written down, this sounds like an awful fever dream, but I can assure you this actually happens. If you avoid the crab, you're all right, but if it bites you, you die horribly. Sadly, Peter Duncan is caught by the crab and perishes, making this his last and most costly episode of *Duncan Dares* (one for the kids, there). Aura asks Barin to keep Flash for a bit, so Ming doesn't find out, like he's a stolen set of bike wheels. Barin isn't exactly enamoured with the idea and accuses her of necrophilia – which to be honest, is an accurate charge – but after a quick snog, he agrees.

Zarkov and Dale race clear of the Mongo kingdom on a rocket scooter, whereupon he reveals that he was just pretending to be mind-wiped and he's actually fine, though now he can't get erections unless he sees Hitler and has hourly nosebleeds. Overall, though, he's euphoric. They couldn't break him because he used his stored knowledge. He recited Shakespeare, the Talmud, Einstein and The Beatles, which sounds like a hell of a Royal Variety Performance. Dale is pleased for him, but their happiness, like all happiness, doesn't last long, as they soon run into a pack of ominous flying Hawkmen.

Barin decides the best place to store his fugitive is in a wooden cage in a swamp. Flash floats the idea of all the kingdoms under Ming's rule teaming up and killing him, but Barin decides that he'd much rather live in a swamp with John Osborne and feed *Blue Peter* presenters to crabs (Simon Groom is going in next week with Goldie). As Flash is lowered into the swamp, he's surrounded by more lizard men, who are clearly fucking awful, as everywhere you go, there's one being imprisoned, tortured or murdered.

Camera angles are important in cinema. They can establish moods, create atmosphere and even tell you if a character is good or evil. Directors have a clear emotional trajectory in mind when they plan their shots, and they pour their creative visions through their pens when creating their intricate storyboards. There can be no doubt that when it came to planning the scene showing the torture of Princess Aura, Mike Hodges really wanted to show us her arse.

Aura will not be broken, even when they tell her that Howard from *Ever Decreasing Circles* will be executed for treason, so Klytus is left with no choice and asks for the Bore Worms, which sends Aura into a terrified frenzy of hysteria – even though the Bore Worms sounds like a *Viz* comic strip about a family of lumbricina who sit around talking about philately.

Dale and Zarkov are taken to Sky City to see Vultan and his Hawkmen. Sky City looks like a big floating toilet bowl, but they seem to like it, so we'll say nothing. Vultan has a plan to send them both back to Ming and isn't that interested in the idea of going against him – that is, until Dale makes the big announcement. 'Gordon's ALIVE?!' Vultan bellows in disbelief. Zarkov puts more wood on the fire of rebellion by telling him that Barin is helping Flash in Arboria, and there's never been a better time to strike. If he were a rich man, he'd even put money on it.

Flash, meanwhile, has been taken to the test of manhood by playwright John Osborne. The tension is high, the stakes even higher. Flash must put his hand into the tree-stump hole and try to avoid the fat crab (aka 'Woodbeast'). He refuses at first, but Barin changes his mind by calling him a coward. They each take turns plunging their hand inside the *Blue Peter* presenter killer, taunting one another, testing their manhood, jousting with their egos. Just when it seems like things are going his way, Flash recoils in agony, pulling his hand out of the hole and plunging to the floor grasping his wrist. Barin tells him death is certain, accompanied by tortured madness, which feels like a nice summary of life itself. Flash looks up and asks, with all the dignity he can muster, to be finished off. Barin pulls out his sword and agrees to help, but it was all a ruse. Flash announces, 'Tricked you, Barin,' as he pushes him over and swipes his sword away. Does he use Barin as a hostage to get a spaceship and escape from the swamp planet? No. He pushes him over again and then makes a run for it in the swamp before being eaten by a big fat jelly monster. Told you, this bloke's thick as shit. As Flash wallows in jelly Barin arrives to once again finish him off, but before he can, the Hawkmen appear from all angles and take them both away.

Once at Sky City, Barin reminds Vultan that, under Ming's law, no prince of Mongo shall be offered for ransom without trial by combat. He demands to fight Flash to the death. Flash, rightly, looks around and wonders why everyone is so fucking insane. He literally can't move without someone wanting to fight him or kill him; it's like being in Croydon. Before he can truly contemplate the madness, Dale and Zarkov appear, and Flash embraces the travel agent. Within moments they're engaged, smooching and talking about their future kids. Obviously feeling sick, Vultan declares that the trial by combat must begin, and Flash and Barin make their way to the centre of the room to the spinning disc of death and spikes.

As the battle commences, Zarkov has done his sums. He tells Dale that they only have fourteen hours, nine minutes and twenty seconds before Ming blows up the Earth, so once again Dale dons her embarrassing soccer mom persona and shouts, 'FLASH, I LOVE YOU, BUT WE ONLY HAVE FOURTEEN HOURS TO SAVE THE EARTH,' so no pressure.

The game of death rages on with the fury, savagery and red-hot anger one would expect. However, something happens that Barin wasn't expecting: not only is he defeated by the Earthling, Flash also saves his life when he has the chance to end it, leading to a moment of beautiful harmony. Barin grasps his hand lovingly, looks into his eyes and tells him, 'Where you go, I follow.' He then gets to his feet and tells the room, 'There is something finer in this galaxy than Ming's law,' but before he can elaborate on his new utopia, Klytus arrives to do a big shit in the punchbowl and starts to throw his weight around to show who is in charge. He's just about to issue orders when Flash and Barin combine to kill him, throwing his wobbly body onto a big spike and causing his eyes to dribble out like wet eggs and his tongue to bulge like fried bacon. Vultan isn't best pleased at this, as it's like getting a parking ticket and then murdering the traffic warden. He knows Ming will be livid, so he orders his Hawkmen to evacuate and refuses to join the new rebellion. He orders his men to fly for their lives and leaves Barin, Flash, Dale and Zarkov behind, at which point we know he's more of a chicken than a hawk.

Ming's ship arrives, and he orders Barin, Zarkov and Dale to be taken aboard while he goes down to run a deal past Flash. He tells him he's never met someone so brave and heroic (*really?*) and offers him Earth. How would he fancy lordship over his own planet in exchange for a bit of loyalty? Just a little bit of loyalty. He can have all the gold he can eat, keep the pubs open all day and have Noel Edmonds as a jester. The only downside would be that, after the earthquakes and floods, everyone will be more 'tractable', easier for him to rule, like the audience at a recording of *Mrs Brown's Boys*. He then tells Flash that Dale will be his wife, but they can take turns having a go if he likes and send their offspring back to Earth to work at Lush. Flash doesn't even think about it. He's out. It's a no. So, Ming orders Sky City, and Flash, to be destroyed.

Ming's rocket fires on Sky City, sending it collapsing, burning and disintegrating around Flash. Luckily, he falls down a hole and finds a rocket cycle. He jumps aboard, fires it up and escapes before Sky City is destroyed, then gets on the radio and calls up Vultan. He's flying blind on a rocket cycle here and could use the help of a bunch of chickenshit middle-aged fat losers with wings. He tells them that Ming has Dale, Zarkov and Barin, and they should go and save them. Vultan agrees and thanks Flash for 'giving a dumb old bird a second chance', which is a line lifted from an Elizabeth Taylor telegram to Richard Burton.

Dale is being prepared for the wedding when Aura is brought in, and they begin to have a pillow fight that is wholly necessary for the narrative. Aura reveals she's due to be executed in the morning and has met the Bore Worms. Aura gives Dale some poison and tells her that every time her father makes love, he drinks a 'power potion' beforehand – which you can get over the counter now. Dale refuses as she gave her word to be a nice wife in order to save the lives of Zarkov and Barin. She tells Aura that being true to her word makes her better than anyone on this shithole of a planet, and she's probably right. There's a lot wrong with Dale, but her heart is in the right place. A handmaiden appears and tells them it's time for the wedding.

While Ming and his crew prepare, an ominous announcement is made in the operations room: 'Flash Gordon approaching on a rocket cycle.' General Kala orders the dispatch of war rocket Ajax to kill Flash and bring back his body. The last time Flash and Ajax went head to head, 50% of my kitchen was better than the other. As the rocket approaches, they discover it's a trap when the Hawkmen ambush them, which is like watching a drunk darts club try to take over a bus.

'Tell me more about this man Houdini,' Barin asks Zarkov as they stand chained in the dungeon, and I'd love to hear how this line of conversation started. There can be no doubt that this dungeon is flooded with the worst banter, and you'd beg for the fucking Bore Worms, honestly. Suddenly, Aura arrives to rescue them both. Barin tells her he's a changed man and that they should get married, and that if he promises to stop killing *Blue Peter* presenters, she can stop shagging sitcom doctors. She doesn't seem convinced, sadly. Barin releases his anger by shouting the greatest line in the film, 'Freeze, ya bloody bastards,' at the staff of the operations room as they take control. General Kala refuses to 'freeze', or indeed be a 'bloody bastard' (she's worked with Visconti and Chabrol, so get to hell), and instead attempts to kill Zarkov, but Barin shoots and kills her – and she melts into a pool of water, obviously having retention issues, bless her.

'That must be one hell of a planet you men come from!' Vultan announces as Flash refuses to leave a now laser-battered war rocket Ajax as it makes a final suicide run at Ming's palace. Yes, Vultan, it's full of weird lunks who make baffling decisions. With the wedding now in full effect, Flash flies the rocket ship into the city's wedding hall and manages to impale Ming on the nose (good shot), thus winning Bully's star prize. Ming drags himself off the rocket nose and slumps to the floor, oozing green blood everywhere. Flash brandishes a sword and offers to spare his life if he will stop the attack on Earth. Ming is deeply offended, telling him his life is not for any stupid Earthling to give, at which point he essentially commits suicide by pointing his ring at himself and disappearing in a haze of red, with the ring dropping to the floor. You have to admire that he's a man of deeply held principles.

Flash hurriedly checks the time left to save Earth just as one of Ming's floating droids announces that the planet is saved, following it up with a lovely 'HAVE A NICE DAY'.

A huge victory celebration ensues. Barin and Aura become the new leaders in Ming's place, and Barin names Vultan the general of their armies. He offers Flash, Dale and Zarkov a chance to stay, and presumably swing, but Dale tells him she's a 'New York girl' and wants to get back home. Zarkov says he doesn't know how they will get back, but they will try, which is deeply un-fucking-reassuring – thanks for all this, it's all your fault, you maniac.

As the Hawkmen fly in formation to spell out 'Thanks Flash', applause ripples through the throne room. Indeed, thank you, Flash, for pointing out that we could have overthrown Ming at literally any point. We literally hadn't thought of it, somehow.

As the celebrations pulse and soar, a gloved hand is seen picking up Ming's ring and cackling with laughter. A caption appears reading 'The End?', which is a bit presumptuous, to be honest, as sadly the numbers didn't stack up and a sequel never came to fruition. But isn't that a good thing? Frankly, no sequel would top this. It's lightning in a bottle, and quite rightly remembered as a Cult Classic, with capital Cs.

As Queen's rip-roaring 'The Hero' blasts out over the credits, you can't help but feel all is well with the world and that Flash Gordon is out there, somewhere, being weird, awkward and thick while simultaneously, somehow, saving the world.

THREE

SUPERMAN II

1980

THE MAN OF STEEL IS BACK, AND BETTER THAN EVER!

The story of *Superman II* is a tale of three agents of chaos, malevolence and evil. A trio who only seek to destroy something beautiful and who will stop at nothing to break the will of the people of Earth. I speak, of course, of Pierre Spengler, Alexander Salkind and his son Ilya, the *Superman* producers who had everything and threw it away.

Richard Donner had shot 75% of *Superman II* while also making the first film, and the production was ready to recommence after *Superman: The Movie* had been released. But things had not run smoothly between the director and the producers. There'd been petty squabbles, simmering feuds and heated arguments along the way.

Then news broke of them not wanting to pay Marlon Brando what they had agreed, and after settling out of court for $15 million, he was dropped from the sequel altogether, which must have been galling given that they'd already filmed key scenes with him (which you can now find on the 2006 'Donner Cut').

With nothing left to lose, Donner gave the producers an ultimatum: if he stayed at the helm, he demanded complete control over everything in order to get the film finally finished. No more meddling, arguing or interference. So, they fired him and brought in old (cheaper) friend Richard Lester. In terms of directing styles, you couldn't have found a more different guy; whereas Donner had a distinct tone and multi-layered vision for the film, Lester was more of a flamboyant and loose filmmaker (which is no bad thing if you like stuff like *Help!*) who preferred chaos and anarchy over the calm order of what came before. Out was Donner's verisimilitude and in was Lester's radical, zany comic-book tone, with many odd visuals and comic moments arriving like corpses in the post.

'I liked him tremendously,' Reeve later said in his autobiography. 'But in my opinion, it was unfair to ask such an accomplished director to imitate the tone and style of someone else's work. Nevertheless, he succeeded in bringing his own brand of humour to it.' Which feels like a very polite way of saying he thought everything was shit, but Christopher was a nice boy.

Donner was out, and with him went Marlon Brando, writer Tom Mankiewicz, John Williams and Gene Hackman (though the scenes he'd already shot stayed in the movie). Could the film survive without them?

We return across the gulf of space to Krypton, before it blew up, obviously. A crystal room (honestly, Krypton, get some interior designers in) is guarded by an officer dressed exactly like a Snow Trooper from *The Empire Strikes Back* (which confused me as a child no end). Non (Jack O'Halloran) strides into the room and breaks the neck of the guard while General Zod (Terence Stamp) and Ursa (Sarah Douglas) enter to remove a red crystal from the podium, break it and look very pleased with themselves. It's never quite explained what this red crystal does, but I can only assume that it contained all Zod's nudes.

Their joy is short-lived, however, as the room is plunged into darkness, and the three villains are placed in two Hula-Hoops that undulate disturbingly. A random voice (not Marlon Brando, as he was too expensive) tells the trio that they are traitors, and they are then sent into the Phantom Zone, which sounds less like a prison and more like an Aldi aisle where you can buy a ghost.

As they spin into space, trapped in a mirror, the credits arrive, and already we can see that despite the fact that the first film was a hit, they've spent less on the sequel. Whereas the first film had gigantic crystal letters that rushed at the screen, dazzling the eyes and befuddling the senses, we now have bog-standard white type floating about with a shadow and very little energy behind it. As this half-arsed effort dribbles over the screen, we are treated to an extended montage of the first film, for anyone who didn't see it or had a head injury before the projector rolled. With John Williams gone (after apparently not seeing eye to eye with Lester), the mighty Ken Thorne was brought in to replace him, as he and Lester had worked together before. Thorne essentially just does an extended covers set from Williams' first score, albeit with a much smaller-sounding orchestra (think school band), as we catch up with what happened when Superman saved the world last time for FIVE MINUTES AND THIRTY SECONDS.

Clark Kent (Christopher Reeve) walks through the doors of the *Daily Planet* office ready for work, and as usual everyone ignores him/hates him, but on top of that, things seem oddly quiet, so he pops in to see Perry White (Jackie Cooper) to find out what's happening. It turns out some terrorists have taken over the Eiffel Tower and, as well as taking hostages, they also claim to have an atomic bomb. Lois Lane (Margot Kidder) has gone via Concorde to report on it, so Clark rushes out to get his cape on. (On a side note, the Superman transformation here is my very favourite. The smooth run through the back alley, the beautiful colour-morphing effect, ending in the graceful swoop out of shot as the theme swells. Perfection. As I mentioned, young me had a very cool poster on my bedroom wall of the whole transition that came with a magazine of the time, and I'd love to get it back.)

Lois arrives on the scene in Paris to overhear the briefing from an official. When he mentions that the terrorists have an atomic bomb, she points out that it could blow up all of Paris, like he hadn't thought of that. As the briefing ends, she manages to sneak past a French police officer and clamber under the lift in order to get to the top of the tower and find out just what these terrorists want – and the news should be that one of them is played by Richard Griffiths, which just goes to show that between-work actors sometimes have to do any job they can get, even if it leads to Paris being levelled.

As the terrorists begin to arm the bomb, Lois becomes trapped under the lift when her handbag gets caught, and she's forced to listen to the inane ramblings of these boring mad men with a stupid plan to extort money while actually possessing a real atomic bomb. They soon end up with oeuf on their visages, though, when they arm the bomb in the lift and the French police blow the lift mechanism, sending the active bomb and Lois hurtling towards the ground at great speed. Bravo! French police. I hope this segment appears regularly in hostage negotiation videos.

As Lois's life flashes before her eyes, presumably scored by Ken Thorne and his School Hall Allstars, much like the opening montage of the film, her prayers are answered as Superman arrives to stop the lift and tell Lois that she can get off – but not with him, as he needs to get rid of the bomb. With great speed he pushes the elevator right back up the lift shaft, through the roof of the beloved structure, all the way into space, where it explodes, sending shockwaves through the galaxy. In something that NASA scientists would describe as 'the last thing we wanted to happen', the aftershock from this Paris-saving explosion sadly breaks the Phantom Zone wide open and releases the Krypton Three. After not really questioning what they'll do, now they're floating in space, they decide to head towards Earth.

Of course, this all depends on which version you happen to be watching, as the 'Donner Cut' (Donner's abandoned footage edited back together in 2006) has no Paris sequence (Lester shot that), the missiles from the end of the first film exploding in space instead freeing Zod, and Lois throwing herself out of a window in order to prove her hunch that Clark is Superman.

Lex Luthor (Gene Hackman) and Otis (Ned Beatty) are in jail, and not a very nice one by the looks of it. A sort of mix of Shawshank State Penitentiary and the one in *Paddington 2*, it makes you wonder which event is more likely to break out: a song-and-dance number with accompanying marmalade sandwiches or a brutal gang bang in the showers. It could be both, especially with Lex telling a prisoner he wants his Liberace record back. Lex is confident of escape, though, and he keeps talking about his 'little black box' that is the key to their escape. But fear not, he isn't talking about pimping his anus out in exchange for a map, he's talking about a special box that tracks alpha waves: alpha waves that will lead him north – to Superman's secret fortress.

Meanwhile on the Moon, Zod and his lads arrive and stumble upon a NASA mission of time wasting. While Cliff from *Cheers* sits in Houston and chats with the astronauts as they collect moon dust and find Stanley Kubrick's lighter, the evil Kryptonians arrive to kill everyone and smash things up, with Ursa in particular seeming to have the most fun: toying with them, stealing a badge from one as she watches him die and then kicking his body into space. Like a Tory-funded space programme. As they survey the damage, the Kryptonians realise that they suddenly have superpowers, unlimited strength and great haircuts. Ursa tells Zod that these people come from a place called 'Houston', and she points at Earth in the distance. Zod declares that they will go there and rule, so off they fly.

A guard at the prison (Angus MacInnes – a veteran Canadian screen presence in British-filmed movies) goes through the lights-out procedure at the prison but notices that a lone cell isn't co-operating. As he attends to it, he sees cellmates Luthor and Otis playing chess and not listening to his commands. It's only when he enters that he discovers, to his horror, that they are a holographic projection.

The real Lex and Otis are out in the yard, looking like they're about to join the *Band On The Run* album cover. Lex, who calls himself the greatest criminal mind in the world, is planning to escape via hot-air balloon, and it arrives right on cue, piloted by Miss Teschmacher (Valerie Perrine), but in a moment right up there with Willem Dafoe's death in *Platoon*, Otis is too fat to hold on to the ladder and is abandoned in the jail as the balloon sails away and the alarms ring out, where presumably he will be forced to do the accounts for the warden and be molested in the showers. Otis is never seen again after this moment, so we can only assume he was murdered by his new cellmate.

Meanwhile, Lois and Clark have been sent to Niagara Falls to investigate a honeymoon scam being perpetrated by the Honeymoon Haven Hotel. I guess someone else will be covering the huge act of terrorism that happened yesterday. Scamming honeymoon couples is probably more important than the guys who nearly blew up Paris with an atomic bomb.

Antony Sher, of all people, pops up as the bellboy showing them around their sex-people hotel room. There's a pink bearskin rug, a 'tub for two', a fire that you can turn on with a switch and a bed that looks like it's seen hell. All in all, the room just screams 'Peter Stringfellow's Mind Palace'. Lois is livid about being given such a rubbish story and bemoans the fact that she'll never win a Pulitzer now, which I could have told her after she nearly got vaporised in Paris. Clark tries to cheer her up by telling her she looks nice, but sort of ruins the mood by sitting on the bed and basically orgasming when it begins to vibrate.

They decide to stretch their legs by the falls, just in time to witness the world's worst mother not paying attention to her son dangling himself over the barrier and plummeting to a watery grave. Luckily, Clark has been sent for hot dogs, so can quickly change out of sight and swoop in to save the boy, who demands another go. The mother then reprimands the boy for making her look bad. Social services should drop by and take that kid away from a giant pool of death and a mother who should be in court in the morning.

It's at this point that Lois begins to suspect Clark may be Superman. Her hunch is based on two key points:

1. He's never around when Superman is here.
2. He looks exactly like Superman.

Meanwhile, at Superman's fortress of solitude, Lex and Miss Teschmacher arrive, completing their long journey via balloon and snow bike. They wander into the snowy compound, and Lex, being the greatest criminal mind, obviously begins to play around with the crystals until he finally gets a tune from them. Susannah York appears as Superman's mother and, in much the same way Sacheen Littlefeather showed up to decline Marlon Brando's Oscar, delivers his expositional speeches for a reduced fee. She explains that three Kryptonian villains are out in space somewhere, floating in a fancy mirror, livid about their life choices. Rather than being utterly terrified at this news, Lex is impressed by the idea of three immortal gods heading his way and, as we cut to a Lester-directed scene, a body double on a snow bike tells Miss Teschmacher that he's been seeing three alpha waves on his little black box. It's always a fun game playing 'spot the reshot scenes with Luthor', as he is placed well away from shot, back turned, and his voice sounds like a very bad impression of himself.

With Lois being a top reporter, she decides to test her working theory of Clark Kent being Superman. She decides that she'll throw herself in an angry river and see if he drops his disguise and flies in to rescue her. 'If I'm wrong, you've got yourself one hell of a story,' she says. You can imagine the headline now: 'FUCKING STUPID *DAILY PLANET* REPORTER JUMPS IN RIVER'.

Clark watches on helplessly as she drops into the watery abyss, following her down the stretch of babbling stream, clucking like a

Bee Gee with a stutter. While she's fighting for her life, and slightly distracted, he lasers a big tree branch into the water for her to grab and use to swim to safety, and as she washes up on the riverbank, looking like Ted Kennedy after Chappaquiddick, she is forced to concede that Clark may not be the Man of Steel.

Later that evening, however, as they dry themselves off in their fancy hotel room and Lois moans about how stupid she was to jump in a river, Clark, after all that effort and all that hassle, trips on his way to pass something to Lois. He lands with his hand in the fireplace. Lois checks his injury and, on closer inspection, finds no marks. So, Clark basically whips off his glasses and reveals that he is actually Superman, which he could have done by the river, and just makes me think of Michigan J. Frog only revealing his secret dancing and singing when there's no one around. It's another fine example, though, of Reeve standing to his full height and dropping the Clark persona. Another sweet underline of just how perfect he was for this role, and how it could have easily been shit. He gave it such heft and weight that it literally stands tall when he switches back into the red boots.

Lois can't believe her luck. Not only is he Superman but he also fancies her and wants to take her somewhere else. No, not the honeymoon suite they're already in, or the bins behind Waitrose, but his home: a giant frozen cave where she must pack light, wrap up warm and continue to have a haircut that switches between bangs and partings – another reminder of the continuity nightmare that two directors bring.

As they depart for the north, the sound you hear is Perry White smashing up his office wondering where the fuck this honeymoon scam story is.

As Zod and his gang arrive on Earth, they spend a while getting familiar with our practices and cultures. They walk on water, like Jesus. They kill a snake with their laser eyes, like Steve Irwin, and they force a watching Gordon Rollings in a fishing boat to do a double take with his Thermos of tea and throw it away – like Jesus, again, probably.

There can be no doubt that they're up to no good and seek to take over the world, enslave the human race and probably murder us all. Usually, this would be very bad, but it's something I can really get behind when Clifton James once again steps into a film to play a sheriff and ruin it. Even Zod tells him he's annoying, and as he sends his deputy to deal with the terrible trio, we get our first instance of 'made-up powers'. There are a few of them in this film in particular, and this is just the tip of the iceberg. Zod uses his laser eyes to heat up the deputy's shotgun, which is fine. This is consistent with heat and lasers. The shotgun then floats through the air into Zod's waiting hands. Hang on. Superman can't do that. It's the sun that gives you guys extra strength and powers, and our gravity allows you to fly. There is nothing on this green earth that allows you to be David Copperfield/Paul Daniels. Zod then shoots himself with it (obviously he's seen *The Man with the Golden Gun*), but, alas, he does not die. He's still here, and thankfully he quickly moves on from Clifton James and wanders off towards a small town to create more bland mischief.

'Pick Up The Pieces' by The Average White Band crawls out of the speakers of a southern-looking diner as Zod and his chaps enter. 'Hey, sweet thing. Sit them buns down here,' one dirty cowboy says to Ursa as he pats his lap like a craven sex offender. She instead challenges him to an arm wrestle and defeats him immediately, but there's no Brundlefly-style gore. Outside, Zod points his finger at a redneck gentleman and sends him floating into the sky (made-up power no. 2), forcing his young son, with a southern English accent, to beg him to let his 'Daddy' down, sounding more Oliver Twist than *Hillbilly Elegy*.

'This is a very special place for me. I wanted you to see it,' Superman says to Lois, as he shows her around his big white load of nothing. There's no TV, no stereo, not even a basic Atari. He instead shows her his boring crystal collection, like some weird bloke you'd meet at a covered market. Lois pretends she loves it all, though, which is very polite of her. I don't think I'd be able to keep it inside if my girlfriend took me back to her place and it was essentially a chest freezer. Superman races out and grabs dinner items in a brown bag, and some flowers, then asks if she wants to eat. As there's no oven or utensils, I'm guessing it's crisps for dinner.

Zod meanwhile has found himself on live TV news making the US Army look like tits. They try attack after attack, and he, Ursa and Non repel each one with consummate ease. It's embarrassing, to be honest. Watching on from Washington is the President (E. G. Marshall), who wants to know where Superman is, like he's David Goyer or something.

If you must know, Mr President, Superman is in bed with Lois, post-coitus, having lost his virginity, and it's probably a bittersweet moment for Lois, as, yes, she's just shagged Superman (and she didn't die), but it was probably also really shit. In fact, it was probably more shit than it should have been, as he's also just relinquished his powers in order to be able to have sex with her. His mother warned him over and over that there's no coming back from this, but he so wanted to have it off, he gave it all away in a big crystal booth and stepped out with floppy hair and flared disco pants.

Zod and his gang, meanwhile, are causing more dull havoc, and fresh from carving their faces into Mount Rushmore with their laser eyes (made up power no. 3), they attack the White House and demand to speak to the manager. Powerless to do anything, the President kneels before Zod and wonders just when dirty boy Superman will get bored of shagging.

Newly laid and powerless, Clark joins Lois on a road trip back to civilisation, and, yes, like you, I also often wonder where they got the car and what they had to do to get it, but we'll let that go – maybe the Fortress of Solitude has a Hertz Car Rental. They arrive at Don's Diner for some much needed hot food after all those crisps. While Clark pops to the toilet, truck driver Rocky (ex-wrestler Pepper Martin) comes in and sits next to Lois, referring to her as 'sweetheart' as he does so, like a chauvinist pig. Clark emerges from the bathroom and takes exception to this, telling

Rocky someone needs to teach him some manners, obviously forgetting he's as likely to win a fight now as a small child who sounds like Oliver Twist. To say that Clark gets his arse handed to him is putting it mildly. Rocky lives up to his name and puts Clark in a pile on the floor, covered in blood. As Rocky leaves, and Clark is comforted by Lois, the President appears on the TV in the diner asking Superman just where the fuck he is and if he fancies stepping up to help with this Zod problem anytime soon. Clark dutifully abandons Lois and takes the long walk north again.

The evil Kryptonians idly dwell in the Oval Office, obviously bored now they're in charge and probably close to breaking out a game of Trivial Pursuit. A white handkerchief waves in the doorway, and the arm holding it belongs to Lex Luthor, who has a deal to run by them. Obviously their first instinct is to tear off his arms and put them up his arsehole, but Lex has important information for them. It turns out that he knows the location of the son of Jor-El. The son of their jailer. The son of the man who is too expensive and legally difficult to be in this film. Lex fills them in on his powers, telling them he has the same abilities as they do but is only one man, whereas they are three. He says he can take them to him and, in exchange, he'd like a small beachfront property: Australia.

Perry White is confused. Whereas Superman usually turns up for a cat stuck in a tree or a small, stupid child falling into a large body of water, he's suddenly, at the worst possible time, vanished. Lois smokes nervously in the corner, obviously not wanting to tell everyone she got him laid and therefore caused him to lose focus. She calms everyone down by reassuring them that he'll probably be there, but no one seems convinced, especially when Zod, Ursa, Non and Lex arrive via smashed holes in the wall and shattered glass. Perry White is knocked senseless, and Lois is injured trying to punch Ursa in the mouth. Lex reassures Zod that Superman will arrive as he and Lois have a special relationship, much like the UK and America.

Things are looking bleak, and just when it looks like Zod is going to let Non put all of them up his own arse one by one, Superman arrives and perches on a flagpole outside the window, demanding that they all step outside and have a fight.

It's here we meet *Daily Planet* employee, and Zod sympathiser, Leueen. She seems to love the fact that Zod is in charge and takes great pleasure in trolling Lois whenever a Kryptonian is beating up Superman. 'The big one's just as strong as Superman,' she says with hungry, immoral eyes. All in all, she's a character that we can all get behind hating, and I am hoping that once the dust settled, she was arrested and thrown in a jail cell with an angry bear.

The street fight is packed full of portentous signs of the shape of things to come with Richard Lester's next Superman outing. Among the fun action, there's a lot of gags involving a very strong wind: ice creams fly out of hands to hit a man in the face, someone on roller skates in a glittery vest is zooming around awkwardly in the street, a man and a woman lose their wigs, a man carries on his phone call in a booth as it blows away around him, and a guy plays trumpet on a street corner. Remember this hilarity, as it will be back in the next movie.

Eventually, Superman realises he's outmanned, so he flies off, seemingly in disgrace. Zod is over the moon, Leueen thinks it's hilarious (her card is well and truly marked), and Lex tells them he knows exactly where he's going: north.

The gang all fly there, with Lois having to ride on Non's back and Lex's body double on Ursa's, probably hoping beyond hope he doesn't get an erection. 'A sentimental replica of a planet once vanished,' Zod says snootily as he arrives, sounding every inch like Kim Woodburn in a dusty two-up two-down. Superman steps out and declares that he expects better manners from his guests, forcing Non to attack him and fall victim to made-up power no. 4, as Superman throws his 'S' and wraps the villain in a giant plastic replica of his logo, forcing him to the ground and basically confusing everyone in the room, including Superman himself.

After some further, frankly bizarre, parlour tricks, Superman realises he can never win in a three versus one contest, so he agrees to surrender. Zod, too, has had enough of Lex's weird banter and declares that it's time he was also killed, and presumably given to Non as a fleshy fuck toy. Supes whispers to Lex that if they can get Zod and his guys in the crystal booth, he can zap their powers out of them, in the same way that he did earlier, but with Lex being an arsehole, he tells Zod of this idea and that he knows how to work it.

Zod forces Superman to enter the crystal booth, and a distraught Lois watches as the power is sapped from Superman's body, in much the same way as she did earlier that day while he was bearing down on her. After a multi-coloured lightship appears, an emotional Son of Jor-El steps out of the booth and kneels before Zod. Taking his hand as he promised he would.

It cannot be overstated just how incredible a moment this is. It's a supersonic ride up the spine, a crashing rash of goose pimples, a field of hair standing up at the back of the neck and a shot of purest, uncut adrenaline. As Superman's hand closes tightly around Zod's, with the loud crunching of bone sound effects, combined with Terence Stamp's guttural shriek of pain and the *Superman* theme breaking out of its box, you're in heaven, pure cinema heaven. Zod is defeated, and one by one the Kryptonians fall, as Lex realises that Superman switched it. He was safe inside the booth while the others all lost their powers. (Fun fact: in a deleted scene you can see Zod and his gang being arrested.)

A triumphant Superman returns Lois to her rooftop, and she promises she will never tell anyone who he really is. 'I know, Lois. I know,' he says, flying away and leaving her in darkness. At work the next day, things are mildly awkward. Lois says she didn't sleep and sat up all night crying, obviously burdened by the fact that her boyfriend is a god. She says she's jealous of the whole world, making this potential pairing very much like Joe Orton and Kenneth Halliwell, but instead of late-night cottaging, it's stopping bank robbers. To reassure her, Clark tells her he loves her, removes his glasses, then kisses her, removing all her memories of his secret identity (made-up power no. 5), which is a very worrying ability. Lois awakes from her dizzy spell and is consoled by Leueen, who should really be in a camp of some sort.

With Lois back to her hectic self, Clark cracks a wry smile as he leaves the office, knowing he's well and truly single again, and while he's riding the high, he nips back to Don's Diner to beat the shit out of Rocky in an act of the pettiest revenge possible. Yes. This is my Superman.

After a promise to the President that he'll never have sex again (with someone else), he once again flies up into the orbit and leaves us with the goodbye of that beautiful smile and a quick turn towards the sun.

FOUR

CONDORMAN

1981

THE FLYING SUPERSPY – AMERICA'S ZANIEST SECRET AGENT!

Before Disney had their renaissance – the golden years of the Marvel Cinematic Universe (MCU) – they had their discombobulating Dark Phase, when projects such as *Tron*, *The Black Hole* and *The Watcher in the Woods* littered the hallways of the Magic Castle like weird squatters spraying graffiti and warming their hands over a fire in an oilcan in an abandoned, once-great mansion. While they were all interesting and visually attractive in their own way, they were arguably too dark and too thought-provoking, and they all flopped to one degree or another. There's a common theme of fear beneath the surface of each, a terror of the unknown and a mild excavation of the uncomfortable – and that's not exactly going to sit well on a spinning teacup ride.

But hidden within this dark pocket dwells a project so terrifying and blood-curdling that even Disney themselves like to pretend it doesn't exist (it still doesn't appear on their streaming service).

Condorman.

Based on the book *The Game of X* by Robert Sheckley, the film follows the same basic plot, but 'Special Agent X' becomes 'Condorman', and, as an adaptation, it feels like an odd fit for Disney. But these were dark, strange times.

It is no exaggeration to state that the opening credits contain more excitement and promise than the rest of the film. A golden Reichsadler, branded with our hero's name, drops into view and surely represents the majority of the budget. A cartoon rendition of our hero leaps around with annoying energy and misplaced confidence before thankfully being euthanised by the falling block of gold brandishing his name. Legendary composer Henry Mancini is on board and has dug out a heroic theme that fires up the adrenaline but after a few bars feels like that meme of someone being threatened by a knifeman.

Woody Wilkins (Michael Crawford) is a frustrated cartoonist/psychopath/twat who has decided to test the veracity of his comic-book creation 'Condorman' – a man who dresses up as a bird and stops crime – by dressing up as a bird and jumping off the Eiffel Tower. His friend Harry (James Hampton) is roped in to take photos of him making a cock out of himself, and rushes to the bridge below to get into position.

'Who can save Princess Juliet, held captive by the evil Count Lorca? Who can save the city? Who? *Who*? This is a job for Condorman!' Woody says to himself as he unleashes a set of giant, ungainly orange wings that look as aerodynamic as bricks and drops from the tower, slowly drifting in the sky like a turd on a string. The music swells as Woody glides along until one of his wings breaks and he plummets into the Seine like a massive tool.

At Harry's flat, a soaked Woody can't understand why the stunt didn't work – obviously apart from the fact that jumping off a sky-high monument carrying a giant pair of unwieldy wings sounds like something even Franz Reichelt would say was questionable. Harry, like all good friends should, gives it to him straight. While he's obviously a great writer and comic-book artist, he's a shite bird, and he could have killed himself. Woody tells him that that's how he creates, that 'if Condorman can't do something in real life, then I won't have him do it in one of my comic books,' and these books already sound appalling. Woody says that kids all over the world love Condorman and they know if he's faking it. Woody, you're doing *drawings*. In a *comic book*. I think kids will understand. Jerry Siegel didn't jump to his death to prove Superman can fly. There's also the fact that Woody can pin all sorts of awful behaviour on it being something Condorman has to do in the comic. 'No, I wasn't having sex with your pie. It's something Condorman does in the next issue, and it has to be real. The kids know when I'm faking.'

Harry mentions that, for Condorman's first assignment, in the comic, he has to help the French government, which is why Woody is with him, to gain lived-in experience. Which begs the question as to what the other issues of this beloved comic have been about?

Condorman, Issue 3. Condorman has a wank in the bath.

Woody is more excited about Harry's job, as he's a spy (and Teen Wolf's dad) and a highly exciting one in his opinion. He imagines he's engaging in all sorts of cloak-and-dagger activities, probably jumping out of planes while having sex with *Playboy* girls and driving cars that shoot hot dogs. That is until Harry is compelled to point out that he's just a simple file clerk for the CIA (why he's in Paris to just do a menial filing job is anyone's guess; maybe he just really likes onions on strings). Harry does have something that Woody can help him with, however, and this might pad out another *Condorman* adventure: the CIA need some harmless papers swapped over in Istanbul, but for some reason they want a civilian to perform the drop, which makes literally no sense. Harry has been tasked with finding a normal civilian to do the job, so of course he thinks of Woody, his profoundly mentally ill friend. He's just the man to perform a simple task and will in no way act like a massive annoying tit in the process.

Sadly, Harry arrives at the train station to find Woody dressed like Humphrey Bogart and generally acting like a deluded prat. Harry removes Woody's hat and sunglasses and reminds him that he's merely a civilian. There's no need to do any impressions; he just needs to get on the train, have a drink, a nap and exchange the docs. A nice simple job. Woody then essentially comes in his pants as Harry handcuffs the important documents to his wrist, tells him again to not be a dick and waves him goodbye.

Istanbul. A city of unique historical and cultural riches, and end of the line for Woody's train. He steps into a typical restaurant: gaudy wallpaper, oversized plants, belly dancers and music that warbles and wobbles – a package altogether as authentic as Crawford's American accent.

Immediately, Woody trips on a step and shoves a waiter, who very nearly stabs a man to death with a giant flaming shish. As Woody apologises, he falls onto Natalia Rambova (Barbara Carrera) and immediately falls in love. She tells him she tripped him on purpose as she thinks they can give each other something. Of course she's talking about the document exchange, which she emphasises must be discreet, but Woody's barely listening. Instead, he's talking over her, telling her how beautiful she is, that he's not a civilian but is actually working as a top-level operative in international espionage. He asks her if the name 'Condorman' means anything to her, and why the fuck would it?

Carried away in his dangerous derangement, Woody starts to believe his own hype, ending up in a fight with a group of hoodlums who are there to get Natalia. Some 'clumsy-fu' ensues, a movie martial art perfected in the silent era that involves moves such as bending over to pick something up while someone jumps at you or accidentally knocking out three guys by moving your briefcase around.

Natalia is grateful for his help in ridding the restaurant of the bad guys, albeit accidentally, and as they exchange papers, they also exchange saliva. As Woody watches her leave, he gingerly touches his lips and rests his fingers there with a yearning desire. This is the woman he now loves, and if there's one thing you can be sure of, it's that this unhinged fantasist will now make her his latest obsession.

Moscow. Dense snow cascades in the darkness. Natalia arrives home and makes her way into the living room, only to find Krokov (Oliver Reed) waiting for her under a lamp, nursing a red wine and gripping a cigarette. He wants a full update. She tells him her suspicions about the swap were right. They didn't send a civilian, but a top operative called Condorman, and although neither has heard of him, they agree that the way he handled himself was impressive. Krokov is displeased that Natalia went to Istanbul, especially as she was compromised. She can no longer join him in Monte Carlo to meet their Arabian friends, and she requires some re-education.

Back in Paris, Woody is drawing pictures of Natalia, over and over, while playful music plays, soundtracking his descent into further compulsive behaviour. He finally settles on drawing her in Spandex, with the title 'Laser Lady', and pats himself on the back for it. You get the feeling that, had this not been interrupted, Woody would have made various video diaries of how much he loves Natalia and then eaten a bullet.

Harry's boss, Russ (Dana Elcar), has just one question: 'Who is Condorman?' Harry explains that he's from a comic book and not a real person, then goes on to explain that, as a general rule, comic-book heroes aren't real people, just drawings, and looks at Russ like he's worried about his wellbeing. This confuses Russ. A Russian named 'The Bear' has been in touch, they've decided they'd like to defect to the US, but they'll only do so under the supervision of this 'Condorman', as they trust him over all others. Harry then takes a moment and realises exactly what's happened and who could be using that name. Before you can say, 'You dumb turd,' they're in Woody's room telling him what's happened and what he needs to do. Suddenly, Woody is worried about how he could get killed helping out and refuses to do so – until Russ reveals just who 'The Bear' is. It's Natalia Rambova of the KGB. Woody changes his tune but has demands: he wants a specific list of equipment and gadgetry, or the deal is off. After an initial period of 'Are you fucking mad?', amazingly, Russ agrees.

Yugoslavia. A country that no longer exists but just screams 'spy' all the same. Woody negotiates a hilltop, making his way through long grass, past rocks and boulders while wearing the clothes of a goat farmer, as well as a fake beard, hat and the face of Geoff Capes. He meets Natalia in a pre-arranged bush. She is dressed as a Romany lady, which was apparently Woody's idea (ahem). He tells her she'd look good in anything, but before he can ask to see her bra, they're immediately captured by two of Krokov's men. They are told to hand over their weapons, but Woody tells them Condorman does not carry a gun, instead, accidentally activating his walking stick, which begins erratically firing off bullets. In the chaos, Woody grabs Natalia, and they make their escape in his battered old Romany truck.

As they wind their way through the meandering country roads Woody asks her why she defected. Natalia explains that she has been mistreated for too long by Krokov, and it's time to escape from under the terrifying thumb of late seventies Soviet oppression for her own safety. Woody interrupts her tales of abuse and hardship to ask if Krokov is her boyfriend. He's over the moon to hear that he isn't, promising her that she'll love America – especially when he locks her in his basement pit and makes her rub the lotion on her skin.

Learning of their escape, Krokov orders Morovich (Jean-Pierre Kalfon), an evil weirdo with a silver eye, and the Prognovieh, his team of bad bastards in black Porsches, to seek out and destroy Condorman at once, and so they race off in unison, like a team of angry, extra murderous crows.

As Woody and Natalia reach the small town of Palovnia, things seem quiet – almost too quiet – and before Woody can ask any further personal questions, they're set upon by Morovich's gang of gits. Woody, though, being a massive child, has an ace up his sleeve. There's no way they can outrun them in their old Romany truck, but with the quick flick of a switch, they descend into the 'Condormobile', a sleek, modified Nova Sterling, with rockets on the back, that's packed full of gadgets to outwit and outmanoeuvre the Prognovieh – which he does, one by one. The fugitives leave the area in the manner of *The Spy Who Loved Me*, speeding off a jetty into the water, the car now a high-powered hovercraft, leaving Morovich stranded on dry land and everyone wishing they were watching Roger Moore.

The entire driving sequence was performed by the outrageously brilliant, and much missed, Rémy Julienne and his equally brilliant team. In the hands of these geniuses, these sequences become more than just a game of cat and mouse on four wheels, but instead a game of Mousetrap on four wheels, with intricate pieces falling into place with perfect timing, to create something incredibly memorable. And let's face it, it's the best sequence in this film – the one everyone remembers.

Krokov is not pleased with Morovich. Not only did he let Condorman escape with Natalia, he's since found out that Woody isn't even a spy, but just a slow lad who likes to draw ladies. He's worried they'll be the laughing stock of the intelligence community. He slumps in his chair, livid, but Morovich asks for another chance. He can get Natalia back and kill this Condorman once and for all. Krokov agrees, telling him they'll be in Italy by now, and he emphasises this by hitting a map with a riding crop in the campest way imaginable. There can be no doubt that Oliver Reed is having fun in this film, especially as he seems to spend most of it in Monte Carlo. The words 'pig in shit' spring to mind.

Upon arriving in Italy, Woody and Natalia are arrested for murdering a man in Monte Carlo, which seems odd to them as they've never been there. There's no doubt that Krokov is behind this, and they're as likely to get out of jail as Charles Bronson.

A strange pipe-smoking man arrives to take them away. Woody begins firing insults at him, blathering on about how the world isn't a vacuum, and is only minutes away from bringing up George Soros when the pipe-smoking man effectively tells him to shut the fuck up and reveals himself to be Harry in disguise.

They escape, and, once again, Morovich is left to explain to Krokov that his quarry has eluded him and he has no idea where they'll be heading. But Krokov is ahead of him. He's been reading Woody's comics, and they contain all the elements of his escapes thus far: the rocket car, the hovercraft and one where they escape over the Alps. This is where they'll be going next.

Natalia loves the Alps. The mountains surround their log cabin like a blanket over cold shoulders. She walks out to take in the view and is instantly surrounded by excited children. They know her, but not from a jazz mag or leaked video, no, from the comic books. She *is* Laser Lady, and it's here that Natalia learns the disappointing fact that Woody is not in fact a James Bond-esque top spy, but Stan Lee ordered from Wish by way of a psychiatric ward.

After much thought and some talking to Harry, Natalia realises that maybe a spy is the last thing she wants. Over dinner she realises that she loves Woody for who he is, even if he is fucking insane, and that when they reach America, maybe they can be friends with benefits, or swing, or maybe he'd be cool if she banged better men? Who knows?

The next day they reach their point of escape: a cute little ski-lift contraption that Woody has designed, that allows them to whizz up the mountain on a cable and escape over the border. Everything is wonderful, and Mancini plays out a jaunty melody as they slowly climb up the steep precipice, but like most things in life, bad news is just around the corner or, in this case, just across the valley, where Morovich is perched with a sniper rifle waiting for the green light. Krokov watches the ascent, slowly leans into the walkie-talkie and softly utters: 'Shoot.' The valley rings with the sound of a bullet, and Woody and Harry's swing takes the hit, sending them plummeting miles down into the thick, deep snow. As Natalia is captured and whisked away in a helicopter, Woody and Harry sit up from their would-be snowy graves and reassure us that they're OK, more's the pity.

Monte Carlo. The place Herbie once visited before he went bananas. Natalia is imprisoned in a luxury room. She refuses to eat, refuses to sleep and doesn't welcome visitors. Krokov pops in to check on her wellbeing, and she tells him she hates him and wishes he'd killed her. He lays out the plan to her: she pretended to defect to draw out Condorman and kill him, they'll kill Morovich to preserve the truth, and she'll be saved from a slow death in a Siberian slave hut – or Pontins, as it's now called. The oil ministers arrive in the morning, and Krokov needs her to be the perfect hostess; if not, he'll have her killed.

The following day at the Russian embassy, a party is assembled for the Arab dignitaries. There was one at the casino the previous evening who caught everyone's attention. Apparently the seventh richest man in the world, he's now wandering around the party exchanging hellos from behind a pair of Aviator sunglasses. There's no doubt in my mind that this man is definitely from the Middle East, and not Michael Crawford in brown make-up and a fake, hooked nose. No. He's joined by another Arab dignitary with a full beard, sunglasses and kaffiyeh. Again, this man is definitely from the Middle East, and not Harry in disguise.

The first Arab finds Natalia alone in the garden. She's brimming with melancholy and clearly in mourning for the mentally deficient man she once loved. He makes gentle small talk with her in his gruff Middle Eastern accent before whipping off the glasses and excitedly telling her the cavalry has arrived. However, Natalia tells him she can't go, that she's changed her mind about defecting. She tells him of Krokov's plan, thereby shattering his pathetic loser dreams by basically calling him a virgin and telling him that she's going to be with Oliver Reed now. And who can blame her? He's a total babe. As she walks off with Krokov she lets slip a line they exchanged during their restaurant love-in: if he brings the dip, she'll bring the Dostoevsky. Woody watches the happy couple leave with tears in his eyes, but then realises that that last bit was code and that she does want saving after all. She really does want to be whisked away to New York to live like an American in his dungeon. Harry then pushes his button (not like that), and an explosion rattles the compound.

Woody breaks free of his disguise, rescues Natalia and takes her to the roof, where he unveils his final form: an orange suit covered in drawn-on feather effects, a pair of goggles with a yellow nosepiece and massive, unwieldy outstretched wings that offer little to no aerodynamic benefit. He tells Natalia to hold on tight, and a watching Krokov simply cannot fathom what he is seeing. Woody and Natalia glide away from the roof, over Monte Carlo harbour, and drift down to a waiting, souped-up rocket boat to make their escape.

However, Krokov isn't giving in that easily. Once again he unleashes the Prognovieh (Aquatic Division), who give chase and open fire on Condorman's superboat. Woody takes out most of them with a mounted laser, but one remains: Krokov and Morovich's rocket boat. Mercifully, a helicopter arrives and lifts Woody, Harry and Natalia to safety, causing Krokov to bale and Morovich to crash into a cliff and explode. Our heroic trio wave at the villain as he bobs up and down in the water, laughing at him like they've learned nothing.

A Goodyear blimp hovers over the Dodgers' stadium in Los Angeles, with a message welcoming Natalia to the USA. There's baseball going on below, a sport that couldn't be more American if it shot everyone. Woody sits next to a beaming Natalia, who's still pinching herself that she made it. She can have as much democracy as she can eat now and drink a big cup of the American Way. She and Woody embrace and kiss, and she tells him he's not bad at it, which sort of suggests he was once very bad, but they need to work on the fact that he's clearly out of his tiny mind. Harry interrupts the two lovebirds with a message from Russ up in the blimp. He leans forward and says to Woody, 'Have you ever thought of taking Condorman to . . .' As we try to decipher what he's asking, the words 'The End' spring up on the screen like a middle finger. One can only imagine where Condorman would have gone next. Space? Ecuador? The Falkland Islands? Up Russ's arse? We'll never know.

Condorman made $9.5 million on a $14 million budget, so that's probably why. But with a project this brave and stupid, it was always going to be a swing and miss, though I do wish Disney+ would find the ball and let the world see him again.

Who can save Princess Juliet, held captive by the evil Count Lorka? Who can save the city? Who? *Who*? This is a job for Condorman.

FIVE

SPIDER-MAN: THE DRAGON'S CHALLENGE

1981

THE AMAZING SUPER HERO BATTLES THE MASTERS OF KUNG-FU

Long before the Spider-Men we know today, Nicholas Hammond was Peter Parker. He had no skateboard, sweet backflips or rad bicycles. This Parker was armed only with flares, a disco haircut and a camera. This was the seventies, a time of grime, crime, corruption, and crime again. Yes, he was once a von Trapp and ran away from the Nazis, but he's grown so much as a person since then (but still tends to run away). He had his own TV series, for two seasons, with this 'movie' being a two-part TV story (*The Chinese Web*) cut and shut together to form an 'exciting' motion picture.

Hong Kong. A huge, bustling city, with a port busier than your mum and vast sums of money pouring in and out of Victoria Harbour like the inevitable ebb and flow of the South China Sea. Min Lo Chan (Benson Fong), the Chinese Minister of Industrial Development, boards a plane at the airport, watched by an evil-looking man dressed like he's on standby for a porn shoot that afternoon. He watches the plane kiss the sky, then travels back to his boss on various forms of public transport (he is clearly not on expenses), the evil Zeider, to pass on the news that Chan has jumped on a plane to America.

Zeider (Richard Erdman) is a middle-aged American man with a great deal of influence and money. He's sitting in lavish opulence on the roof of his fancy building, having his portrait painted while dressed like a Ribena berry. He's haggling with Mrs Brent, a posh antiques dealer, on the legitimacy of her goods and the prices she sells them at. The idea that he is a real bad guy with money, power and influence is being pushed, but in reality he seems like a drunk pantomime extra who's watched too much *Lovejoy*.

When Zeider hears of the minister's departure to New York, he is surprised, as Chan has charges levelled against him. His henchman informs him that there are people in New York who can prove that he's innocent, and this is bad news for Zeider. If he's found innocent, Chan will award the contract for construction of a steel mill to the Canadians – an outcome that would make even Thanos shit his toga. Zeider suggests that if Chan never leaves New York, then all his problems will be solved. What an evil man.

Chan's first port of call once he arrives in New York is his old pal J. Jonah Jameson (Robert F. Simon). Jameson immediately compliments him by mentioning that he looks younger than him, which wouldn't be hard, as J. J. looks about ninety here. Chan fires back, saying that Jameson looks 'distinguished', which is a very polite way of saying 'old as fuck'. Jameson reveals that they went to college together, probably rooming with Moses.

Chan asks for help. In 1946, before he came to the US, he was a Chinese spy. He gave some information to the US government – to three Marines in particular – via an old schoolteacher friend, who was later murdered. He was offered money to do it but turned it down. So, he asks Jameson to help him find these Marines. No one must know about this, not even the government, as he reveals that he's been charged with selling state secrets, and murder, in China. These men know he's innocent, and their testimony will get the charges dropped. I heard this was the original plot to *Infinity War*, but it was dropped as it was too scary.

Jameson remembers that Peter Parker recently did a story about a Marine officer – he literally says this out loud – and may have a way to get the information without alerting the state department. This thrill ride must never end.

Just when you think you can't handle more excitement, who should stride out dressed in military finery, but Ted Danson, as Major Collings. He approaches his car looking like a barrel of sex that's been gently warmed by an open fire, only to be greeted by Peter Parker, who needs his unofficial help on finding the three Marines from 1946. Collings tells him he will get it for him the next day as Parker's article about him was very good (sort of suggesting that it mentioned how handsome he is). Parker is careful once again to underline the fact that no one must know he's looking for this information, as a man could die (of boredom).

Armed with the information, Parker takes Chan to the dingiest underground newspaper archive in the world, to look for the whereabouts of these men. He confirms that Ted Danson came through for them with names, but Chan isn't really enjoying the vibes down in this weird basement. As he goes on to express that he's essentially shitting himself, Parker suddenly stops what he's doing while his eyes flash like insane Belisha beacons.

Worry not, this is his 'spider-sense' kicking in, even if it comes across like he's possessed by the devil himself and, rather than help Chan, will stab his bum with a crucifix before throwing himself out of a window. His sight-beyond-sight has spotted a big, burly man with a gun heading their way, so quick as a flash he makes his excuses to Chan and appears from behind a filing cabinet in his full Spider-Man regalia: the tight red Spandex suit, the baffling utility belt, the silver wrist brace and the milk-bottle-top eyes. Yes, the suit looks pretty ropey, but as a child I thought it was incredibly exciting.

As the gunman takes aim, Spider-Man leaps into action and pushes some cabinets over before running away accompanied by rather lovely disco music. Despite being able to crawl up walls, stick to the ceiling and swing wherever he wants, the Amazing Spider-Man loiters on a staircase and blindly looks around to see if the gunman is anywhere nearby (that spider-sense seems to have abandoned him when he really needed it) before jumping out on him and having a mild brawl with the would-be killer, that he barely wins. As the attacker lies unconscious, Spidey shouts that someone needs to call the police, then runs away.

After the police have done the bare minimum possible and left, there's talk of writing an amazing story about the altercation, but Jameson kills it, saying that they need to keep everything they're investigating secret, and if I were Parker, I wouldn't want people knowing that a portly man nearly beat me up. Jameson wants Parker to carry on finding the Marines and report to Emily Chan with his results.

Zeider is feasting upon a succulent Chinese meal when he gets a call from his henchman Evans (Hagan Beggs) to tell him the hit has failed. Zeider is not concerned with the details; he tells Evans to just get the job done by any means necessary and at any cost, though he will not be paying for this long-distance call. So, Evans and his associates storm Chan's house while he's entertaining his niece and Parker, with the latter running away in the middle of the break-in. Secret identity or not, that just makes you look like a chicken. As Chan and his niece cower in fear, knowing that they will soon come to harm, Spider-Man jumps in through the same window Parker exited and fights off the intruders (although Evans gets away) while jumping around the room like a stuntman on cocaine. Chan thanks him for his rescue, but then tells them both that he thinks he's having a cardiac arrest.

Parker arrives just as the bad guys are being arrested and Chan is being carried out on a gurney by ambulance men. His niece basically tells Parker he's a gutless coward and that everyone would be much happier if he just fucked off and never spoke to them again. He insists that he ran away to get the police, but it doesn't wash with her. She's done with him, and this news hits him hard. If only he could tell her that he ran away to get changed and then came back and beat everyone up, even though he could have just done that anyway. A policeman tries to console him as the ambulance drives away, but he's too upset. He leaves the scene, presumably to go and lay an egg.

Parker engineers a chance meeting with Professor Dent (John Milford), a lecturer on Far East history at the university, as he's leaving for a dentist's appointment. He tells him his lectures have really had an effect on him, and then we get some incredible dialogue.

'I've been working for a paper for a year or so. I've encountered some really fascinating people, interesting stories. It's amazing, you know? Some of them are funny, some of them are not so funny.'

'Yes.'

Before they stop to pick up their Emmy, Parker gets to the point. He asks Dent about Min Lo Chan, and the name causes him to freeze on the spot. Dent served with Chan in the Marine Corps in 1946. The professor turns to Parker and tells him to drop it, and that he's going to pretend this conversation never happened. Parker watches in anguish as he walks away in anger. Gone now are the chances of finding out what happened, and gone now, surely, is that Emmy.

On the way back from the university, Parker notices he's being followed, so he darts into a parking lot and changes into Spider-Man. He waits in the darkness for his pursuer to find him. It's another of Evans' henchmen. He's wielding a gun and has orders to kill Parker. Spidey webs him and then tells him he's going to get charged with a felony for carrying a deadly weapon. The villain, as it hilariously turns out, can't afford another felony on his record. He'll go away for a long time if charged, so he spills his guts: Evans will kill Chan in the hospital the following night and he's also sent two guys to pick up some microfilm that will give them the location of the Marines. Spider-Man tells him he will tell the police he was very cooperative and then runs away, leaving this man webbed to the back of a random car, alone in a car park, with no consideration whatsoever for that car owner maybe having to leave in an emergency.

Parker races to the hospital to warn Emily Chan, but she doesn't want to hear a word of it. She's still hurting from him literally jumping out of a window to save his own life when hers was in danger. He emphasises that this information comes direct from Spider-Man, that they're friends, which Jameson backs up, telling her he gets pictures from him but no porn. 'I don't see what you two have in common,' she says, heavily implying that Parker is a big old shitty chicken. The gang decide to proceed with the plan to print a false story in two newspapers announcing Chan's death – but it has to be a noble death, like a mild heart attack or saving the regiment, and not that he fell on a loose dildo on a slippy bathroom floor. Emily agrees. They tell Chan, and he makes Emily and Parker promise that they'll work together in finding whoever is behind all this. He offers to pay for sending the Marines to China to testify to his innocence. Emily isn't that keen to go out into the field with a man who is basically a full-feathered coward but promises her uncle she will do her best.

Spidey foils the robbers trying to get the microfilm but is shot in the back while running away. Does this idiot not know he has web shooters and can swing in the air? How long will this fraudulent fucker operate by jumping on people and then running away? The robbers return to give Evans the bad news, only to find that he's happier than a pig in a river of shit. He holds up a newspaper with the headline that Chan is dead, already excited about returning to Hong Kong as a hero.

Parker tries again with Dent, but this time returns armed with receipts; Dent stole money, killed a schoolteacher and received a dishonourable discharge from the Marines. He's their last hope as the other Marines are either dead or dying. He must search his heart and help a man in dire need of assistance. Dent realises that it's no good resisting any more, but he also wants to clear his name. He didn't kill the schoolteacher or steal the money – another Marine did, and planted the evidence on him to ensure he got the blame. Parker is doubtful (as that Marine is dead), but Dent says that, before he died, he sent a letter taking the blame, including pictures, and with Parker's assurance that the newspaper will back his case, he agrees to testify.

Evans returns to Hong Kong like a dog with two dicks, desperate to see Zeider and tell him the great news, but Zeider is not impressed at all. He's found out that Parker, Emily and Dent are coming to Hong Kong to testify and clear Chan's name, and why would they want to do that if he was dead? He proposes that if they allow them to do just that, Chan will mysteriously come back to life. Evans sits through all this like a cat watching an episode of *Twin Peaks*. So, Zeider has to spell it out to him: they can't allow them to succeed. He can't lose that deal. Once they arrive, they must be stopped, and they will select the greatest 'Kung-Fu Men' Hong Kong has to offer.

Upon arrival in Hong Kong, Parker and his friends immediately receive a message telling them they must go to a different location. Although he's immediately suspicious, Emily tells him he needs to chill out: they're in Hong Kong now and therefore much safer, even though they have been assigned with two men to keep them safe. Parker suggests that they should keep away from crowds, as they could still be in danger. Dent tells him that he needs to relax. He's agreed to testify, and he has two days in Hong Kong that he doesn't want to spend in his hotel room. There is no doubt in my mind that Dent has decided that he has thirty years of sex tourism to catch up on, and it's worth dying for.

The following day, in broad daylight, in a busy area of Hong Kong, they're attacked by Kung-Fu Men, and Dent is kidnapped, and I hope that hand relief was worth it, sir. Now, not only will Parker have to find you, he will also have to work out how to say 'I fucking told you so' in Cantonese.

He immediately changes into Spider-Man and awkwardly runs along the dock watching the Kung-Fu Men loading Dent's unconscious body into a boat. He then gets in a boat of his own and follows, in full costume, which is like watching Superman queue at departures. They manage to lose him, so Parker returns to Emily and tells her that, luckily, before Dent was captured, he put a tracking bug on him, so they'll be able to find him easily.

After yet another bungled attempt at being Spider-Man, he's fished out of the river by locals, having taken a tranquilliser dart in the arm and fallen off a roof. Emily is at his bedside as his rescuers decide to remove his mask, I guess to check that it isn't Norman Wisdom in there. She's shocked to see it's Parker, having pegged him as an almighty fucking loser, and can now reconcile all the facts about why he went missing. He isn't an almighty fucking loser after all, just an almighty fucking loser who dresses up in Spandex. He comes to and sees Emily's confused face looking back at him. She says she feels like a fool for doubting him and tells him Dent is being held at a tower, but that he should rest. He refuses to do so and suits back up to try and save the day.

A lone hero climbs the walls of Jardine House, a vast, looming skyscraper that stands proud by the harbour. The hero makes his way up the exterior wall, floor by floor, barely touching the walls with hands or feet, as if pulled by unseen ropes, while sexy disco music keeps the beat and a mounted camera chills the blood regarding how high up it really is. He reaches the top and, using his scanner, makes his way to where Dent is being held, dispatching Kung-Fu Man after Kung-Fu Man as he goes – and with the disco backing track and low-grade film, it all feels a bit Dirk Diggler.

Dent is tied to a chair, his face covered with a blindfold. Across the room, Evans and Zeider kill time having a chat, presumably about how they're the worst fucking international criminals since John Darwin and his wife. Silence is broken, though, as Spidey jumps in through the window and zooms across the table on his stomach in one sweet, sleek motion, taking out Evans with one loud bundle. He then uses his webbing to fling a door in Zeider's face, which is hilarious. It knocks him out cold, thus ending this whole sorry, pathetic nightmare.

With Zeider and Evans safely in jail, Chan's name is cleared, and Emily thanks Parker for all his help while also reassuring him that his secret identity is safe. She won't tell anyone he's Spider-Man or that he's fucking useless. She's going to stay in Hong Kong and learn what it is to be Chinese.

'Will you ever come back to Hong Kong?' Emily asks as he's about to board his plane. 'I have a reason to now,' he says, which is a very polite way of saying no. They exchange a short kiss, and Parker then does what he does best: leaves immediately. He'll head back to New York, once again to assume the mantel of 'Friendly Neighbourhood Spider-Man', where he'll jump on criminals and then run away, leaving New Yorkers safe in the knowledge that they'll always be safe, if they learn to take self-defence classes of their own.

This was to be the last Spider-Man film for twenty-one years, and the last outing on screen of Nicholas Hammond's interpretation, but if you're around my age, you'll always remember him as the very first live-action Spidey and, like me, you'll probably never forget those shiny milk-bottle-top eyes, the Kenny Everett sketch and that very unique, and adorable, wall-crawling.

SIX

SWAMP THING

1982

SCIENCE TRANSFORMED HIM INTO A MONSTER.
LOVE CHANGED HIM INTO EVEN MORE!

'Not long ago, in the unexplored reaches of an unmapped swamp, the creative genius of one man collided with another's evil dream, and a monster was born.'

In 1980, uber-comic-book fan and comic-book writer now turned producer Michael E. Uslan managed to secure the film rights for a relatively new property over at DC: *Swamp Thing*, the tale of a scientist turned living plant-man created by Len Wein and Bernie Wrightson.

Uslan wasted no time in securing a director, turning to someone who was used to documenting misfits that roam the unmapped underbelly of America: Wes Craven. Craven had never heard of the character but liked the idea; he saw it as a great story, as well as an opportunity to break back into the mainstream. He'd made *Last House on the Left* the same year *Swamp Thing* was born and had spent the remainder of the decade pumping out grimy horror movies. They have all become cult classics for good reason, but here was a chance to show the world that he wasn't just about weirdos hanging around in unmapped areas of wild America . . .

Oh.

Out in the derelict wastes of boggy swampland sits an old, abandoned church. Lost to a levee break fifty years ago, with its exterior long drowned, it now serves as a research facility. Alice Cable (Adrienne Barbeau) has arrived from the government to serve as a replacement for a scientist who died recently. While she may come over all corporate in her lanyard, skirt suit and heels, and complaints about the lack of good restaurants, she's got what it takes. Alice knows everything about the equipment in the facility, which doesn't go unnoticed. She's introduced to Harry Ritter (Don Knight), a gruff man from the north of England who is basically Crocodile Dundee by way of *Coronation Street*. He takes her to the top-secret underground lab, where she meets Alec Holland (Ray Wise of *Twin Peaks* fame), a sexy scientist who has a love for all things green. A lovely guy, with a smooth demeanour, but you know things aren't right when his sister Linda (Nannette Brown) drops a 'You don't have to be crazy to be around him, but it helps'. He tells Alice that he'll give her a tour of the swamp, an idea she's not that keen on, but he uses his suave, handsome ways to talk her into it.

As they skirt around the wetlands, he professes his love of the place, of the trees, of the animals that live in harmony with nature, and he tells her that there's so much beauty in the ugliness of the swamp, if only you open your eyes to it. Oh, Alec, why don't you just marry the damn swamp? She's not so convinced. She really hates bugs and her predecessor was literally killed by the swamp. Alec disagrees – it was sad, sure, but it was only an alligator doing its thing. Bloody hippie.

They return from their pleasant little jaunt with a broken sensor to examine. But they're met by the ire of Harry Ritter. He's livid that his top scientist has been taken out into the world by a 'stupid broad', as their top-secret project could be jeopardised. Alec tells him it was all his idea, but Harry stomps away barking that a woman has no place in the swamp, and he is so lucky there's no HR department there, or he could well be up before a tribunal.

Alice must be wondering what she's in for over the next few weeks, stuck in a fucking soppy nightmare with a horny hippie environmentalist and a drunk misogynist from Manchester.

Scientific progress has been made, in a way, though. Linda and her brother seem to have accidentally invented a new form of nitroglycerine that's lime-green, which they seem chuffed about, but their superiors are not so impressed. That's not the purpose of their studies. Alec explains to Alice that they've been developing a way to combine plant and animal, to create an exciting new being that's never existed on the planet before, and the first question should be: why? It turns out that good old Alec wants to use this technology to evolve ways that food can grow in the most inhospitable areas of the globe in order to solve world hunger. Isn't he just a dreamboat?

They place their new exploding sample under a microscope and are flabbergasted by how quickly it grows and multiplies. It would seem this formula is able to create rapid growth, though they just need to work the kinks out regarding the drawback that it also explodes. Alec is so happy that he pulls Alice in for a snog, which she seems to accept, though once again, HR would probably see this differently.

Things couldn't be better in the lab that night, so it's a real shame that a group of armed mercenaries crash the party, knock out Alice and ruin everything. As Linda and Alec are held at gunpoint, Harry walks in to ask the armed men what's taking them so long, and Alec cannot begin to fathom the levels of betrayal at work here. But there's a bigger surprise.

Harry peels off his face to reveal that he is actually Anton Arcane (Louis Jourdan), the smooth French leader of a paramilitary organisation (the PlantRA, if you will) desperate to steal their research and use it for their own nefarious ends. He wants all the materials relating to their work and, when Linda tries to resist, he has her shot to show he means business. Overcome with grief, Alec tries to escape with a beaker of the formula grasped in his panicked hands, but he's tripped up and he drops it all over himself, leaving the lab to erupt in flames. He climbs to his feet, covered from head to toe in angry fire, and slowly staggers out of the lab as a one-man Pink Floyd album cover while everyone watches, mouths agape, checking their watches and wondering just how the fuck this is taking so long. As his burning body races over the dock and leaps into the water, it's clear that it's going to take more than the tube of Savlon from the lab's first aid kit to fix him up.

It's a very impressive burn, nevertheless, performed by stuntman Anthony Cecere, who performed an equally impressive act in *A Nightmare on Elm Street* two years later.

The following morning, with the lab now a heap of smouldering ashes, Arcane's men place a beleaguered Alice in a boat and take her out to the middle of the swamp in order to drown her in the fetid water, and as Ferret (David Hess) clamps his hand to her head, the struggles cease underwater and it seems the job is done. That is until a giant green man surfaces with incandescent anger, flips the boat into the air, killing most of the men, and then vanishes back into the marsh.

The original intention was to have Ray Wise play the Swamp Thing, with Dick Durock serving as stuntman, but their body sizes were so different that they decided to go with Durock as the monster.

Arcane perches in his leather armchair, a cultured smile beaming. He's poring over the captured research books through his enormous glasses while sipping a cup of coffee. With these books he can begin work immediately, and power absolute will be in his hands: the world must either bow or starve. As he reaches the final paragraph of the sixth book, he notices a problem: it's not the last book at all, it's from two weeks ago, and it's a drawing of a pair of tits and an unfinished sudoku. Without the missing volume, he can't proceed, and all that murder will have been for nothing.

Alice finds a rundown gas station in the middle of nowhere and meets a precocious boy named Jude (Reggie Batts) sitting outside on a rickety chair drinking a bottle of Coke. He says she can use his phone, so she makes a hurried call to Harry, as she has no idea he's actually dead. Arcane picks up and puts on his best northern accent, telling her he's been down t' pit all day flying whippets and about how great Eric Cantona is. He asks where she is and if she managed to take anything before she got out. She confirms she has the missing book and that Arcane is behind it all.

After another attempt to snatch her is foiled by the mysterious green man, Arcane asks for a full description of it, what its behaviour is like and what its ideal Sunday is. He's told it's big, angry, green, can withstand bullets and is basically a walking tree (the Incredible Mulch). It's immediately clear to Arcane what is going on: this 'Swamp Thing' is obviously a pure element created from the formula itself, and he wants it captured in one piece for study. His men are confused: just how are they supposed to find this thing? It always manages to disappear. But Arcane, being clever, sexy and French, knows exactly how: get the woman, get the monster.

The Swamp Thing walks through the wreckage of his lab, touching stuff and remembering happier days. On finding his sister's necklace on the floor, he opens it and finds that it contains family portraits. Alice is smiling. He looks normal. Tears well and tumble down his viridescent cheeks. Where once was a handsome, toned face is now a green belt of empty country. His body, now a big arterial map of despair, with vines and veins protruding all over, is the sort of thing Monty Don would make if he did his own *Weird Science* film.

This place of advanced creation is now the dictionary definition of destruction, and as he slowly wanders around the ruined laboratory trying to utilise the unbroken test tubes and beakers, he has no idea

Alice is watching. His hands are unable to hold the delicate glassware, and so, in a fit of rage, he finishes the job and destroys the rest of the room himself, roaring like a monster. Alice has seen enough. She races to the back of the building to grab the book she stashed, and as she and Jude escape by boat, Swamp Thing emerges from the fog and watches them go, saddened by the fact that he'll probably never get that shag, not even green fingers and tops.

With yet another attack foiled, Arcane and his men are forced to concede that maybe this creature isn't as stupid as they are. It seems to be able to second guess every move they make and get out of every trap they set. Like a brilliant chess player, he's always one step ahead, so it's time to take his queen.

Alice watches helplessly as Jude's lifeless body floats down the river in their boat. She screams his name as she's dragged away by soldiers, and as the boat bumps against the bank Swamp Thing arrives. He cradles the dead boy in his arms and looks on forlornly. There's blood on Jude's face, and his eyes are closed, bereft of life: nothing can be done. He places his hand on the boy's face, and within moments a green glow emanates from the ends of his fingers. Rather than turning Jude into a bunch of lilies, he brings him back to the land of the living. Jude recognises him as the person who saved his life about 300 times in the last twenty minutes and asks if he's a friend of Alice's (not sure if that's a euphemism). When he nods, Jude tells him he has the missing book and that he can't think of anyone safer to leave it with than him.

Ferret has momentarily lost Alice, again, like the bellend he is, and is chasing her through the woods when he stumbles, again, upon the man in green. This time, instead of running away, he uses his brain and pulls out a machete, chopping Swamp Thing's arm off. He enjoys the moment, but his joy is short-lived, as the monster responds by crushing his head and breaking his spine. Life is full of fleeting victories.

'That's very kind,' Alice says to the man in green when he offers her a flower. They're sitting in a picturesque corner of the bog, in a pocket of calm, suffused in shards of sunlight and a world away from the recent explosions and carnage. He begins to speak, slowly, shakily and awkwardly, telling her that there is much beauty in the swamp if you know where to look. And it's then that the penny drops, and she realises who he really is. He is Alec Holland, and he's now a fucking cheese plant on legs. She asks, understandably, if this is all a dream, and Alec soon asks himself the same question when she steps into the water in the nude to do some gratuitous bathing. He watches on like John Belushi on that ladder, but soon snaps out of it and decides that, rather than standing there watching her wet naked body – and probably, hilariously, growing an extra stump – he'll leave her to it and go for a walk. He's clearly forgotten that in this universe, as soon as his back is turned, Alice is snatched by Arcane and his men, which is exactly what happens. As he rushes to save her, he's smothered in a net and taken away for testing.

With the beast in chains and Alice in a dress, Arcane has decided to hold a celebration dinner. He stands to speak to his very stupid army, raising a toast to their hard work and mourning the loss of those who couldn't be there, with the line, 'Regrets are trifles, when one considers the grand design' – a delivery of such aplomb that it deserves a round of applause. Apparently, Louis Jourdan was very hands-on with his own dialogue, and it shows. Every time he speaks it's like a vintage Bentley purring into a demolition derby. As the toast is imbibed, he lets slip that the first compound is ready and has already been consumed. Alice asks if he has taken it himself, but Arcane tells her that Bruno (Nicholas Worth), his loyal henchman, has just drunk it. Everyone then watches in curious terror as he writhes, wriggles and screams while turning into a small monkey man with big ears. Not sure Nobel will give a prize for that, my man.

'Why doesn't Bruno have your strength?' Arcane asks Swamp Thing as he sits chained in his dungeon room. He explains that they followed his notes to the letter, but instead of a hulking mass of strength and intelligence, they've created Bob Hoskins if he fell in a tumble dryer. He's given an ultimatum: either he explains what went wrong or Alice dies. As he watches her being chained to the wall, thus giving birth to a grunge band, he explains that there's no trickery or missing extra ingredient; the formula just amplifies what lies beneath. Bruno clearly has a little monkey inside of him, and that's what he ended up with, but we don't talk about Bruno.

Arcane accepts this explanation, suggesting that because Bruno was thick as shit, he transformed into an Oompa Loompa with male-pattern baldness, but if a genius were to drink it, then he would become 'monumental in body, as well as spirit'. So, he shuffles upstairs to his study and pours himself a goblet of magic compound. He takes his poison and then steps out onto the verandah to speak to himself, with yet another soliloquy that has no place in a film about a man who turns into a shrub: 'Not to be the phenomenon, but the thing in itself. Eternal, absolute beauty, absolute strength and power, physical and spiritual. To be the world, and own it.' He then sits down in a chair and turns into a wolf-fish-pig on two legs. Legend has it that it was supposed to be a simple werewolf, but the filmmakers were worried that everyone had 'werewolf fatigue' after the recent spate of films, so they went with this fucking mad thing instead.

Swamp Thing and Alice escape back to the swamp via a secret door, and they're about to embrace sweet freedom when they hear a disconcerting sound. Rising from the water and dry ice is the Arcane wolf-fish-pig, and he's got a fucking sword. They fight, wrestle, punch, roll and swim their way through the swamp, but in the end Swamp Thing is the victor, plunging the sword right through the weird aberration and then carrying Alice away to safety.

As he leads her to dry land and turns to leave, she asks if she can come with him and help him start his work again, but he reminds her he's got fucking rhododendrons for hands, so there'd be no point. 'You need to tell our story,' he says before reminding her that he'll always be out there if she needs him and he'll see her soon and she's definitely not allowed to get another boyfriend.

As Jude arrives and embraces Alice, they both watch as Swamp Thing trudges back into the undergrowth to be alone with his beloved swamp, at one with his precious flowers and at home among the trees he calls his best mates. He'll be bored stupid within five minutes and may come back for a chat, though.

Wes Craven didn't work again until *A Nightmare on Elm Street* two years later, which sadly meant that this step into comic-book science fiction didn't pay off, but who remembers that now? He went on to bring the world another burnt man out for revenge, succeeding far beyond his wildest dreams, ironically. As for Michael E. Uslan, this disappointment didn't last long, either. He also co-owned the movie rights to another DC hero called Batman, and within seven years that investment would end up paying off rather handsomely.

SEVEN

SUPERMAN III

1983

IF THE WORLD'S MOST POWERFUL COMPUTER CAN CONTROL EVEN SUPERMAN . . . NO ONE ON EARTH IS SAFE!

'What do you go and see? Pictures, comedies mainly?' legendary talk-show host Johnny Carson asks in his usual warm and charming drawl from behind his world-famous desk. It was 20 May 1981, and guest Richard Pryor, slouched in his chair, baseball cap perched on head and wearing mainly beige, sheepishly confesses that he really wants to see *Superman II*. As he goes on to explain to Carson what it's about and how excited he was seeing the previews, his whole demeanour changes. He visibly lights up (not in a freebasing accident way) and gesticulates madly, eyes awash with excitement and boundless giddy adventure. He concludes his statement by pumping the sky and shouting, 'Yay, Supe!'

Carson chuckles and cuts to the commercial, unaware that many miles away, the producers of *Superman* were most definitely watching, and were now hatching a new idea for their next foray with the Man of Steel. What if Richard Pryor could meet Superman? What if they could harness Pryor's massive fame and box-office appeal and combine it with the power of the last Kryptonian? Pryor was contacted and given a cool $5 million to join the team, an offer he happily accepted. Gone now were the plans of Dudley Moore becoming Mister Mxyzptlk or Supergirl turning up to help. The focus was now well and truly on Pryor and how he could fit within the 'Big Apricot' that is Metropolis.

The original plan for the third film was for Richard Donner to hand the reins to Tom Mankiewicz, stepping back to be the producer, but seeing as Donner was fired midway through making *Superman II*, back-to-back with the first film, this was now scrapped, and Richard Lester was once again brought in to oversee the production. The producers were happy with what he brought to the table in the second film, and seeing as he was cheaper and lived in England, it was a no-brainer.

Lester was now able to make the Superman film he wanted to make, and it would be 100% his project. This is immediately obvious with the opening 'slapstick' routine, which is like a knackered clown car slowly driving through a burning old folks' home. It's a bizarre, elongated set piece pulled from Chaplin's bin, or Laurel's arse: a blind man confuses a giant road-marking machine for his own, much smaller and non-metal dog. Another man has a paint bucket land on his head and seems utterly incapable of removing it while falling over people who were just moments ago enjoying a lunch and are now having to deal with this fuckwit rolling around in their lap with a bucket on his head. Custard pies are being delivered somewhere and end up in faces. This already feels about as far away as you can get from Marlon Brando doing Space Rumpole. However, despite the desperately sparse banquet of LOLZ, it must be admitted that it's all quite charming, or at least it seemed so if you were a child in 1983.

Gus Gorman (Richard Pryor) is unemployed, and seemingly unemployable after having his benefits stopped, so he takes up the opportunity to 'retrain for cyber'. Within minutes of him sitting behind a vast computer, he's made it make beeping noises, a feat he is unable to explain to his supervisor, who for some reason is incredibly impressed by the chirping cursors that fly across the screen like Horace Goes Trepanning. The film is not so subtly trying to tell us that computers are evil and shouldn't be trusted, as they are not born of love and can't go to the pub. Even the drinks machines tell you what they are pouring, and I reckon if we don't watch it, they'll become self-aware and take over the world, maybe even putting Superman in a ball bag.

During this comedy funeral, Clark Kent emerges for the first time, trying to buy a newspaper from a vending machine, but in his usual bumbling style, he rips it in half. After a moment of quiet contemplation, when I am sure he wonders why he's bothering with this shambling alter ego, he simply puts half the paper under his arm and moves along whistling, knowing full well that he will soon be caught up in this clusterfuck of broken jokes. It's not long though before Superman emerges during the mayhem. Clark dashes into a photo booth to change, and as the pictures fall out of the machine, it's a nice touch that the boy who collects them is played by Aaron Smolinski, who played Clark as a tiny infant in *Superman: The Movie*. Superman takes the Clark pictures and hands the boy the rest before flying a few yards to rescue a man who has become trapped in his car and is seemingly unable to open any doors.

Reeve was not best happy with how this film turned out. Despite interviews at the time where he sounded overjoyed that Pryor was on board, he would later say in his autobiography that, although he liked the 'Evil Superman and good Clark Kent' scene, he felt overall that the film sacrificed too much for the sake of being silly.

Talking of people who weren't happy, over at the *Daily Planet* Lois Lane (Margot Kidder) is asking permission to go to Bermuda and is thus waved out of the film in one swoop. Retribution for her part in the minor mutiny that occurred when Richard Donner was fired, and there may as well be a scene where the producers help her pack and drive her to the airport. The real talk in the room, though, is all about Ross Webster (Robert Vaughn), a Lidl Lex Luthor, a character who, if played by anyone else, would be instantly forgettable, but in the wise hands of Vaughn is heaps of fun. It seems he is causing quite the stir after being nominated as Humanitarian of the Year. Jimmy Olsen (Marc McClure) attended the ceremony and spent all evening taking pictures of Lorelei Ambrosia's (Pamela Stephenson's) tits. One supposes that such an action would have been forgivable if he were still 'Young Jimmy Olsen' – a sort of youthful exuberance – but the fact that he's now in his mid-thirties should probably be a sign that he needs some sort of intervention, maybe a ban from hanging out with the lads from Porky's and some time away from the camera. It's at this point that we are also introduced to Ross Webster's sister, Vera (jazz singer Annie Ross), with a picture of her face that makes everyone physically sick, which must have been a nice bit of the script for her to read. Clark Kent appears to ask Perry White (Jackie Cooper) if he can go back to his old Smallville school and write about a reunion, which frankly sounds as boring as shit, but Perry seems to be saying yes to everything today.

Clark is punished ultimately, however, as he's forced to travel by coach to Smallville with Jimmy Olsen. Jimmy has a minor affliction, in that he won't shut the fuck up. Luckily for poor, weary Clark, there's a chemical factory fire, so the bus must pull over and let the passengers out. Now they can all stretch their legs and presumably breathe in the toxic chemical gasses and die of cancer within two years.

Clark races into his Superman costume and within moments is on the scene to help the firefighters (led by Apone from *Aliens*, fact fans) put this raging fire out. However, it quickly becomes apparent that they're having problems with their hoses (it can happen at that age) and may need to seek an alternative water source. To make matters much, much worse, a scientist then tells Supes that the jars of beltric acid he's protecting will create deadly travelling clouds of melting death if they get hot – plus there's a hose-pipe ban. So, time is of the essence. After providing a slide for some trapped boffins made out of a dangerous chemical chimney that probably gave them all leukaemia, Superman flies off at top speed to a nearby lake to freeze it and bring it back like a tray of fog. As he lets go of the icy lake, the heavens open, and torrents of rain put out the blaze, again, presumably, releasing further deadly fumes, with Superman being heralded as the hero that he most certainly is.

Jimmy, meanwhile, has broken his leg, after sticking his nose in where it doesn't belong to take a picture of some fire, only to then fall off a ladder like a big twat, so no school trip for him. He'll be taking his bad pictures from his hospital bed, probably of out-of-focus arses.

Gus has got himself a fancy job. He's put his magic beep-beep computer skills to good use and secured employment with Webscoe Industries, a company owned by Ross Webster. Things seem to be going great, with Gus probably applying his beep-beep technique all over the place. Coffee machine broken? Just have Gus point at it with a computer pen, and it will soon go beep-beep. Problems with the photocopier? Beep-beep will sort it in a flash.

Gus is sunning himself in the warm glow of his genius when he gets his first pay slip. That bright mood suddenly turns dark when he realises that he has to pay tax. A co-worker explains that it's money for when he retires, but Gus says he'd rather have it now while he's 'young', so he can 'boogie-boogie' – which historians now know means 'consume excessive amounts of cocaine'. His colleague goes on to explain that in the process of paying workers, there are half-cents floating around in the financial cosmos that no one can be bothered to collect, which makes many lightbulbs appear over Gus's head. He decides it's time to do some good old-fashioned embezzling. With beep-beep computer pen in one hand and pay slip in the other, he drags those half-cents from the ether and ends up a very rich man. (On a side note, I have always enjoyed that this is part of the plot of the Mike Judge comedy *Office Space*.)

It's the Smallville High School reunion, and Clark wanders around looking lost while The Beatles' cover of 'Roll Over Beethoven' plays – a collector's item of a Beatles song getting played in a film. Lester had been given the nod by the remaining three Fabs due to their previous working relationships (he directed *A Hard Day's Night* and *Help!*). Brad Wilson (Gavan O'Herlihy) is regaling fellow alumni with stories of how great he was as a footballer when he was young – and not of the fucking loser he is now – thus making him the patron saint of school reunions. Everyone knows they're awful. If I wanted to hear about what everyone is doing where I used to live, while talking endlessly about the past, I'll just visit my mum.

As the adults dance about, Clark runs into Miss Bannister, an old teacher who keeps telling him how great he looks, but he isn't listening as he's just seen Lana Lang (Annette O'Toole), the girl he once held a torch for, or at least I think it was a torch. He asks Miss Bannister to excuse him, which seems to upset her – I think she thought she was well in there with Clark, and you have to admire that optimism.

Lana and Clark hit it off immediately, like they have never been apart, and there's a certain pathos attached to their lives these days. She probably would have liked him more as a teen, but in those days, he looked different and ran like he was on strings. However, after the reunion he helps her clean up, and they have an interesting chat about what they've done with their lives. Lana had a child, the father left her, she had to sell her diamond ring, and she's now stuck in Smallville – a prison so effective that she was still there in the late nineties.

Clark has to bite his lip. He can't really mention that since they left school, he spent decades at the North Pole, saved the planet twice, lobotomised a woman who fancied him with his lips and beat a violent trucker half to death. Probably best say he's a boring journalist. The scene is lightly seasoned with the sweet and lovely sounds of Clark tinkering on the piano, eventually giving us a sudden cute burst of 'Earth Angel' – played by Reeve himself and yet another reminder of how bloody great he was.

'Run it by me just one more time,' Ross Webster asks, from behind his vast desk, in his personal trophy room of an office. Simpson, his assistant, tells him that $85,000 has been taken from the account, embezzled it would seem. While sister Vera rages and steams, Ross seems impressed by the act, reminding everyone that they are 'yesterday' and whoever pulled this caper is 'tomorrow', which is difficult to take on board when you see the state of Richard Pryor in this film. Before any decisions can be made, Lorelei enters to offer Ross a massage. He introduces her as his 'psychic nutritionist', and it's evident that Vera is not her biggest fan – think Ma Boswell to Lilo Lil. Simpson is sure that our embezzler will slip up, but Ross is of the opinion that he will lie low for a while and won't do anything to draw attention to himself – unless he's a compete moron. As the words leave his lips, a red Ferrari, playing very loud music, arrives in the car park (not actually parking in a space, just being abandoned), and out steps a very happy-looking Gus Gorman.

Clark is helping Ricky (Lana's son) to get better at bowling. Ricky's friends seem to think he's a bit of a loser, and they might be right, as he is proper shite at bowling, but Clark would like to have sex with Ricky's mum, so he needs to help out quick smart. However, a pair of drunk eyes at the bar can see what Clark is doing, and they're not best pleased. Brad steps forward and tries to take the ball from Ricky to show him how it's done, but Clark believes in valour and decency, and basically tells Brad to get fucked while handing the ball back to the lad. Lana looks on with loving eyes, and there can be no doubt that Clark has sealed the deal with that act of kindness. As Ricky steps up to bowl another ball at the pins that will probably end up in the gutter, Clark trips over a tray of powder, which causes him to sneeze and send Ricky's bowling ball flying at the pins with all the speed and power of Orson Welles at an All You Can Eat buffet in 1976.

Gus is summoned to the top floor to answer for his crimes. He explains to Ross that he's worried he'll go to jail and meet 'robbers and rapists, and rapists that rape robbers' (this is a kids' film, lads). But Ross wants to use Gus's skills to make his company number one. So, there'll be no *Casino*-style hammer to the hands or blowtorch to the testicles. He simply wants to utilise Gus's skills (that he's only had for a matter of days) to devastate Colombia via weather. While that sounds mad to you or me, it turns out Ross has access to the Vulcan satellite, or something, that you can programme to 'make weather', or something, and decimate any country with just the push of a button. Ross explains that 'Colombia has two major exports, and one of them is coffee', and their biggest customer for their other produce can really help him out of a bind, as Colombia is the only country that will not deal with him and his coffee empire, so he wants them wiped off the map and destroyed down to the last bean (but leave the coke, yeah?). So, Gus is sent to Smallville to access their computer (as they assume that will make it more untraceable?) and begins executing the kind of baffling plan you make while sitting around a lazy Susan covered in cocaine.

Clark and Lana go for a picnic next to a cornfield on a heavily overcast day, which seems to stretch the boundaries of reality somewhat. I can take the flying man from space, but not going on a picnic when it looks like it's going to piss down. Little Ricky runs off on his own while Clark flirts with Lana and eats some dog food (I shall be passing this footage on to social services). Ricky falls over, knocking himself out on a rock, so Superman flies in and rescues him, giving the stink eye to someone driving a combine harvester, like he was responsible for what occurred here, and not some prick who was picnicking on a grey day and eating dog food rather than watching over a child. Ricky and Lana are very impressed that they saw Superman, so Clark throws a wet blanket over their enthusiasm by telling them he sees him all the time as he's from Metropolis, but the joke is on him, as Ricky wants an autograph (at this point it may just be better to launch young Ricky into space).

Gus has arrived at Webscoe in the dead of night, greeted by Brad, who is already hammered and telling long, winding tales of why he needs to get inside – an eighties trope also appropriated by Axel Foley and Fletch. In this case, it's to install a booze cabinet, and Brad follows behind like a drunk erection. Gus's plan is to blast out some Roger Miller and outdrink Brad while talking shit. This could go one of two ways:

1. Gus could quickly die of alcohol poisoning while Brad, the seasoned drinker, would be largely unaffected and have to hide the body in a skip on the other side of town, then try to continue living as normal a life as possible while always knowing he definitely helped kill a man. Who knows? This may be just the ticket to get him to quit drinking.
2. It could work like a charm.

It works like a charm.

Gus then accesses the highly elaborate Webscoe computer (that looks like it controls nukes), and, presumably because he's drunk, the computers of the world suddenly become stupid: a cashpoint begins vomiting money, Sandra Dickinson gets assaulted with a fruit, and, worst of all, the green man and red man on a set of traffic lights turn into cartoons and start having an actual fist fight while traffic below turns to chaos. No man should have this much power. Now he am become quite sick, mild manipulator of worlds. Gus manages to get his hands on the weather satellite and is somehow able to strike Colombia down with the worst storm the world has ever seen, all via a computer from 1983. Highly impressive, as I remember around this time we had a BBC Micro at school, and all we could do was make a tortoise robot go in circles.

Ross Webster is over the moon with the news that Gus has succeeded in his plan. He cackles with joy as he takes coffee on his rooftop ski slope – which feels like it would be against all building regulations as the only thing stopping Ross from plummeting 200 feet to his death is a rickety fence. But no one ever accused a billionaire of being clever. As he helps himself to some mulled wine, Vera tells him he's thinking too small. Why stop at coffee? Why not get the oil too? She tells him that if Gus presses the right buttons, they can have it. It's at this point I feel we should have some sort of Microsoft Paperclip appear and explain how that would work exactly. Could Gus maybe get the cartoon men from the traffic lights to step out of the road sign and start an oil company? Could ATM machines start spurting oil? Is Sandra Dickinson oil?

None of this matters anymore, though, as Gus arrives on the rooftop repeating the phrase 'It's not my fault', like he's just been forced to murder someone. He goes on to explain that the Colombia plan has failed, as Superman arrived and tidied everything up – and to demonstrate how, Gus puts on skis and a blanket. To say Ross is annoyed would be an understatement; he's positively livid. With his plan ruined, he turns his attention to how to stop Superman. After a brief brainstorm, he declares that he wants Gus to find pieces of Krypton in order to stop the Man of Steel, and the scene is then abruptly ended with Gus tumbling off the roof on his skis and somehow landing safely in the traffic below. Presumably leaving everyone on the roof to just assume he's dead?

Fact: Christopher Reeve HATED this scene. He said in his autobiography: 'I did not think the scene of Richard Pryor spoofing Superman by falling down a skyscraper's edge on skis, with a pink tablecloth snagged on his back, was particularly funny.' Happy now, Richard Pryor? You've pissed off the actual Superman, well done.

Gus, with no injuries from his fall, races off to the nearest computer and asks his friendly satellite to locate some kryptonite and scan it so that some boffins at Webscoe can duplicate it in a lab on Earth. Lasers spurt out from the satellite and send back the readings, except there's immediately one problem: there's an 0.57% element of the components that the computer cannot identify. Gus simply looks at the packet of Camel cigarettes that he's smoking/advertising and notices that there is tar in them. So, he uses that to fill in the blank. Sort of like in *Jurassic Park*, but instead of using frog DNA, they use Bernard Manning.

Clark gets a call from Lana, and it turns out that massive pain-in-the-arse kid Ricky has been running around school saying that not only is he friends with Superman, but Superman is also coming to his birthday party, thus making Superman sound a bit weird and groomy.

Rather than silencing Ricky for ever, Clark, who wants to look good to Lana, proudly announces that Superman will be there, as he and Superman are great friends. It's all getting a bit pathological, this. Of course, tongues wag, and when Superman arrives in Smallville, it's become a massive welcoming ceremony, with even the mayor basically saying, 'Come and stay, and have sex with all our women – or men, if that's what you're into, no worries whatever way,' while also presenting him with a big key and a cake for saving 'Your Pal Ricky' and putting out the chemical fire. While the town applauds, an ominous jeep arrives, and out steps Gus dressed bafflingly as an army general. He barks out a bizarre speech about plastics and thanks Superman for his factory heroics. At the end of this deeply shit monologue, embarrassing for all involved, he hands Superman a solid rock of kryptonite that the boys in the lab made, hoping it will kill him, but it doesn't. He just puts it down and carries on being celebrated.

Gus instantly gets on the phone to Ross to tell him the bad news that Superman didn't drop dead, and receives the best line reading in the film: 'I ask you to kill Superman, and you're telling me you couldn't even do that one simple thing.' In the hands of any other actor that line may get attention, but in the hands (or mouth) of Robert Vaughn, it's like watching an alchemist fashion pure gold out of thin air.

But Ross need not be too disheartened, as, instead of killing Superman, the tar-kryptonite has actually caused him to be smelly, dirty and horny. First, he tries to seduce Lana, rather than saving a falling truck, then he goes on a spree of pranks such as making the Leaning Tower of Pisa become upright, blowing out the Olympic torch and probably joining Johnny Knoxville and the boys to get his testicles nipped by a snapping turtle.

With Superman out of the picture and causing mayhem, Ross agrees to Gus's demands to build a giant computer, the biggest computer in the world. It can do anything you want it to do. If you attack it, it will defend itself by sensing your weakness. Ross is impressed until Gus hands over his blueprints, scrawled on bits of paper and cigarette packets, so fuck knows how this machine will really be assembled. The supercomputer's construction continues apace, with the builders seemingly able to make sense of the notes and somehow avoid a 'Tiny Stonehenge' situation, so hats off.

Ross dispatches Lorelei to the very top of the Statue of Liberty to pretend that she's going to jump. Dirty Superman arrives to tell her that he doesn't save anyone any more, which seems like a long journey for a humble brag. He also says he'd love some sex that could possibly blow her insides out. She agrees but with one proviso: that he takes out some oil tankers for her. He duly obliges, before returning for some out-of-this-world, next-level rumpy-pumpy.

The following day, Dirty Superman is in a bar, looking like he smells of Lynx, sex and shit, and probably reflecting on the fact that he's become a very dirty sex boi. The other bar folk don't seem to be at all shocked or ill at ease that a man who could rip them to pieces or kick them into the sun is sitting at the bar drinking heavily.

He flips over a bowl of peanuts and begins flicking them at the booze, smashing bottles and making the bartender think about what he can possibly do to stop this from happening, as if some sort of wild elephant is swinging its trunk around the room and you have to ask it to leave. After melting the mirror with his laser eyes, Dirty Superman steps outside. To make matters worse, Ricky has arrived with Lana and is going on about how Superman is probably just ill in his whiny little voice while his mum pushes him towards an intoxicated god. After telling everyone to stop looking at him, he flies off in great discomfort, like he's just necked three pints of Imodium. The workers in the junkyard run like their lives depend on it when Dirty-Horny Superman lands in their midst and begins to roar in anger.

I can't be alone in this, but at the time of writing I am forty-five and I am still not too sure what happens here. If we were able to get hold of the CCTV, is he throwing himself in pools of acid? Throwing tyres on himself to break out of? Strangling himself to soberness? Or did an actual other person step out of his arse and fight him? We'll never know, really, but the end result is the same: nice Superman is back, and he's ready to right all the wrongs in the world. He hopefully relights the Olympic torch, repairs the oil tankers he pulled open (somehow blowing the oil back in) and knocks two verses off 'American Pie'.

Ross and his gang have relocated to the Grand Canyon, as this is 1983 and a computer this powerful needs acres of land to function, whereas these days it would probably be the size of a lap dog. This computer is incredible, though. Not only can it detect weakness, it also has games. As Superman approaches the giant computer, he is set upon by various missiles controlled via joystick. While many people will tell you that the game sequence was made by Atari for an abandoned game, the truth is Atari (who were owned by Warner Bros. at the time of filming) created the graphics as a fancy animation rather than a functioning game. But it worked, as six-year-old me got a massive kick out of a video-game Superman fighting missiles. That's how stupid we all were back then. Supes deals with every missile quite easily, apart from a final Thunderbird one that knocks him out.

As Superman's body flops down on a rock, Gus arrives late to see his giant baby being used for nefarious tasks. He seems to be upset about this, which leads one to ask just what the fuck he thought it was going to be used for? A mobile disco? Hard maths? A cocaine grinder?

Superman walks into the cave and demands they turn off the computer and go home. Lorelei stands up to wave at Superman in a way that sort of says, 'That sex the other night was great,' but Superman is having none of it. He gaslights her viciously by saying, 'I don't know you, lady,' and goes on to say that the man she had sex with was 'someone else'. I mean, yeah, but no, it was definitely you, Supes. We all saw you do it. Lorelei sits back deflated, like she was the victim of some elaborate prank.

As he waves threats at Webster, the computer analyses his body and begins its attack. It first puts him in a giant floating scrotum, and all the villains begin to cackle and speculate how long he can go without air. Lads, this fucker flies in space all the time, he'll be fine. Sure enough, he breaks out of the nut sack by using his laser eyes, but before you can say, 'What the fuck was that scrotum meant to be?', he's met with a red-hot beam of kryptonite. 'This time we got it right,' Vera proclaims to Gus, as he begins to waver and have second thoughts. Yeah, Gus is responsible for some awful deeds, has embezzled money, hurt people and nearly wiped out a whole country, but he's no killer, and with his freshly acquired conscience, he heads down to the guts of his supercomputer and removes one red screw.

A red screw that on the surface may look like a normal red screw, but it has a red rubber head and for some reason it's one of those props that has lodged itself in my brain for forty years, especially when Gus swallows it. I'm not alone in this by the way. I've spoken to lots of people in my life who tell me that that screw is something of an obsession. It may be the fact that it represents the beating heart of the computer or that it just looks like it might taste nice to a six-year-old. I have no idea, but every time I see this film, I welcome the sight of the magic red screw.

With the screw removed and eaten, the computer shuts down, and Superman is able to slowly gather his strength as the beam of green light vanishes. Before Ross can chastise Gus for eating metal, though, the computer begins to fire back into life on its own. It has become self-aware, and it's pissed off. The green beam once again fires down onto Superman's flailing body, and while everyone flaps around trying to figure out how to stop it, Gus declares that 'it wants to live!', and we're treated to a montage of Metropolis being plunged into darkness while the computer feeds on electricity from every US state. Gus races into frame with an axe and destroys the computer's kryptonite beam but is fired across the room for his troubles. Superman rises to his feet cautiously and then races away at speed, leaving Lorelei to plead with him not to leave them alone – a plea he ignores, once again leaving her to feel rejected.

Ross calls for his women so they can escape too, but as they both race out of the computer, Vera is sucked back in by force, and in a moment that broke the collective psyche of a generation of children, she is reconfigured and Frankensteined by Gus's evil contraption. As her voice gurgles and wobbles in agony, strips of chips, boards and silver strings are bolted to her. Her skin turns silver, and her eyes, turned into shiny balls of evil, open.

Now resembling Rod Stewart if he joined Kraftwerk, she takes her first strides out of the metal cave. A malevolent, deadly machine of shimmering robotics, Robot Vera first pins Lorelei to a high wall and then plunges Ross to the ground with beams of forceful energy. Just when it feels like all is lost, Superman suddenly reappears. With a quick palm he directs Robot Vera's energy back onto herself, sending her into a pit where she explodes. He's holding something behind his back, some sort of tube, but the computer senses no danger, like an idiot, and goes in for the kill, sending out tentacles of wires to pull Superman inside its complex maze of computer guts.

As he becomes enveloped, he pulls out his tube and removes the lid, revealing it to be some of the beltric acid from the chemical factory near Smallville, which, as you'll recall, can go completely mental when heated. As Supes disappears inside the computer, the acid turns into hot, thick jam and wildly ejaculates hot blobs of liquid death in no particular direction, causing the computer to fizzle, burst and break down in quick succession, eventually becoming one huge, fused mess of stone, glass and steel.

As the smoke rises from the debris, a lone hand emerges and pushes a giant rock out of the way. It's Superman, and he's fine. He sees Gus's hand hanging out of a hole nearby and pulls away the wreckage. They see each other and smile, then exchange possibly the most embarrassing handshake in film history, a sort of white accountant trying to do a rapper kind of handshake. 'Thank you, brother,' Gus says, as we all look away in hot mortification.

Superman and Gus fly off together and have a chat about how the computer didn't sense the acid was dangerous, which seems like a massive load of bullshit, and then a joke is cracked about it dying of 'acid indigestion', which gets a rightful sigh. It's then revealed that Ross, Lorelei and Vera will have to face the police, and presumably Superman has left them in the middle of the Grand Canyon buried under rubble, which seems a bit fucked up. Is Vera still a robot? Is she all right now? Questions that have remained unanswered for decades.

They land at a coal yard and are greeted by Larry Lamb, making this his third *Superman* appearance, which is a lovely pub quiz fact. Superman asks him if his boss has a computer; if so, he should hire this bloke who embezzled thousands of dollars and nearly destroyed humanity. While Gus takes in what just happened (and turns down the job), Supes looks around for a big lump of coal, crushes it in his hand and produces a perfect, massive diamond.

Lana and Ricky are living in a hotel room in Metropolis. She's left Smallville for the Big Apricot, and she wants to start again. She's tired of smalltown life, and she wants to live in the city that never sleeps. Though their spirits may be high, they seem to be generally having a bad time there, with Ricky eating from a wooden bowl of sadness and Lana pining for Superman to come round and have dinner with her. There's a knock at the door, and it's Clark. He has bad news: Superman can't make dinner as Lorelei gave him chlamydia, so he's sent Clark instead to give her a massive diamond ring that's nearly as big as her whole hand. She puts it on, and the music swells, just as Brad arrives out of nowhere – a subplot the film doesn't address, with Brad just turning up in Metropolis like some awful stalker. He assumes that Clark has proposed and tells him that he hates him, has always hated him because he's so nice, and then he takes a swing at Clark, misses and is propelled via a fold-out bed onto a room-service trolley and into a lift, where presumably he will just dust himself down and come back? There needs to be a scene where Superman threatens to break his cock off if he even goes near Lana again, but sadly we don't get it.

Lana, though, gets a job at the *Daily Planet* as Mr White's new secretary, which is nice, and Lois rejoins the film at the end covered in fake tan to remind us she's still alive and has only been on holiday. She asks Clark for lunch, but he sadly dumps her in favour of Lana, and as she looks at the two of them, she knows that she's yesterday's news and may as well go out with Jimmy fucking Olsen.

As Superman arrives in Pisa to re-lean the tower, he can finally wash his hands of his many misdeeds and fly into space to rejoin the stock footage from the end of the first film, beaming at us from Earth's orbit and reassuring us once again that all is well and Christopher Reeve has one hell of a smile.

Yet, as he flies out of shot, there's a lingering doubt in the air that he'll ever be seen in those tights again. He didn't have a nice time on this film, and in his autobiography criticised the majority of it as 'poor taste' and a 'misconception' – and who could possibly argue with the Man of Steel?

EIGHT

SUPERGIRL

1984

ADVENTURE RUNS IN THE FAMILY!

In 1982, the Salkind family announced that they would be making a film of Supergirl. Not only that, there was more exciting news: she was also to feature in the upcoming, and highly exciting, *Superman III*. The plot was to centre around Superman battling against both Brainiac and Mister Mxyzptlk, with Supergirl dropping in at some point to lend a hand in saving the day.

Obviously, history tells us that this version of the film never left the ground once Richard Pryor indicated he wanted to appear, so plans were abandoned. Instead, it was decided to pack all the exciting energy and audience goodwill that would inevitably be accrued from Superman's third adventure and pay it forward. Sadly, there was little to none, but they pressed ahead anyway. Richard Lester was sounded out, but he'd already started making *Finders Keepers*, a quirky comedy starring Michael O'Keefe. So, they went for *Jaws 2*'s Jeannot Szwarc, who was recommended to them by Christopher Reeve himself. He'd enjoyed working under the French director on *Somewhere in Time*, though whether this was in the same conversation where he told them he had zero interest in appearing in *Supergirl* is anyone's guess.

An unknown actress was sought to play the role of Kara Zor-El, and after seeing a cast of 350 women, they picked nineteen-year-old Helen Slater, who in fact was the very first person they saw. The 'Making of' documentary (introduced by a very stern-looking Faye Dunaway) features not only her screen test (where she wears the comic-accurate costume complete with headband), but also the moment she is told she has the part, and it's all rather adorable. She was then placed on a vigorous fitness regime (running, trampolining and weight training) led by stuntman Alf Joint.

As with *Superman: The Movie* in 1978, there's a very impressive opening title sequence (that apparently cost $1 million), with giant flying words careering towards the screen from the depths of space; only this time, they're chrome, rather than ice, and look like alphabet spaghetti in a lava lamp. There's also a very impressive and memorable score composed by Jerry Goldsmith that evokes the unique sense of awe and wonder that he's able to wrangle from even the most mundane spectacle.

Argo City. A white Christmas tree of a thing that looks more like a model of the ArcelorMittal Orbit fashioned from snot than a working planetoid. Perched on a rock in the middle of space and lit only by a revolving system of stage lighting, it's immediately obvious that whoever created this godless carbuncle was really taking the piss.

Inside, it's no better. This huge, soulless branch of IKEA, with bland, hanging drapes, thick white cobwebs and a network of labyrinthine bunk beds, beanbags and blankets that all scream 'sex people', is where young Kara Zor-El calls home, and it's here that Zaltar (Peter O'Toole) also unfortunately calls home. His purpose is unclear, but he seems to be part Argo 'super', part wizard, dressed as he is in head-to-toe knitwear, and bearing the studied insouciance of a man who's seen and done everything while also presenting *Rainbow*. Kara finds him making something called a 'tree' with his special orange wand, a creation that confuses her. 'A lovely thing which grows on Earth,' Zaltar explains in his unique façon de parler, which sends a lightbulb flashing in her head; that's where her cousin went, though how she knows this is unclear, seeing that, as soon as he left, Krypton exploded, so there wasn't really time for a postcard. Zaltar tells her she's correct and that one day he'd like to go there too, as he's constructed something called a 'Binary Chute', a small spaceship that looks like it was built at the Early Learning Centre. He confidently predicts it will allow him to 'zip-zap' his way off Argo City and, presumably, into the first pub he finds. Kara finds the idea of planets confusing, so Zaltar gives her a quick exposition hit: Earth and Saturn are in outer space, but Argo City is in 'inner space', which potentially means they're up Martin Short's bumhole. The city has two great power sources, one being the all-powerful Omegahedron – a spinning ball with an internal light source which Zaltar just happens to have in his pocket. He's 'borrowed it for the afternoon', without the knowledge of the city government, and is very much enjoying the chaos. I can only presume his orange wand is the other source, but let's not dwell on that. To demonstrate the exciting power of the Omegahedron, Zaltar points at his newly created tree, and the ball makes it pulse with living light. Kara is deeply impressed, but he laments that, although it seems it can create life, it's only really an illusion.

Kara's mother, Alura (Mia Farrow), interrupts the fun to ask Zaltar if the rumours of his leaving Argo are true. As he explains how fed up he is on this lonely old rock and how he'll probably head for Venus, he hands the orange wand to Kara and allows her to have a go at creating something fun, which is exactly what she does. A beautiful giant dragonfly proceeds to flutter to life and pierce a hole in the Clingfilmed walls of Argo City, sending the Omegahedron flying out of it like shit in a wind tunnel. The elders are angry at Zaltar: without the power source the city will fade and die. He promises he'll go and retrieve it, though it's clear that he's very pissed off about all this, as it will put a real dent in his plans of getting pissed every day for eternity on Venus. Heated arguments persist about just how he will achieve this, but none of them notice a clearly guilt-ridden Kara climbing into the Binary Chute and powering it into life.

As she hurtles out of the city and into the shadows of inner space, Zaltar calms her weeping parents by telling them that she'll be safe due to gravitational radiation – a pathway that leads to outer space that will keep her alive and well. As they mourn her loss, he turns the subject to himself, declaring that as he was the one who lost the power source, he should be sent to the Phantom Zone. 'Your suffering will be short, mine . . . forever,' he says, ever the narcissist. He's literally just lost their daughter FOR EVER, and he's asking them to feel sorry for him, when it's all his fault and he was leaving anyway.

Schoolteacher Nigel (Peter Cook) and Selena (Faye Dunaway) are picnicking by a beautiful lake. A sumptuous spread of champagne and pineapples rests on a tiger-skin rug. They are discussing just how long it will take to master black magic. Selena wants to rule the world as the most powerful witch, and Nigel can assist her, as he's something of a warlock. Dunaway seems to be something of a reactor in this film: feeding and storing bad energy and outputting maximum evil power while bathed in the softest focuses available to man. Peter Cook obviously fancied the money and had been recommended by Dudley Moore after his Mister Mxyzptlk role fell through. He had no preconceptions as to what he'd signed up for, commenting in the 'Making of' documentary, 'It's not stretching me enormously. I have to stand upright, walk about, say some lines and be fairly sarcastic, vaguely unpleasant and nasty, so I don't have to act, just be myself.'

As Nigel spouts further warlock stuff to Selena, he reminds her that she needs to be patient when it comes to learning the secrets of black magic from the ancient grimoires, but before he can get his spirits too high, the Omegahedron falls from the sky and lands in some dip. Selena picks it up, and it immediately spins in her hands, so she begins asking it for eternal life. Nigel asks what it is and what's going on, though that may just be Peter Cook off mic. She tells Nigel she no longer has any need for him, and as she speeds off, leaving him by the lake, we hear on the radio that Superman has left Earth on a peace-seeking mission to another galaxy, which is a very roundabout way of saying Christopher Reeve had less than zero interest in appearing in this film.

Meanwhile, across the gulf of inner space, the Binary Chute has reached its destination. Kara, dressed in an all too familiar costume of red, white and blue, shoots out from within and bursts from a lake to land on its shore. It's here that she discovers her powers: the ability to crush a rock, grow a flower with her eyes and, last but not least, fly. As Jerry Goldsmith conjures magic from his orchestra, the audience watches some sublime wire-work. Supergirl tumbles, rotates and glides amidst trees and around the lake with balletic precision, before taking off to fly over a herd of galloping mustangs and up into the clouds – all of which demonstrates that the same visual effects team who made you believe a man can fly have now done the same for a woman.

After Kara lands in Midvale, she's instantly greeted by two pervy truck drivers (one played by future Max Headroom, Matt Frewer) who tell her they're out looking for a good time, whether she likes it or not. Really? If there's one thing a children's film primarily aimed at young girls doesn't need, it's a scene where two men are intent on violently raping the hero. They've picked on the wrong person, however. Supergirl quickly blows one off his feet and boots the other through a wall, before flying off, leaving them to agree that they'll keep the events of this evening to themselves. After all, it will not do for others to find out that they're in a Ted Bundy tribute band.

Selena, who lives in an abandoned fairground and has set up home in the ghost train – incredibly on brand – is throwing a party for her fellow warlocks and witches. Nigel is at her ear as a constant menace, wanting to hear all about the magical ball she inherited. Is it electrical? Is it hot to the touch? Where is it? He warns her that her plans for world domination may have hit a snag, as when he was walking back from the lake, he saw a blue and red figure flying through the sky. Selena isn't worried, though; with this ball in her possession, no one can stop her. Perhaps she should look up a little word called 'hubris'. After all, it wasn't that long ago that a little man called Hitler also had one ball and a plan for world domination, and look what happened to him.

Kara observes schoolkids from the bushes next to a playing field (it was a different time). She sees girls her own age playing baseball, talking about the hunky groundsman and having fun, so she decides to join them. Somehow she manages to transform from a blonde girl in red, white and blue superhero gear to a nondescript brunette in a perfect replica of the school uniform. She walks into the school, straight into the principal's office, and by using the classic method of scouring the walls for inspiration, picks the name 'Linda Lee' after a picture of Robert E. Lee, the Civil War general – and presumably a packet of vegetarian sausages. The principal asks for her letter of recommendation, and when he's distracted by Peter Cook complaining about the little monsters who have nailed his desk shut, she springs into action, typing one out at superspeed, filing it in the cabinet and then pretending it was written by her cousin, Clark Kent.

'Linda Lee, meet Lucy Lane,' the principal announces as he leaves her to settle in her new dorm. There's already a connection between the two girls, as their relatives work together at the *Daily Planet*, and while Lucy (Maureen Teefy) isn't thrilled about having a roommate, she's very excited by the fact that this new girl is Clark Kent's cousin. As she shows Linda around the room and points to her bed, the eye can't help but be drawn to the pin-up photo of Prince Andrew: a portentous warning from the past that through the prism of the 21st century transcends that of an innocent snap and takes on the appearance of a man peering in through the window of a girl's bedroom and then writing a cheque for £12 million as he walks away.

'My sister's got something going with the big guy,' Lucy says as Linda spots the Superman poster on the wall, and the music swells with the theme from Krypton as Linda reaches out a hand to touch the poster.

Selena has fallen in love with groundsman Ethan (Hart Bochner, Ellis from *Die Hard*) and has already spent many a Diet Coke break observing his work methods, noting his manly contours and longing to have a look at his mighty oak. She decides that she'll get him to visit her ghost train (not a euphemism) on spurious grounds and concoct an overly elaborate potion that, once drunk, will cause him to fall into a trance and then in love with the first person he sees. As the potion takes effect and Ethan face-plants the sofa, Nigel, dressed like a Cornish fisherman if he appeared in *Thriller*, arrives to see Selena. He informs her that she's playing with fire, that she needs to learn to walk before she can run with that ball. But she's not interested in his advice or the explanation that the bizarre suit he's wearing is his 'leisure suit'. He has three days off, he tells her, and he intends to let his hair down, presumably by heading to the nearest old folks' home. Ethan, meanwhile, has woken up in a dazed state and is now staggering around the streets of Midvale.

Jimmy Olsen (Marc McClure) has been invited by Lucy to meet her at Popeye's Chicken, and as Linda joins them, it all feels like an elaborate episode of *To Catch a Predator*, seeing as Jimmy now looks about thirty-nine in his tank top and bow tie, and really shouldn't be hanging around with schoolkids. Lucy tells her there's an all-night party at a guy called Eddie's house and she should come as his folks are out of town, but all this talk of potential sex offences is put on hold when they both notice Ethan wobbling through traffic, particularly when Selena, who has by now realised he's gone, sends a magic-powered bulldozer to retrieve the object of her lust, which proceeds to trash the entire town centre. Supergirl swoops in and saves the day, whisking Ethan away to safety. As he regains consciousness, he opens his eyes and sees Linda telling him everything will be OK, and with the potion now in full working order, he tells her he loves her, much to Selena's intense disappointment. 'A bird of free and careless wing was I through many a smiling spring. The cold repulse, the look askance, the lightning of love's angry glance, stay,' he says in mild bewilderment before embracing Linda and kissing her softly. She is taken aback by a man considerably older than her wanting to kiss her and tells him she has to go back to school because she is a child in the eyes of the law.

Selena is livid that her sexy plan has been foiled. She sends a dragon to take care of Linda, but because this is a pre-CGI world, the 'dragon' is invisible, a fact that has always annoyed me. As the tension ratchets and the sound effects rumble, we're forced to watch Supergirl fighting a blank space that occasionally leaves a footprint and bends a lamppost. Selena and her gobby friend Bianca (Brenda Vaccaro) watch on at home, and they're left asking themselves just who this woman in blue is who is wrecking all their wicked plans. Using a special tracking bracelet, Supergirl traces the power source of the magic to the fairground. There, she encounters a smitten Ethan toting flowers and chocolates like a terrible TikTok groomer. 'Oh no, not now,' she moans as he quotes more poetry and asks her to marry him. Selena breaks up this touching scene, introducing herself as 'Selena, Diadanus of Catania, Priestess of Sekhnet, I am the ultimate Siren of Endor' before telling Supergirl she's trespassing and getting heavy, once again, with the magic. Supergirl foils her again, of course, and escapes with an unconscious Ethan in an airborne dodgem car.

A mountain has appeared on the edge of Midvale. Not just any mountain, either. A mountain with a castle on top. Selena's plan for world domination has taken a big step forward, thanks in no small part to her magic consultant, Nigel, and his conjuring of pure, unadulterated evil, that has also brought Ethan back to her chamber in chains. For his payment, Nigel's made to look dusty and old and covered in lipstick, sort of like Mick Jagger in 2003. Supergirl races at speed to confront Selena in her new fortress, only to find that she's cast two further spells: one to encase her in an invisible mime-proof glass box, the other to turn Ethan's heart in Selena's favour, leaving Supergirl powerless as she watches him necking with sexy Grotbags. She screams for him, but he is lost to magic, not even noticing as she is sent hurtling into space, deep into the Phantom Zone.

It's a cold, dark, desolate place. The roaring wind is the only sound that can be heard, and her powers of flight and superstrength no longer function. She screams for help, for any sign of life, but there are no replies. As she stumbles around the barren landscape, she's plunged deep into a pit of thick green goo. Hope is all but lost.

Back in Midvale, Selena has taken over and is parading down the main thoroughfare in an open-top Rolls-Royce accompanied by a private militia all dressed in black. Ethan sits next to her, semi-comatose, dressed in a white suit, and Nigel is chained to the rear bumper. The citizens of Midvale are brandishing signs protesting her evil rule. Lucy mouths off about freedom while Jimmy holds her back, suggesting that it's not a good time to express herself, the gutless wimp. During her rant, she mentions that Linda went missing the day the mountain showed up, which leads to Selena realising what no one else seems to be able to.

'Squirt?' Zaltar says, spraying a liquid that is undoubtedly heavily alcoholic into his open mouth. He's pulled Kara out of the bog, is clearly pissed out of his fucking tiny mind and has lost all hope of escape. His knitwear has also given up the ghost. Gone now are the cool patches of pale blue, replaced with sad, hopeless, smudgy brown. He's at his lowest ebb, and you still get the feeling that he's one of those people who will always have it worse than you. Eventually, Kara manages to draw him out of his self-pity, and he admits there may be a way to escape, but it will not be easy. He's right about that: he dies while helping Kara through the maelstrom of the Quantum Vortex and leaves her with the haunting last words, 'I am with you.' I am amazed his last words aren't a complaint about a bad back. After watching her mentor spiral down into the vast nothingness, Kara stretches out her arms and flies like a bat out of hell through space and time before crashing through Selena's fortress window and freeing Nigel, Lucy and Jimmy from their dangling cages.

Supergirl demands the Omegahedron. But Selena is now fully powered up, and she unleashes a shadow demon on Kara, stretching her, twisting her, destroying her will and sapping her energy, a feeling shared by the viewers of this prolonged and agonising end sequence. She's about to lie down and give up hope when she hears the words of Zaltar ring through the pain and suffering, with his deeply inspiring message: 'You can! On, girl!' This gives her the fortitude to fly out of the demon's clutches and create a powerful whirlwind, sending Selena spiralling into the hands of evil, screaming as she and the demon become one within the mirror.

With the Omegahedron safely back in her hands, Supergirl says her goodbyes and flies back, somehow, to Argo City, bringing the lights back with her as she approaches, and even though the people in there had it as hard as can be and couldn't breathe the air for ages, they can take comfort that Zaltar probably had it worse, as he tumbles for eternity, squirting into his open mouth.

Supergirl was not the hit they had expected it to be. The critics disliked it, Faye Dunaway and Peter O'Toole were nominated for Worst Actress and Actor awards, audiences felt it was too long (hence the many cuts of it that can be found), and it made less than half its budget at the box office. All in all, it convinced the Salkinds that their Superman journey had well and truly come to an end, and the following year at the Cannes Film Festival, they sold the rights to Cannon for $5 million.

This can only be good news, right?

NINE

HOWARD THE DUCK

1986

TRAPPED IN A WORLD HE NEVER MADE

During the making of *American Graffiti* in 1972, George Lucas stumbled upon Steve Gerber's niche comic book about a duck called Howard from outer space that had somehow ended up in Cleveland. He thought it was funny and could make a great movie. He imagined it as a film noir with a wacky spine running throughout it and discussed the possibilities with his old film-school buddies, the co-writers of *American Graffiti* Gloria Katz and Willard Huyck. They all agreed it had potential, but within a couple of years Lucas would become tied up with his dream project (you can guess which one), and it was put on the back burner.

In 1984, the project was dusted off when Lucas decided he wanted to produce more films. He called up his buddies, and wheels began to be set in motion. Initially planned as an animated film, Lucas eventually insisted it be live-action and pushed for his own company, Industrial Light and Magic, to bring it to life. With that, the egg was hatched.

Duckworld. Two pink moons nestle in the sky above a sprawling metropolis of skyscrapers and high-rise blocks. Downtown, a tired citizen returns to his homey apartment and switches on the light. His name is Howard T. Duck, and as he hangs up his umbrella and throws down his coat, the eye catches the various decorations of his flat. Among the pictures of women with beaks and copies of *Rolling Egg* magazine, there's pun-movie posters galore, such as *My Little Chickadee* starring Mae Nest and W. C. Fowls, *Splashdance* and *Breeders of the Lost Stork* featuring 'Indiana Drake' – the new hero from the creators of *Beaks* and *Fowl Wars*. Already I want to die.

Howard (Ed Gale) cracks open a bottle of Budweiser, which for some reason remains free from puns, and flicks through the TV channels. There are game shows, soap operas and infomercials, all of which leave him yawning as he puffs on a cigar. He turns off the TV, unwraps his new copy of *Playduck* and unfolds the centre to reveal 'Miss October', the first of two ducks with their tits out that the film wants us to admire. Suddenly, the room begins to shake, and quite without warning Howard and his armchair are pulled with a heavy invisible force through the building – momentarily revealing the second pair of duck tits, a woman singing to herself in the bath, as he crashes through her wall – and out into the sky, shooting like a star into space. Howard is voiced by Chip Zien, hired for his dry, nasal performance, but initially the job was given to Robin Williams, who quit seconds later. According to Zien, in an article in the *Hollywood Reporter*, Williams hated trying to fit his voice over the animatronic beak, apparently saying, 'I can't do this. It is insane. I can't get the rhythm of this. I am being confined. I am being handcuffed in order to match the flapping duck's bill.'

As Howard drifts through the endless vacuum of space, without any oxygen, a narration begins: 'The Cosmos. Countless worlds upon worlds. Worlds without end. In these galaxies every possible reality exits. And what is reality on any one world is mere fantasy on all others. Here, all is real and all is illusion. What is, what was and what will be start here with the words. In the beginning there was . . . Howard the Duck.' It truly is a word salad, and basically an advert for cocaine.

Howard sinks like a stone through the Earth's atmosphere, hits everything on the way down and somehow lands injury-free in an alley. What a very different film this would be if someone just found a crushed giant duck at the side of the road.

As Howard gets his bearings, he's instantly set upon by a street gang who drag him into a music club, telling the bouncer that he's their date, which is something that gives off horrific mental images. After being thrown out for being a child in disguise, Howard is presented with the harrowing night life of Cleveland – dangerous women on motorbikes, chasing police cars, random violence – all taking place to a soundtrack by Cherry Bomb, a music act put together by Thomas Dolby, who also wrote all their songs for the film.

Beverly Switzler (Lea Thompson) is merrily making her way home from another awesome gig, where she and the Cherry Bomb girls have well and truly rocked the party, and life couldn't be better. Shame, then, that she's accosted by two street punks looking like Droogs who shop at Top Man. They loved her show, so naturally they want to drag her into the darkness and sexually assault her. She fights back and knocks one of them down, but is dragged away by the other, and just when things look like they can't get much worse, Howard leaps out of a bin, declares that he's had quite enough and tells them he's a master of Quack-Fu. The two punks declare that they've obviously had too much 'toot' and run away in terror, as you would if accosted by a three-foot-tall talking duck wearing a suit.

Beverly is grateful for his help but genuinely freaked out by the appearance of a talking *anas platyrhynchos*, especially one with such a sassy vocabulary. Feeling sorry for him, she offers him a makeshift bed at her vast warehouse apartment.

Howard says that, like her, he used to write songs and play music but eventually had to get a proper job as an advertising copywriter. He then proudly tells her one of his catchy slogans. Beverly tells him he's a massive sellout and should have stuck to the music, even though just minutes ago she was complaining that her manager takes all their money and they're basically playing for free. How's that going to put food on the table, Beverly? How about you grow up and get a proper job? Howard has always been sure that he has a special purpose and fate has something in store for him, and Beverly suggests that maybe that's the reason he's arrived on Earth. Howard contemplates this logic but swiftly drops into a deep sleep while John Barry's 'You're The Duckiest' begins to delicately seep out over the images: a piece of music so fragile, endearing and soothing that it really has no business being in a film about a cheeky, horny duck.

Beverly covers him with a blanket, touches his feather-hair and then proceeds to go through his wallet, observing his 'Bloomingducks' card, family photos and a condom (human penis-shaped) – and we really have to pause here and think long and hard about why the ducks in this film have cocks and tits.

Beverly has come up with an idea: her friend Phil (Tim Robbins) is a scientist and works at the museum. Maybe he can help. The next morning, she sneaks Howard there in a bin liner, like he's a fresh Mafia kill, and places him on Phil's table. Phil is a fucking shambles of a man, a baffling cocktail of stupidity, and when he's not talking to Howard like he's a moron, he's making quack noises to his face, which in the duck world is basically racism. It turns out that he's not a scientist at all – he's a mere lab assistant – so Howard is rightfully pissed off by this turn of events, especially when Beverly tells him that if he thinks his situation is bad, her career is mildly suffering. So, having seen two samples of humanity that in no way do us any favours, Howard decides to storm out and follow his own path, terrifying passers-by as he roars in their direction.

After going to the employment office, he's bafflingly given a job as a janitor in a disgusting sex club, but he only lasts a short while, quitting after being forced to clear a blockage in a hot tub while two people carry on fucking next to him. He may be a horny duck, but he has principles.

While Beverly rocks the joint on stage, her sleazy manager, Ginger Moss (Tommy Swerdlow, who would go on to write *Cool Runnings*), pockets the band's fee and tells the promoter that he'll give her the money after she agrees to have sex with him, because apparently she's been holding out on him. Howard doesn't like what he hears and threatens Ginger with an ice pick, telling him he's no longer their manager. He takes the money owed and tells Ginger that if he comes anywhere near them again, he'll give him 'SPACE RABIES', which sadly took so many of that generation.

Beverly cannot contain her excitement and appreciation for Howard's hard work in freeing the band from their evil manager. She invites him back to her apartment again, only this time she has more on her mind than going through his wallet. She wants Howard to be their new manager and duly invites him into her bed, where they both dance very close to the red-hot flames of bestiality.

Luckily, Phil arrives, and by 'arrives', I mean walks right into her apartment as she's about to fuck a duck. He's reached out to contacts and has brought in a pair of experts – Dr Walter Jenning (Jeffrey Jones) and Phil's friend Carter (Miles Chapin) – the latter of whom is physically repulsed by what he sees, and the former seems sort of down with it, which speaks volumes when you check his Wikipedia page. They may have some idea of how Howard got here. Jenning is in charge of a lab that, on the night that Howard arrived, was testing a new laser spectra scope when some unknown force deviated the target and instead shot the beam at Howard's planet, just missing a pair of tits. After the beam cooled, a single white feather fell into the lab, which they have tested and are sure came from Howard's head. Howard demands that they repeat the test but flip it around so he can go home, and Jenning heads off to set it all up, making history for a second time.

Upon arriving at the lab, Howard finds that not only has the lab exploded and Jenning is missing, but the police want to strip-search him. There's no way he's travelled millions of miles to have some police officer stick a rubber-gloved hand up his Aristotle, so with the help of Beverly, he manages to break free of the cops. On their way out of the facility, they bump into Jenning, who looks like he's just snorted John Belushi. He explains that when the spectra scope exploded, he blacked out and found himself in the wreckage. Luckily, he has a car waiting outside, so they all jump in and escape. As they break clear of the facility and head to the freeway, Jenning begins to warn them both that he thinks he's about to become someone else, but not like *Stars in Their Eyes*. His voice suddenly bottoms out into a low growl, like George Burns trying to pass a massive, unwieldy stool, and he tells them something evil is growing inside him, replicating his organs, changing his brain and taking over his entire body. So, they stop for a coffee.

'The transformation is complete. I am now someone else,' Jenning tells them, in his demonic voice and, as they are seated, he tells Crystal the waitress that the world is about to end and be replaced with a new one. He then reintroduces himself as one of the Dark Overlords of the Universe and informs them that he was summoned by the laser beam and he will summon his brothers and destroy the planet soon. Howard and Beverly then watch in terror as he goes on a laser-eye frenzy, blowing up condiment bottles and causing most of the diner to lynch Howard, dragging him into the kitchen presumably to chop him up or give him to Errol Flynn, so he can make another 'duck centipede' (look it up: he really did this).

Jenning goes full nuclear and begins to paint the restaurant with wild electricity, raging fire and that fucking voice. As the diners scramble, Howard attempts to escape with the keycard that works the spectra scope, but Jenning is too crafty for him. He throws

Howard across the room with his laser eyes, grabs the key and Beverly, and steals a truck. He's heading back to the lab, where Beverly is told she will have a lord put inside her, like it's a 10 Downing Street party during lockdown. As the truck speeds down the freeway, Jenning tells her he needs more energy. He unleashes a tongue at least two feet long that buries itself in the cigarette-lighter hole and begins to charge his growling, aching body. I'm sure he's merely exchanging long protein strings. If you can think of a simpler way, I'd like to hear it.

As the police comb the area looking for Howard, he bumps into Phil, who accompanied the police to the crime scene, which literally makes no sense. He breaks Howard out, and they both hide in a nearby junkyard that happens to house a small two-man plane. Phil is very excited as he's sure he can put it together and get it started. Howard tells him about a saying they have on Duckworld: 'If God intended us to fly, he wouldn't have taken away our wings.' Presumably this explains why they also have tits and cocks. With the police gaining on them, Phil gets the aircraft started, and they soar away, with the alternative wind of Sylvester Levay carrying them away – and not John Barry, and the difference is marked. For this scene of wacky sky-high japes it was probably felt that Barry's laid-back, Bondesque, jazzy feel just wasn't exciting enough.

As Howard and Phil fly alarmingly close to the ground, taking out duck hunters with much hilarity, it's alarming to read that for some of these shots, it is actually Ed Gale and Tom Robbins flying on their own. Obviously, precautions were taken, with military-style precision, but it's still a hair-raising watch when you know that it's just them in control as they dive-bomb over wetlands.

Phil and Howard arrive back at the lab to find that Jenning now looks like the dad from *Bread*. He's inhaled a whole nuclear plant and is at the peak of his powers when they arrive. He has Beverly strapped to a table under the laser and is busy programming the coordinates. Luckily, Phil remembers that they have an untested (why are they always untested?) weapon in the store room: the

Neutron Disintegrator. Jenning isn't pleased to see them and begins powering up like never before, with shades of red and blue firing from every inch of his body. So, Howard races towards him on a small, motorised cart and sends every atom of the Disintegrator in his direction, causing a huge explosion.

Jenning wakes up back to normal and explains that he isn't evil any more, that the Dark Overlord must have escaped but is still in the room somewhere. (I wonder if he said the same to the police and if they bought it?) From the broken walkways of the shattered laboratory it emerges: the Dark Overlord, now a beautiful puppet. Not stop-motion as some may think, but very much a Phil Tippett 'go-motion' creation. Go-Motion was a technique invented by ILM that incorporated a blur within the movement, thus making each creation seem less unsteady and awkward. The subject will typically move while the shutter of the camera is still open to give the illusion of a smoother set of movements. The technique was getting better and better each time it was utilised, but within a few short years *Jurassic Park* happened, and go-motion was made extinct.

The Overlord is a scorpion-like monster with a giant mouth stacked full of teeth and a pair of arms finished with deadly pincer claws. It makes you wonder just how that got inside Jenning, but it probably paid for dinner. After a quick roar (voiced by Brian Steele) he reactivates the laser, subdues Howard and throws a forcefield around Phil and Beverly. More of his Overlord brothers are on the way, riding the laser to join him on Earth in two minutes, and upon their arrival they'll probably get inside the nearest human like a stag do in Magaluf. Howard frees himself, gets back on his buggy and fires another laser right into the face of the Overlord, this time extinguishing it for good. There now just remains the simple task of destroying the laser itself, with Beverly reminding him that if he does, he's stuck on this planet for ever. In the end, it's an easy decision, and Howard destroys the machine, frying the remaining Overlords as they near the end of the barrel.

Beverly digs his scorched body out of the wreckage after the inevitable large explosion, and such are Howard's sassy ways, he can't resist pretending to be possessed by an Overlord, which makes Phil shit his pants, before admitting he's fine and getting a cheeky cuddle from Beverly, as they all celebrate saving the world.

The Cherry Bomb ladies have a new song, and they're debuting it tonight. It's called 'Howard The Duck', and it has lyrics that tell the audience to get his planet on the phone and tell them he ain't coming home, which really feels less like a cheeky song and more like a disturbing message from a kidnapper. Howard, though, is very happy, and loving his new role as band manager, sometime guitarist and on-off fuck machine for the girls. In terms of management style, I'm hoping Howard will adopt the Peter Grant of Led Zeppelin approach and supply an endless buffet of drugs, groupies and mud-sharks while randomly battering anyone who dares come near them.

Howard the Duck was not a success, financially or critically. In fact, over the years it's become yet another stick with which to beat poor old George Lucas, but is it that bad? No. I'm sure readers of around my age remember it as fondly as I do and still think of it as a sort of cultural hug, a nostalgia blanket, a film that contains enough quaint nutrients to soothe upon revisiting. You can at least argue that Lucas never played it safe, though rumour has it that, following a test screening, Universal executives Sid Sheinberg and Frank Price had an actual punch-up over who actually green-lit the film – neither of them willing to take the blame for it, and both unwilling to join Howard for a duck-walk across the stage.

'What can I say? It sucks,' Steve Gerber would say in a 1997 interview with Kuljit Mithra from *Man Without Fear*. 'In retrospect, though, after eleven years that have brought us so many worse films, it's not quite as sucky as the reviews might have led you to believe.'

And amen to that.

TEN

MASTERS OF THE UNIVERSE

1987

A BATTLE FOUGHT IN THE STARS . . .
NOW COMES TO EARTH.

There are few films in history that seem to miss the point as much as this one. The plan surely was to cash in on a popular franchise and have fans of He-Man queuing around the block to see their favourite toys in live action, but by 1987 He-Man was, if not actually dead, then on the last blips of life support. Releasing a movie based on Prince Adam and his chums in 1987 was less 'after the Lord Mayor's show' and more 'after the Lord Mayor's funeral'. Any normal movie studio would look at the figures and probably walk away, but this was no normal movie studio. This, my dear friends, was Cannon, and they needed this film to be a hit. (Spoiler alert: it wasn't.)

It's clear from the opening titles that this is a magpie of a production. Rather than leaning into the already established mythos from hours of the cartoon, they've decided to grab a bit of *Superman*, a bit of *Star Wars* and, most alarmingly, a bit of *Death Wish 3*.

An opening narration informs us about Castle Greyskull, which I've always felt was the Elgin Marbles of Eternia. It's a big castle with a skull on it, a grey one, and it should really belong to Skeletor, if we're honest, but he's forced to squat up at Snake Mountain and plan just how he can get his house back. Eternia should do the decent thing and offer reparations.

The basic premise of the narration, aside from being pointless, is to say that whoever gains control of Castle Greyskull will gain the power to become Masters of the Universe, which would be fine if that is what plays out, but it isn't.

Bill Conti is on board to score the film, and it feels like he's been shown a picture of John Williams, played a cassette and told, 'Just do that, yeah?' It's a reasonable score, but it feels very TV parody.

Skeletor (Frank Langella) marches purposefully through Greyskull accompanied by a piece of music that could have been lifted from *Star Wars*. He's being saluted as he strides past black stormtroopers and speaks to Evil-Lyn (Meg Foster, who is clearly having a great time). He pushes her for an update on the war, and she tells him they've nearly conquered the planet, but He-Man and his small band of rebels are still, just, holding out. He tells her he wants He-Man kneeling before him. Evil-Lyn proclaims with extreme pleasure that 'Greyskull is ours', but Skeletor quickly barks, '*No! Mine.*'

There are many who will point at Langella in this film and laugh as he doesn't look a great deal like the toy and cartoon character, but good Lord, is he selling it. The story goes that his son talked him into doing it, and that he decided to approach it as if it was Shakespeare, and I can well believe it. As many problems as this film has, and there are LOADS, Langella isn't one of them. He is immense – very much the cream at the top of this bog of mud.

The imprisoned Sorceress, who is basically part-caretaker part-Debbie McGee of Greyskull, reminds Skeletor that the power of Greyskull isn't his yet because the budget won't stretch to it, so he electrocutes her slightly for insolence and then asks Evil-Lyn to put him on camera so he can broadcast an evil message to those dastardly rebels out in the wastelands.

Those wastelands are smouldering in the shadows of plumes of black smoke. Eternians stand with hands on their heads, resigned to the fate of the black hand of Skeletor. His hologram compounds their sorrow, informing them that he has Greyskull, the Sorceress and is coming for He-Man next (just not outside, as it will cost too much).

Watching Skeletor deliver his evil message is the last defender of Eternia and the strongest man in the universe: He-Man (Dolph Lundgren). He looks angry, or maybe bored, or maybe wondering if he turned off the tap before he left the bathroom. Urban legend has it that Stallone, who had worked with Cannon, recommended Lundgren to the producers, and when he was told they'd cast him in a film, quickly said, 'You didn't give him a speaking part, did you?' Lundgren is mostly fine, as a living doll, and has something of a presence, albeit one more of wood than plastic – though this could be a direct result of Grace Jones, his girlfriend around this time, taking him to one too many ten-hour sex orgies while wearing matching leather pant suits.

He-Man quickly sets about a group of faceless soldiers, and I think I can speak for ten-year olds in 1987 everywhere when I say that his use of a laser pistol, rather than the sword, can fuck off. And the fact that pretty much every interesting bad guy from the toy and cartoon range is absent can also fuck off. The only bad guy who shows up is Beast-Man, and he looks like Chewbacca's meth-addled cousin.

On the good-guy side, however, He-Man is joined by Man-At-Arms (Jon Cypher), who looks like a weird dystopian Scout leader, and Teela (Chelsea Field), Man-At-Arms' impulsive and, frankly, stupid daughter. They clear the area of bad guys and release a small prisoner trapped in a net. Is it Orco? No. It's Gwildor (Billy Barty), an annoying little scientist arsehole – Jeff Lynne as a ZZ Top goblin, covered in pubic hair – with a weird scrotum face. While we can celebrate the fact that Orco will not be joining us, we can also mourn the presence of this ginger bag of shite.

They free him from his net prison, and he introduces himself as a locksmith and inventor, who was being hunted by Skeletor's forces. He-Man asks why, like Skeletor has locked his keys in his Vauxhall Astra again, and Gwildor says he will show them back at his place, which sounds like one of the PSA clips that we used to get at the end of the cartoon. Perhaps he has puppies or candy?

Skeletor is after Gwildor for his invention: the Cosmic Key. It generates tones that can open a doorway to anywhere (as long as it's cheap). Skeletor has one, and that's how he's winning this war, but Gwildor has a prototype, which is fortunate. He explains how he was duped by Evil-Lyn, who used her beauty to fool him into handing over the key, which is very in character as Gwildor looks exactly like the kind of man who would be conned out of large amounts of money by some sexy chat. He-Man asks if the prototype can get them into Greyskull, and he confirms it can, but before they can celebrate, Karg arrives with some soldiers.

Karg looks like Granny from *Looney Tunes*, if she was badly burned in a chip-pan fire. Why they felt the need to invent a new monster when Trap-Jaw and Mer-Man were RIGHT THERE is beyond me, but they did. Instead of those two badass creatures, we have this singed ball of cotton wool with a hook for a hand, who sounds like he's chewing wasps.

Gwildor then reveals he has a secret door that leads to the castle, which is something he could have revealed earlier, to be honest. They make their escape and arrive in Greyskull, where they find the throne room empty and quiet – perhaps too quiet. Is it a trap? Could everyone be out? Or was there not enough money to pay more than four people that day?

They encounter the Sorceress, who reveals she is imprisoned within a forcefield and they should all leave, just as Skeletor and his army arrive in force to tell He-Man that, when the moon rises, he will have 'the power' and the Sorceress will die. This all sounds like a great time for Gwildor to make so much noise they spot that he has an extra key. As a fire-fight commences, Man-At-Arms tells

Superman: The Movie: The one that started it all, and set the bar so very high. *Alamy*

Superman II: Another boring editorial meeting at *The Daily Planet*. *Alamy*

Flash Gordon: On Mongo, hot pants are a sign of respect. *Alamy*

Spider-Man: The Dragon's Challenge: Anyone need someone to kick someone up the arse and then run away? *Alamy*

Condorman races to show us the only bit worth watching. *Alamy*

Swamp Thing: "Photosynthesise this, bitch." *Alamy*

Superman III: You either die a hero or live long enough to see yourself become trapped in a testicle. *Alamy*

Supergirl: Get witch or die tryin'. *Alamy*

Howard the Duck and the cinema showing they can both put their bills up their arse. *Alamy*

Superman IV: "Hands up who deeply regrets doing this film?" *Alamy*

Masters of the Universe: "I am not an animal, I am a He-Man being." *Alamy*

Batman: "Clowns to the left of me, Joker to the right." *Alamy*

The Trial of the Incredible Hulk: "I'm out of order?! You're out of order! The whole trial is out of order!" *Alamy*

Captain America: "I'm sorry I pretended to feel sick and then stole your car." *Alamy*

Batman Returns: The gang dress up as Batman and the Penguin. *Alamy*

Judge Dredd: "You really should be wearing the helmet."
"I'm not wearing the helmet." *Alamy*

The Shadow cabinet. *Alamy*

Batman Forever: "Chase me." *Alamy*

Violator and Al get the Spawn. *Alamy*

Batman Forever: "I may have made a huge mistake." *Alamy*

Gwildor to get them out of there, so he keys in random sounds, and they all fly out of the throne room through a secret portal that will take them to the cheapest Californian locations possible.

Skeletor is not happy, and he demands that his people hunt them down and find the key immediately, and there's a definite pleasure to be derived from an angry Skeletor, as when Langella breathes heavily, his mask undulates considerably and breaks out in wild nostril flares.

The gang arrive in their new world, a little worse for wear but fine. Their first misstep is to ignore the opportunity to leave Gwildor to drown in a ditch, and, to compound this, once they rescue him, he reveals that he has no idea where they are and he's lost the key during the portal jump. So, until they get it back, they are lost on an alien world (it's Earth). As they set out to look for it, they encounter a cow in a forest. Why would a cow be in a forest? When did YOU last see a cow in a forest? It's just silly.

Meanwhile, at Robby's Ribs 'n' Chicken, Julie (Courteney Cox) is working her last shift before she moves to New Jersey because both of her parents died in a plane crash – though they might well be hiding. She still has to end things with Kevin (Robert Duncan McNeill), her musician boyfriend, who is a big fan of the song 'Living In A Box'. She's leaving in the morning at 8.30, so Kevin asks if she can watch his soundcheck. Oh, Kevin, love, no one gives a shit about your band. She agrees and gives him free ribs, for his pleasure. She then asks if they can stop by the cemetery to say goodbye to her folks, which must be the ultimate in boner killers.

Apparently, the location used for the ribs place is the exact spot where Rodney King was later beaten half to death by the LAPD – so that's something fun you can look out for when you watch.

Julie and Kevin stand before the grave. She keeps saying that the plane crash was her fault because she didn't go with them on the flight, which is probably true. Kevin tries to reassure her but quickly forgets about her grief when he uncovers the Cosmic Key in a bush. He decides it's a Japanese synthesizer and begins jamming on it frantically within feet of Julie's dead parents, with the same energy as Alan Partridge at Lynn's mother's grave.

Unfortunately, Kevin's jam session has alerted Skeletor to the location of the other key, so he orders his mercenaries to assemble, and, oh boy, do we need to talk about them. First off, we have Beast-Man, an actual He-Man character, so there's one point in the plus column, despite him looking like David Bellamy as a werewolf. Next, we have the aforementioned Karg (the old man's pube wig on legs – no action figure required), followed by Saurod, a creature that sort of looks like your friend rendered his pet lizard in cardboard in order to enter him into *Robot Wars*. Saurod is not too bad, and eventually became a legitimate toy, so well done. He's also played by Pons Maar, who frightened children will remember as the lead Roller in *Return to Oz*. Finally, we have Blade – no, not that one, but a white, bald man with a sword and an eye patch. He was played by Anthony De Longis, Frank Langella's stuntman and the sword master for the film, so it's sweet that they made a role for him, but it's just not a very interesting one. These mercenaries are said to be Skeletor's 'finest warriors', and they are hand-picked to go to Earth to find the key and bring He-Man back alive. They should have mailed it to the Marx Brothers.

Kevin tinkers with his Rhodes Chroma Polaris keyboard, asking Julie to listen while he farts out awful key licks. The banner running along the school-hall stage reads 'Illusions', the name of his band, and a small wall of amplifiers is stacked behind him. Clearly, this will be a palace of rock once the Illusions assemble. Julie looks on, bored as fuck, as he tickles the keys, but still tells him it 'sounds great'. Kevin jumps away from his groove and decides he wants to amp up the 'Japanese synthesizer'. Before you can say 'Jean-Michel Jarre', it begins to play a haunting melody while also producing an optical effect of flashing lights. Kevin proclaims that they need to take it to Charlie, his friend who runs a music shop, but Julie wants to stay behind at the school hall on her own 'to say goodbye to the place'. Sorry, Julie, but you're a real drag.

Her peaceful reminiscence is soon broken, however, when the mercenaries arrive, eat a janitor, set fire to the hall and chase her out into the street. As Julie races for her life in a state of panic, she luckily bumps right into He-Man, who just happened to be passing. He carries her to safety, reassures her she's safe and then leaves her by some boxes in an alley with a handgun. A battle ensues with He-Man facing off against Skeletor's finest warriors. He beats them all up fairly quickly, and they retreat immediately. Pathetic. Julie tells He-Man that Kevin has the Cosmic Key, and they run off to find him.

Kevin has made it to Charlie's music shop with the Japanese synth, and his friend also assumes it's Japanese, which somehow feels a bit racist. They once again try it out and look for the perfect pitch but become distracted by the many police cars and fire trucks screaming by. Kevin quickly figures out the school has burned down and races there to see what happened. He's stopped by Detective Lubic (James Tolkan), who is essentially playing the same role he played in *Back to the Future*. He takes Kevin in his car to find Julie at her house.

The amazing mercenaries arrive back at Greyskull, empty-handed and fewer in number. Ol' Daddy Skeletor is not best pleased, especially when they make up a bullshit story about being outnumbered, so he kills Saurod, which seems harsh, but it might be a 'last in, first vaporised' operation. Skeletor rages and tells Evil-Lyn to go with them and finish the job.

'Stay put, we'll be right there,' Julie tells Kevin on the phone. So, Kevin and Lubic chill out at Julie's house for a bit before deciding to mess about with the Japanese synth again. That is until Lubic performs another mood flip and becomes suspicious about the synth. He announces that he's going to take it away and find out what it is and where it came from. He's not long out of the door before it's blown down and Evil-Lyn and her army arrive. They beat up Kevin and attach a neck brace (the Collar of Aldruber) to him to force him to tell them everything.

This is when things go all Ray Cooney farce. Evil-Lyn leaves, just as He-Man and his friends arrive and find Kevin on the floor, still in his collar and looking like he's had one hell of a power wank. He tells them the same story: that Lubic has the key, but he doesn't know where he's gone. As soon as they wrench off the collar, Kevin panics and tells Julie they're in trouble, so she has to explain that these weird freaks are her new friends, and to compound matters further, Gwildor wanders in dressed like an Australian's nightmare, though, to be fair, this does seem to break the ice. He announces that he's wearing native clothes, but, in reality, he just looks like Harry Knowles after a long movie marathon.

Kevin composes himself enough to tell the gang that Lubic probably took it to Charlie's music shop, so they all head there and arrive just in time to detect that Skeletor's army is on the way. So, the weak Earthlings are sent to the back of the shop while the Eternians, crouched behind synthesizers and pointy guitars, begin battle with the stormtroopers.

As the fire-fight rages, Julie looks out of the shop window and notices her dead mother standing in the alley waving and smiling at her. Any normal person would of course assume that there's no way their very dead mother could be standing there, unless she had a plane wing sticking out of her head, but Julie isn't a normal person. She rushes out to greet her mother, probably to tell her that this is neither the time nor the place for a reunion, but quickly wilts and is overawed that her mother has come back from the dead during an interplanetary battle. Not only to reunite, but she'd also like that Cosmic Key they've all been playing with – presumably she's forming a supergroup of dead parents and wants to wow them with new tech. Idiotic Julie goes and gets it, at which point her mum turns into Evil-Lyn and walks off with the key. Well done, Julie.

He-Man rides on flying frisbees all round the shopping precinct, like some sort of cosmic *Last of the Summer Wine*, to try and get the key back, and Skeletor arrives on a carnival float, flanked by hordes of soldiers and flashing lights. With the key now in his possession, he has the upper bony hand. He forces the surrender of the Eternians, including He-Man, who, while putting up a fight in one of the worst choreographed moments I've ever seen, is soon overpowered. Skeletor now has He-Man as his slave and some top-of-the-range Japanese technology. In a rare moment of clemency, Skeletor agrees to leave the rest alive, in exchange for taking He-Man back to Greyskull, where he'll presumably mount him over the fireplace.

As He-Man is taken away, Teela and Man-At-Arms are left with all the humans, and they must be wondering how much a taxi back to Eternia will cost, but Julie, as per usual, has a problem. She caught some pink lightning from Skeletor on her leg, and it now looks like the back of a wet Gremlin. Only the Sorceress can heal her now, and it looks very much like Kevin will need a new girlfriend. As Gwildor admits that he can't unlock the tones on the spare key because the memory has been erased, and it would take him a thousand years to find the right ones, where's Philip Glass when you need him? Just as all hope fades, Kevin suddenly springs to life and remembers the tones, a simple, six-note melody that, for some reason, Gwildor, the inventor of the key, couldn't remember. Kevin humblebrags that he can remember melodies and it's sort of his gift while also admitting to the fact that he was going to lift it and put it in one of his songs. Gwildor practically begins humping him and excitedly announces that they'll be able to get home.

It's time to talk about Pigboy. In 1986, the toy company Mattel ran an exciting competition, and the winner of said competition would win a small cameo in the new and exciting *Masters of the Universe* movie.

Kids flocked to branches of Toys 'R' Us to fill in entry forms, and the lucky winner was eight-year-old Richard Szponder from the Chicago suburbs, which all feels very Willy Wonka. Richard had no idea what role they'd be giving him, and rumour has it nor did the movie makers. They eventually settled on creating a tiny role for him, which was to be called 'Pigboy'. The role saw

Richard, dressed as a lizard-pig, handing Skeletor his Havoc Staff and watching as he walks past, which doesn't sound like much, but for some reason Pigboy has become an important component for fans of the film and a star in his own right. In an increasingly cynical world, it's a nice story knowing that a fan got to hang out with the cast and crew and watch it all happen, even if that is akin to being on the *Titanic* for a small part of the journey. Mattel also paid for Richard and his family to see Los Angeles by limo, and for a release party at his local cinema, so it's heartwarming that someone had a fun time with this film.

Skeletor stops as he reaches his throne and proclaims, 'I win,' and he certainly appears to be correct. He-Man is in chains, the Sorceress has withered, and he has the Sword of Greyskull and the Cosmic Key. Within hours he will have all the powers of Greyskull and become a Master of the Universe. If only He-Man could somehow throw Pigboy at Skeletor like a javelin, or drop-kick him into his balls, that would save the day for sure, but, alas, He-Man is not only in chains, but is also whipped with a cartoon laser by Blade, a character that doesn't even exist in the toy range. Life is cruel.

Back on Earth, Lubic stumbles upon Kevin and Gwildor building the world's most cosmic keyboard set-up – as if they've hired Keith Emerson and Brian Eno as consultants – and instantly tries to ruin everything by coming in like Popeye Doyle with piles. He ends up travelling through the portal with the rest of them, back to Eternia, back to the future.

Thanks to the collected powers of the universe, Skeletor has achieved his ultimate makeover. Gone is the dour black cowl and cape. Gone is the dark grey Havoc Staff, which did nothing for his eyes. In is the giant gold headpiece, gold cloak and matching staff. Goodbye, Greyskull, hello, Goldenballs. If I have to be critical, though, I'd say he went a bit overboard on the hat – you could get three heads in there, and you'd have to duck through doorways, but as long as he's happy. And happy he is, telling He-Man all about his plans to get rid of everything good and decent and replace them with darkness and evil, sort of like the Conservative Party, right?

But his speech is interrupted by the arrival of our heroes from Earth and that lilting tone of the Cosmic Key. A fire-fight begins, and it quickly transpires that it's not going well for Skeletor, particularly when He-Man breaks free and manages to regain the Sword of Greyskull. Evil-Lyn and her mercenaries slide away as He-Man raises the sword in the air and declares, in his best broken Swedish, 'I have the power!'

There then begins a sword fight with Skeletor, which is mostly shot in darkness, as Cannon refused to pay for any more filming, forcing the director and two main actors to shoot it guerrilla-style while the studio's back was turned.

He-Man breaks the Havoc Stick, and Skeletor reverts to his old shabby-chic look. 'It's over,' He-Man says to a defeated Skeletor, who refuses to be beaten and ends up plummeting off the side of a platform and falling in slo-mo down towards a vast hole, with zero emotion on his face – almost as if he's a stuntman wearing a mask.

The day is won, the Sorceress returns to life, and the people of Eternia can celebrate. Kevin asks Lubic how he's doing, and he announces that he's decided to stay in Eternia and retire. Mainly because he's now got a girlfriend and there's nothing for him on Earth. It should be noted how much of a player Lubic actually is, given that he's managed to secure a hot babe within about twenty minutes.

The Sorceress, now young again, hands Julie a special jewel and tells her Eternia will always be with her. Things get very *Wizard of Oz* as Julie goes from person to person saying, 'Good journey' (an old Eternian saying), careful to not tell Gwildor that she always thought he was an annoying prick. He programmes the key and offers to send them back in time, but Kevin says they don't want that, which is very fucking presumptuous, seeing as Julie could see her parents again. As they step through the portal, Julie changes her mind and tries to ask Gwildor to do what he offered, but it's too late, and they head back home.

Julie wakes up in bed, back home, back to normal, surrounded by birdsong and warm light. She jumps up and heads downstairs to find both her parents alive and well and having breakfast. She breaks into joy and tells them how much she loves them and that they shouldn't get on their plane. They are a bit freaked out, especially when she steals their car keys and runs off outside in her nightie. I must say, it's certainly a bold film that ends with the main character being sectioned. Kevin finds her at the end of her street, and they embrace. Kevin then produces the jewel that the Sorceress gave him and confirms that it wasn't a dream. 'They were there.' They are then greeted by the sight of He-Man lifting his sword once again outside Greyskull and declaring that he still has the power while Lubic walks by behind him with his pants down and asks if anyone's seen his lube.

As the credits roll, you may think about leaving your sofa, but don't. In a move that was decades ahead of time, there's a post-credits scene: Skeletor's head rises swiftly from a purple, misty patch of rough water and declares, 'I'll be back.'

He was wrong.

ELEVEN

SUPERMAN IV: THE QUEST FOR PEACE

1987

NUCLEAR POWER.
IN THE BEST HANDS, IT IS DANGEROUS.
IN THE HANDS OF LEX LUTHOR, IT IS PURE EVIL.
THIS IS SUPERMAN'S GREATEST BATTLE.
AND IT IS FOR ALL OF US.

After securing the rights to Superman at Cannes Film Festival, Cannon Films immediately set to work on making *Superman IV*. But there was a problem: they had no script and Christopher Reeve wasn't interested in donning the tights again. He'd really not enjoyed the process of making the third one and did not want to partake in another slapstick film that flew in the face of everything that had come before. Cannon went away and considered things, then came back to Reeve with an offer he couldn't refuse. If he would do *Superman IV,* they said, he could produce any project he wanted (and he did: 1987's *Street Smart* starred Reeve as a struggling journalist and earned Morgan Freeman an Oscar nomination for his portrayal of a violent pimp) and he could write the story to *Superman IV*. Reeve accepted the offer and work began, but what Cannon didn't tell him was that the promised budget of $36 million was already slashed to $17 million. They had a whopping thirty films in production at the same time as *Superman IV* and decided to 'share the wealth', so Superman's wings were slowly being clipped without him knowing it.

Reeve began to flesh out ideas with Lawrence Konner and Mark Rosenthal. They agreed they wanted to focus on what would happen if Superman intervened in Earth matters, even though his father told him explicitly not to do so. Nuclear weapons for instance – what would happen if Superman tried to stop the build-up of nuclear weapons and give the world peace? They decided that this would be the direction to take and set about writing a screenplay based around this idea, bringing back Lex Luthor as the one man who could capitalise on the arms industry and creating a supervillain to stop Superman, terrifyingly called 'Nuclear Man'.

Created from Superman's DNA, Nuclear Man would be the opposite of him (very much like Bizarro Superman) but just as powerful. He would, in a move that would have been far too reminiscent of the previous film, also be played by Christopher Reeve.

It soon became apparent that the budget wouldn't stretch to even a third of the ideas they were having. A scene in which Superman lands outside the United Nations building in New York and then promises the leaders of the world that he will end the arms race ended up being filmed in Milton Keynes with a handful of people.

The effects budget, the very lifeblood of any Superman film, was also slashed, meaning that all the flying sequences were either one shot reused over and over again – or appalling.

But one thing that the Cannon group had in their favour was the availability of Gene Hackman. He was at a stage in his career when he would pretty much appear in anything – and good thing too, as *Superman IV* needed Lex Luthor. Margot Kidder was also back on board, though with a reduced role.

'Christopher felt that I was too old to be romantic with him this time, so he wanted a younger girl. So, basically I'm in there as a sister/confider, or something,' she told the BBC in 1987 when they visited the set, and she was quite right not to hold back her indignation. 'I don't think I look that old, and I don't think I look that much older than Christopher, and I think it's a big stupid mistake.'

Mariel Hemingway was hired as the other love interest, Lacy, a disposable love interest as it turned out. Mark McClure was also back as Jimmy Olsen, the keen-as-mustard staff photographer. Rounding off the familiar cast was Jackie Cooper as Perry White, who looked as though he was just happy to be paid. Jon Cryer (*Pretty in Pink*, *Three and a Half Men*) was cast, in arguably the most annoying role in the film, as Luthor's mentally ill (it would seem) nephew Lenny, who wanders around continuing his fine Jeff Spicoli-esque Californian brogue. Finally, Cannon took the decision to cast unknown actor Mark Pillow as Nuclear Man, thus putting an end to the dream of Reeve playing dual parts.

The budget problems are clear from the opening credits. Long gone are the hollow, crystal letters zooming out of your screen, shaking the senses. Instead, we are offered a freeze frame of planet Earth with multi-coloured words whizzing past it like some kind of advert for an album that is 'not available in the shops'. It's a kind of monstrosity that clearly cost the production team around £5 to cook up and may well have been done in the back of a branch of Snappy Snaps.

A group of Russian cosmonauts happily drift in space while a comrade outside sings Sinatra in Russian, a soft gentle embrace of the culture of the West, and with the wall just over two years from coming down, he's ahead of his time. Sadly, a rogue satellite races through space and takes him out, sending him spiralling away from his ship (these days Putin just poisons people). Luckily, Superman

(Christopher Reeve) races to rescue him, with an optical shot of him flying towards the camera – that you should get used to – and returns him safely to his vessel, telling him to shut the fuck up, in the nicest possible way.

Smallville. Clark lingers at the empty farmstead. He has a meeting with Mr Hornsby, a realtor, about whether he'll be selling the farm or not. It's empty now, with Martha having clearly passed away, and Clark wanders around soaking up memories. He stops in the barn to retrieve something from the capsule that brought him to Earth.

It's here that production designer John Graysmark (*Flash Gordon*, *Robin Hood: Prince of Thieves*) deserves a great deal of praise for turning lemons into lemonade. Given the budget and location restraints, the fact that he was able to make Baldock in north Hertfordshire even remotely resemble Kansas is quite the achievement.

Clark finds a green crystal containing another message from his mother, and, honestly, it seems that all those fuckers did for the last few weeks was run dictations. She tells him the green crystal is all that remains of the planet Krypton. Once he removes it, his ship will grow cold and silent, and he will be alone. The crystal's power can be used only once, and he should use it wisely, and definitely not as a paperweight or a back scratcher.

Hornsby draws up to the farm to try to change his mind, but Clark gives him short shrift, telling him he wants it to remain as a working farm and not be sold to ruthless developers. Hornsby tells Clark that no one wants farms any more and that he needs to move with the times, but Clark stands firm. If this place is to be sold, it has to be sold to proper farmers, the ones who wear dungarees, wield pitchforks and have those beards without moustaches.

Lex Luthor whistles Mozart's 'Eine Kleine Nachtmusik' to himself as he bends over to pick a flower for the lapel of his prison uniform. He's working on a chain gang in a quarry, breaking rocks in the hot sun (well, the hot sun of Springwell Quarry in Rickmansworth), doing hard time for helping General Zod try to take over the world a few years before. For some reason, this morning he has a spring in his step. He tells a fellow prisoner that he has plans to recreate life itself (which is a hell of a pick-up line) and that no prison can hold him. The guards tell him to stop slouching and get back to work, but before they can bring out the rubber hoses, a mysterious car rounds the corner and enters the quarry.

Lenny Luthor tells the guards he's lost, but they're more impressed with the sound system – a Sensurround 100 with four blunderbuss-style horns pointing back into the car – and they're very keen to try it out. As they sit inside and put on headphones, the driver makes his move, activating the car via Walkman and launching it off the edge of the quarry. He races to Lex's ankle chains and sets him free with bolt cutters, so they can get on with their plan to destroy Superman.

Lois Lane practises her French as she joins the wild rabble of morning passengers flowing through the subway to catch the train to work. Once again, while the production design team have done the very best with what they're given, it's immediately clear that this is a London Underground station (Aldwych), even more so as Lois boards a Tube train.

The train pulls away from the station and trundles into the tunnel as usual, but there's a problem: the driver seems to have suffered a cardiac arrest and has slumped over his controls, sending the train up to high speed, shooting through stations and causing panic.

Clark overhears the screams and darts into a nearby phone booth, emerging as Superman and then flying through the station to stop the train. As the emergency services race to get to the driver, Superman blocks their way and makes an announcement: 'I'd like all the people back there to know that our subway system is still the safest and most reliable means of public transportation. Thank you.'

Let's just hope the driver pulls through and Superman's delay to give that tedious speech didn't hinder his chances of survival. It would be an awkward funeral otherwise. 'As Dad lay dying, emergency services arrived quickly, but they were told to wait while Superman explained that the trains are safe or something. The doctors told me that if he'd been treated just two minutes earlier, he'd have pulled through. So, while we're thankful the people on the train were rescued, we're sad that Dad is no longer with us. Here's a special speech for Dad, read by *Daily Planet* reporter Clark Kent, who has kindly agreed to join us today.'

'Hello, all, I'd just like to say that I think Superman does a bloody good job, and you should all lay off him. Anyway, we are gathered here today . . .'

Thanks to the subway antics, Clark is late for the morning editorial, which is the first from new owner David Warfield (Sam Wanamaker), a Rupert Murdoch facsimile who wants to turn the *Daily Planet* into a tits-out tabloid that no longer cares about the truth. He shows the room the mock-up of the new-look paper, which declares in bold letters that the world is 'on the brink', while also showing a half-naked lady – so on the brink of having a wank? When Clark points out that the headline isn't true and may be misleading, Warfield tells him that it doesn't matter, it will sell papers – and that, ladies and gentlemen, is how Freddie Starr ate a hamster.

Editor Perry is livid about this, referring to the *Daily Planet* as 'a grand old lady' and complaining that he doesn't want it to become one of Warfield's 'bimbos'. On a side note, it seems odd that a newspaper can be taken over by a newspaper tycoon and none of the existing staff knew about it happening. Isn't that sort of their job? To report and investigate news?

Warfield introduces the room to his daughter, Lacy, who thinks the new look for the paper is 'super' and mentions that she'll be 'helping' the editor – with what, though, is unclear. Prostate exam?

As the room clears, Clark gives Lacy a piece of his mind by telling her that a reporter's first allegiance must be to the truth and that they can't let the public down. He walks away with the stride of a giant dork, and Lacy tells Lois that she thinks he's kind of cute. Lois warns her off by telling her that he's a giant Boy Scout, probably a virgin and possibly gay. Lucy, though, is sure that he'll fancy her as she's fucking loaded.

Warfield's storming of the *Daily Planet* is parked for the moment, as the President (Robert Beatty, the Canadian actor who not only played the tanker captain in *Superman III* but also reported on the Blitz to North America for the BBC during World War II) appears on TV to tell the country that, as peace talks have failed, they have no choice but to strive to be second to none in the arms race, which is music to Mr Warfield's ears. There's nothing like a world crisis to increase circulation, after all. Eyes roll, but he's right: the job of a newspaper is to report news, not to sit around and only find out you've been purchased by a media titan when he arrives to tell you.

A teacher turns off the television and turns to face her class. She suggests that, instead of being worried or depressed about the inevitable nuclear war that will cause endless destruction (and cause a middle-aged woman to wet herself in Sheffield), they should try to be positive and discuss anything they can do. The room is bereft of ideas, but one child has an idea. Jeremy (Damian McLawhorn), the class idealist who spends most of the lesson dreaming of a better world while staring out of the window, suggests that they ask Superman to step in and intervene. He did turn the world backwards to get laid, so this should be a walk in the park.

Over at the Metropolis Museum of Modern Art (Winter Gardens, Milton Keynes, Buckinghamshire, now a gym), a tour guide shows off the pride of their collection: one of Superman's hairs. It hangs in a glass case and is able to hold a 1,000lb load without breaking. She explains that they can all have fun looking at it for a bit, but as she escorts the tour away to another exhibit, Lenny and Lex Luthor (the former dressed in a Letterman jacket, plaid trousers, baseball cap and sunglasses – like he thinks he's Danny Baker) emerge from a hiding place, smash the glass and steal the sample, their plan being that they will use his DNA to create a new superbeing that will have eternal allegiance to them and rid the world of Superman.

Lacy has decided that she will seduce and destroy Clark. Summoned to her office, Clark arrives to find her splayed across her desk like a side of beef. She tells him she wants him to write a feature about Metropolis after dark, which is like asking Arthur Negus to go to an acid rave. She tells him that it might help improve his rather stuffy image, plus she's a member of all the right clubs and can come with him in the form of a date, tonight, at the grand opening of the Metro Club. But Clark isn't that keen, especially when he sees a letter Jeremy has sent FAO Superman, asking him to stop the bombs.

Superman flies off to the Fortress of Solitude to ask his mother for her opinion. He knows he can't interfere (again) but he can see parallels between what's happening on Earth and what finished Krypton. Suddenly, loads of other elders, whom we've never seen before, pop up to throw in their two cents, telling him he can always go to another planet if he doesn't like it, and if he teaches Earth to put its faith in one man, he's teaching it to be betrayed, with one elder in particular saying the word 'betrayed' four times with increasing vigour, like he's self-taping for a part in a Neil Breen film. It's food for thought.

Lois has arrived at Clark's apartment with questions, as they're due at the Press Awards dinner and he's not even dressed properly. He's a map of inner turmoil and pained expressions. He tells her he's had a lot on his mind, so he probably won't be joining her, and he goes off to sit in a slump. Lois, obviously worried, shows concern and asks if there's anything she can help with. Clark thinks for a moment, then asks if she'd like to join him on the balcony for some fresh air before leaping off and taking her with him. While in any other film this would be a deeply disturbing course of events, he turns into Superman and takes Lois on a flight around the world, in a cynical retread of the iconic scene from the first film, only with a special effects budget of eighty-seven pence. When they return from pointing at buffalo, gawping at trains and doing that thing where he drops her and catches her, Superman's mind is clear: he knows what to do. But before he can do anything, he once again kisses Lois and wipes her memory, like some kind of real *Men in Black* shit, and you have to ask how many times he's done this to her and under what dreadful circumstances.

Jeremy poses for photographs at a hot-dog stand. Jimmy Olsen takes some snaps, with the hustle and bustle of Milton Keynes Central railway station behind him. In Christopher Reeve's autobiography, he described filming this scene: 'We were hampered by budget constraints and cutbacks in all departments. For example, Konner and Rosenthal wrote a scene in which Superman lands on 42nd Street and walks down the double yellow lines to the United Nations, where he gives a speech. If that had been a scene in *Superman I*, we would actually have shot it on 42nd Street. Dick Donner would have choreographed hundreds of pedestrians and vehicles and cut to people gawping out of office windows at the sight of Superman walking down the street like the Pied Piper. Instead, we had to shoot at an industrial park in England in the rain with about a hundred extras, not a car in sight, and a dozen pigeons thrown in for atmosphere. Even if the story had been brilliant, I don't think that we could ever have lived up to the audience's expectations with this approach.'

Superman has arrived to speak to the United Nations assembly. He has decided that he will indeed step in and rid the world of nuclear weapons, effective immediately, and to do so he'll need a net the size of South America. His plan is to hang around in space and wait for missiles to be launched, catch them in a big net and throw them into the sun. If you or I pitched that to the leaders of the world, we'd be laughed out of the room, but Superman gets a pass, for some reason. The world reacts to this announcement by launching nuclear weapons like there's no tomorrow, and you'd think Superman's announcement would be a deterrent, but it's actually somehow encouraging.

Arms dealers Jean Pierre Dubois (Jim Broadbent), Harry Howler (William Hootkins) and General Romoff (Stanley Lebor) sit around Lex Luthor's luxury penthouse suite. The man himself enters with a sexy lady on each arm (Dixie and Trixie) and a spring in his step. Not only has he clearly just had a threesome with rhyming women, he also has a solution to everyone's problems. He explains that the sun is basically a huge nuclear bomb, and so proposes attaching a 'genetic stew' of his own making to one of the nuclear weapons that Superman hurls into it. The reaction will create a 'Nuclear Man', and he will be Superman's biggest nightmare, apparently. He'll be able to pierce his skin and make him weak, mortal, sick and die, and all that Lex asks for in return is a small cut from all the nuclear weapons that are sold.

Lex and Lenny stand dressed in surgery gowns, slaving over a metal box while test tubes bubble and smoke all around them. The plan is on, and Lex explains to Lenny that the protoplasm he created from Superman's hair cells will duplicate creation itself, and to really sweeten the deal they also inset some fabric into the container, which apparently has a computer inside that will automatically know how much fabric it will take to cover his cock and balls, thus maintaining the high moral standards that modern society subscribes to.

The missile is launched, box in place, and Superman arrives, right on cue, to throw it into the merciless, boiling core of the sun. A reaction begins, a boiling red blob careers out of the fire, and it begins to form into shape. A red baby slowly grows into a man: a man dressed in black, with gold trim, and silver claws: Nuclear Man (Mark Pillow). He takes in his new body, flexing his joints, observing his nails, before pointing his arms towards the Earth and flying in the same direction.

Mark Pillow wasn't the first Nuclear Man. There was an entire sequence filmed with a 'first try' version of the creation: a much simpler, more childlike model, played by Clive Mantle. It involved Nuclear Man 1.0 showing up at the Metro Club Lacy mentioned earlier in the film and fighting Superman, a sequence that I remember as a child as Johnny Ball visited the set to watch it being filmed. It involved a lot of throwing and fighting, and the set piece of Superman and Nuclear Man pushing a line of cars from opposite ends. It was all cut from the final film, though you can see it for yourself on the 2012 box set, where, inexplicably, it has the theme from the Brian Cant show *Bric-a-Brac* placed over it as a temporary track.

In 2018, I hosted a screening and live podcast of *Superman IV* and asked Clive if he had any stories from the time. He sent me quite a few and very kindly agreed to let me share them again here:

'I went through several rounds of auditions for Sidney Furie who could tell that somewhere inside what I was improvising for him was what he wanted. It was bald and uninteresting on the page as I remember, but loosely basing the movement on Lennie from *Of Mice and Men*, which I'd just played in the West End, I just goofed around for him in whichever room we were in, including the wardrobe at Elstree for my final audition. Picking stuff up and being silly basically. I made him laugh and got the job.

'I can just remember standing with Sidney and Gene Hackman in the centre of the set and having Sid's back to me. I was in a dressing gown which covered my painted green body and felt a little left out of the conversation as Sid asked Gene, "So, Gene, how do you want to play this?" He sensed that I was being snubbed and said, "I don't know. Clive, what do you think?" It was a wonderful thing to do for a young actor and I was allowed to offer my thoughts, which they both liked, and that's what we did with the scene.

'The fight with Superman took quite a few nights to shoot, as I remember. It was great fun and was all manageable. I did most of it but was doubled by my long-term friend and stunt double Terry Richards during a couple of tricky bits. Chris Reeve was very friendly and very giggly. We shared a reasonable amount of downtime on set together. He certainly wasn't disappearing off to his dressing room all the time. We played the "movie game" a lot on night shoots, where someone says a film and the next person has to say an artist or director etc that worked on it and the next person has to say another film they were involved with etc. That certainly passes the time while they're rigging a stunt.

'I was only aware that I was cut after I got my agent to enquire about tickets to the premiere. I was doing a TV job in Birmingham and staying on about the tenth floor of a hotel when my agent rang and said that she was about to have her most difficult conversation ever with a client. I was very shocked and was told that the preview audiences hadn't understood the character [you would have to be surgically dead not to understand it] and that I was no longer in the film. The temptation to leave the hotel through that high window did pass through my mind and I don't know for how long I was in that state of mind, before realising it was not the answer. I have never really totally recovered my love or trust for the business as a result. There have been highlights since, of course, but I could never reconcile myself to the fact that through no fault of my own, my world had changed again, this time for the worse.'

Nuclear Man has arrived at Lex's apartment, revealing his full form – Michael Bolton ready for a workout – in the exact costume he had to wear to the royal premiere, where he shook hands with Charles and Diana while looking like he should be in *The Running Man*. He walks across the floor, leaving burning footprints as he goes, booming in his borrowed voice (he was dubbed by Gene Hackman) about how he has to destroy Superman at once. Lenny tells him to cool his boots and that he's just an experiment, a mere freako, which leads to Nuclear Man spinning on the spot at high speed and, sadly, not killing him. Lex reveals that he knows his Achilles' heel and leads him into a shadow that powers him down immediately. He needs to be in direct sunlight at all times or he turns cold and shuts down.

John Williams didn't return to score the fourth instalment. Instead, he suggested his old friend Alexander Courage (the man who created the *Star Trek* theme) and also contributed some new themes ('Nuclear Man Theme', 'Lacy's Theme' and 'Jeremy's

Theme'), all of which help the score stand out as strong work. While the film has a myriad of problems, the music is definitely not one of them.

Lacy has suggested that Clark *and* Superman come to her penthouse for high tea, and they've *both* accepted – I smell a sitcom! So begins a lamentable farce that involves Clark and Superman entering at different times before leaving swiftly, with all exteriors filmed at a building that is now an Argos, which somehow seems fitting. It's on the last of these visits as Superman that he receives a high-frequency message from Lex that he's going to blow up a building unless he comes to see him (again borrowing from the first film), so he races away to stop him. Lacy and Lois are left pondering whether Clark is dead.

'The Dude of Steel, boy, are you gonna get it,' Lenny says to Superman as he enters the wacky apartment to find out about this bomb. Lex confesses it was all a ruse to lure him there. He doesn't just want a chat; he wants to introduce him to Lenny and his newest creation. Lex asks Superman to look closely at the cell structure to see if it reminds him of anyone, at which point Superman should be asking Lex if he's been going through his bins. Lex explains that, with him out of the way, he can make real money and profit from the threat of war for years to come.

The epic battle between Superman and Nuclear Man begins as they tumble down the building, the effects spluttering, juddering and faltering under the weight of their own ambition – resembling a Terry Gilliam segment rather than a major Hollywood spectacle. It's a game of cat and mouse, with Nuclear Man flying around the world breaking things while Superman fixes them, with the pinnacle being the Great Wall of China. Nuclear Man lands and blows out a whole row of the wall with hand blasts. Superman arrives and replaces it with his eyes – another budget victim, with the sequence, as written, calling for him to replace the bricks at lighting speed. Instead, the audience is left wondering what the fuck just happened.

Nuclear Man plucks the Statue of Liberty from its resting place and attempts to drop it on the people below. Superman catches it, and as he flies to replace it, he is scratched on the neck by the new baddie on the block and collapses on the floor in agony. Nuclear Man then lands, takes a run-up and boots Superman into the sky, causing his cape to fly off and float down the front of the statue in a last poignant act.

Warfield has two presents for Lacy. One, she's now the publisher of the *Daily Planet*, and has her own office to prove it, and two, Superman's cape. Someone found it and handed it in. She's just about to freak out when Lois storms in brandishing that day's paper, with the headline 'Superman Dead?', telling them they've both gone too far and she's quitting. She grabs the cape as she leaves. 'Let her go, darling,' Warfield says to Lacy. 'I mean, she's useless.' I guess that means Lois's probation is over. He also tells her to fire Clark Kent as he hasn't been in and hasn't called. Lacy is worried about him, though, and he basically tells her that you should never shit where you eat, and she tells him to shove it.

Clark sits in the dark, a fire raging in front of him. He's wrapped in blankets, feverish yet freezing, pale yet full of colour, worn out, sick. His door is forced open, and it's Lois, checking if he's still alive. He tells her he has a really bad flu, and she explains that everyone has been worried about him as he didn't call the office. She also tells him how sad she is about Superman having gone missing. The world needs Superman, she needs Superman, and she loves him very much, will always cherish the time they spend together, and no matter how few minutes they spend together she's always happy, though she has very vague memories of the time they spend together, as he always wipes her memory. Clark sits there shivering, looking in her eyes, with a face that screams, 'So what?' He tells her he needs to get some more rest, so she tearfully leaves him to his sofa and tissues.

Lex beams a smile that could light the darkest room as he sits behind a vast wall of money. The arms dealers are equally happy:

they've all done very well since Superman left the picture a few days ago. Lex thanks them for their hard work and support, but in the same breath tells them they're out. Nuclear Man is his new enforcer, and he chases them from the room. Drunk on power, Lex speculates on the endless possibilities. With his brains and Nuclear Man's brawn, he could be a king, an emperor or, at the very least, Dom Littlewood.

The sun rises to bring a whole new day, crowning the city skyline with a fresh beam of hot orange. The light reaches Lex's penthouse and washes over a slumbering Nuclear Man. He rises like a phoenix and opens his eyes. On Lex's desk in front of him is a copy of the *Daily Planet* with the headline, 'New Publisher of Your Favourite Paper', accompanied by a large photograph of Lacy Warfield. So, with what can only be described as the 'Nuclear Horn', he races to the *Planet* to give Lacy a good time, stopping briefly on the way to roar and smash up the street – a street on Elstree's backlot, which had low sheds in the background instead of towering steel skyscrapers.

He's greeted at the front door by Superman, now revitalised after using the mysterious green crystal found in the Smallville barn. He tells Nuclear Man to back away, that he'll never let him in to see Lacy, but Nuclear Man has an ace up his sleeve. He begins to make all the innocent people of the city lift (on all too obvious strings) or move backwards as if they were pieces of film put in reverse. Superman has seen enough and agrees to take him to Lacy. As they both walk into the building, Superman bundles him into a lift, where Nuclear Man shuts down immediately, and then dumps him on the Moon. However, Nuclear Man awakes immediately, and they have another battle in the dark of space, where Nuclear Man gets the upper hand. He buries Superman in the grey rock before flying back down to Metropolis to retrieve Lacy and bring her into space. I'm not sure how, but, to his credit, she doesn't die immediately.

Superman has a great plan. He moves the entire Moon (ignoring the extreme weather conditions this would surely cause down on Earth) to block the sun, which shuts Nuclear Man down immediately and allows Superman to rescue Lacy, take her back to Earth and then drop Nuclear Man into an open nuclear core, thus creating an enormous power surge that destroys him – probably causing Chernobyl nuclear reactor Unit 4 to explode, but at least he's saved the day.

Back on Earth, Perry is overseeing the *Daily Planet* being returned to its former elegant glory, much to the consternation of Warfield. Perry managed to convince the city's bankers to put up the money to buy back the paper without the owner knowing until it was a completed deal. 'The *Daily Planet* should be treated like a natural resource,' the editor says before barking one of the strangest line readings in cinema, 'PRO-TEC-TED FROM PRED-A-TORS!' He then informs Warfield that he's now a minority shareholder and he hates tits.

Superman calls a press conference at Milton Keynes train station, to tell the assembled press that he was wrong to think that he could end all wars. It's not his right to do that, it's up to the people to demand it, and he's confident that one day it will come, after all. 'I wish you could see the Earth the way that I see it because, when you really look at it, it's just one world.' A beautiful sentiment from a man who kisses women into silence.

Lex and Lenny try to make a run for it, but Superman finds them, first dropping Lenny at a boys' school run by a priest, to set him on the straight and narrow (I'm saying nothing), and then taking Lex right back to the chain gang he started on. 'Just one thing – how did you beat him?' asks Lex as he's being taken into custody. 'High school physics,' says Superman, telling him he figured out his creature's weakness and exploited it to save the world. It has to be said that a film that has a woman screaming and breathing happily in space while the Moon is moved around should stay away from any mention of 'high school physics' as that's the very last fucking thing at work here.

As the beautiful theme begins to exquisitely manoeuvre into place, the same old end segment from the first film whirs into life, with the beautifully lit Superman from 1978 looking down over the world and smiling at the audience, almost thanking them for watching this and apologising via the medium of a superior film.

If *Superman IV* had been a success, Reeve was apparently told by the producers he could direct the next chapter (though whether he would have wanted to is another matter). As it happens, the film was not well received in any capacity, and it put the final nail in the coffin of the man from Krypton, though it didn't stop Cannon going to Cannes the following year with a poster promising a *Superman V* that thankfully never came to pass as within a few years they'd cease to exist.

I salute you, *Superman IV: The Quest for Peace*. Yes, you are absolutely terrible and one of the worst superhero films ever made, but there's a charm in there, supplied by Hackman and Reeve, that covers it with a sheen of goodwill that puts it just above disaster and well within the realms of a misguided and well-intentioned mistake.

They can be a great people, Kal-El, they wish to be. They only lack the light to show the way.

TWELVE

BATMAN

1989

ONLY ONE WILL CLAIM THE NIGHT

Rising from the ashes of a camp legacy that had long 'gone West', Tim Burton's *Batman* took the Caped Crusader into very dark territory. Shades of blue and grey were replaced by the blackest of black shadows and dense, labyrinthine smoke. Surf guitar music was ditched for themes of pure gothic horror. This was to be like nothing seen before: this was a new Batman, a Batman awash with eighties cynicism, violent undertones and downright abominable people. Not a pun in sight, nor a whimsical, sideways building climb. This Gotham was hundreds of feet tall and full to the brim with crime.

Our first introduction to the new Batman is a trip through a giant bat symbol carved out of stone. Our senses rock as we navigate the many trenches, nooks and crannies, and Danny Elfman's incredible theme purrs ominously and writhes awake from a deep slumber. There can be no doubt that this one is up there with Williams' 'Superman Theme', and maybe even scrapes the same orbital skies. It's the very definition of iconic, and when the final note resonates within the bang of a gong, you realise that this is something altogether very different.

The Gotham set feels alive. It's teeming with extras and absolutely *huge*. Each tower on the broken horizon resembles an arm reaching out to the heavens for some form of redemption, each street leads to avenues of peril, and each sidewalk emanates gusts of smoke like souls leaving their bodies. While Burton generally gets the credit for the look of the film and the dark feeling of it, in most circles, the real architect of this dystopian nightmare was Anton Furst. Furst's career was brief (he was dead, by suicide, within two years) but his impact enormous. He made fairy tales terrifying in *A Company of Wolves* and somehow managed to bring Vietnam to London for *Full Metal Jacket*. With *Batman*, Furst wanted something that would be remembered for ever. 'It has to be unique, like no other film,' he told his friends when he got the job. He talked excitedly of the Futurists, of Fritz Lang, of holograms and 'cosmic reality'. Furst really enjoyed working with Burton. 'I don't think I've ever felt so naturally in tune with a director,' he said. 'Conceptually, spiritually, visually, or artistically [Furst also designed the legendary poster campaign]. There was never any problem because we never fought over anything. Texture, attitude and feelings are what Burton is a master at. We imagined what New York City might have become without a planning commission. A city run by crime, with a riot of architectural styles. An essay in ugliness. As if hell erupted through the pavement and kept on going.' What Furst designed and created was a set that was the biggest since *Cleopatra* in 1963, and it was the last time that that much money would be spent on a set of such a scale.

A father (Garrick Hagon) manoeuvres his wife and son through the streets dripping with crime, fog and extras. A hot-dog cart passes, playing a song by Prince ('The Future'), who had his own album of *Batman*-inspired music released at the time. Jon Peters was a producer on the film and the man who practically invented accompanying pop soundtracks with his work on *A Star Is Born* and *Flashdance*, so this was his genius idea. In a 2001 interview with *Rolling Stone*, Prince said that the original intention was for the album to be shared with Michael Jackson, with Prince effectively playing the Joker and Jackson taking on the role of Batman. Thankfully, it never happened.

The hapless father is having no luck getting a cab and even has to put up with a sex worker propositioning his ten-year-old son, which even for a rundown city seems decidedly uncool. He decides to nip down an alleyway as a shortcut, where he is robbed at gunpoint by Christopher '*Auf Wiedersehen Pet*' Fairbank. As the family run, and the mother screams, a cartoon of Batman's shadow, up on a high ledge, turns and ominously heads towards the noise.

A couple of thieves sit within a nest of stolen things. The guts of a wallet and purse spill out as Fairbank counts the spoils and makes a reference to the American Express adverts of the time – 'Don't leave home without it' – which feels so dated, he may as well high-five the Noid from the pizza ads. The younger of the two (George Roth) doesn't want to hang around. He tells the tale of a friend of theirs who was thrown off a rooftop by 'The Bat', but Fairbank is having none of it. As he mocks the other for talking shit, we see a winged figure slowly descend onto the roof behind them, silent and menacing, like a ninja or an estate agent after an elderly death. He presents himself to the duo, wings akimbo, and after kicking one of them through a door, he hangs Fairbank over the ledge of the building and orders him to tell all his friends about him, especially to mention that he has a massive cock. Fairbank demands to know who he is. 'I'm Batman,' the man in black growls before jumping over the edge and vanishing into the night.

This is no normal origin story. Batman is already suited up and known to the criminals and police of Gotham. While not infamous yet, he is gaining a reputation. The origin story is slowly revealed throughout the film, which, with hindsight, is much appreciated, given that we are now bombarded with modern comic-book films awash with tedious origin tales.

A press conference is being held for Gotham's new District Attorney Harvey Dent (Billy Dee Williams). He's pledging to rid the streets of Gotham of crime, and with the help of Commissioner Gordon (Pat Hingle), he'll be targeting crime boss Carl Grissom (Jack Palance) and shutting down his operations – and, if he fails, he's Tommy Lee Jones. There's an empty spot at the table, set for Bruce Wayne, but he is strangely absent. Probably off doing weird billionaire stuff like promising to end world hunger (and then not), sending space dragons with lasers to Ukraine (and then not) and buying Twitter and making it worse.

Watching this speech on TV is smooth criminal Jack Napier (Jack Nicholson). He's not impressed. He thinks decent people shouldn't live in Gotham, that they would probably be happier somewhere else, like Croydon. He's playing with a deck of cards – and also playing with fire. Alicia (Jerry Hall), the beautiful lady by his side, is Carl Grissom's girl. She mentions that if Grissom ever found out about their affair, Jack would be in trouble, but Jack is an arrogant bastard. He boasts that Grissom is an old man who needs him by his side to run the city and he'll never find out about them. As he preens in the mirror, Alicia comes to his side, takes in his reflection and tells him, 'You look fine.' Jack coolly turns and looks into her eyes. 'I didn't ask,' he counters before wandering off to be cool somewhere else.

Back at the scene of the crime, reporter Alexander Knox (Robert Wuhl) questions Lieutenant Eckhardt (William Hootkins) about reports of a six-foot bat terrorising the criminals of Gotham City. They say he drinks blood, that he can't be killed, that there's absolutely no way he's six foot tall. Knox is a persistent man, and clearly a fine reporter, but Eckhardt is having none of it. He's taking the 'fake news' angle. He then wanders off to have a meeting with Jack Napier in the next alley to collect his pay-off. Jack tells him that he needs to deal with the Harvey Dent problem and, rather than kill him, why not throw acid over half his face? Eckhardt tells him he reports only to Grissom and that Jack is a psycho with no future in the game. As Jack leaves, laughing away to himself, Eckhardt wryly mumbles, 'Where have you been spending your nights?' This either means he'll tell Grissom all about how Jack has been shagging his girlfriend or he's doing an advert for Premier Inn.

Back at the *Gotham Globe* newspaper, Knox walks through the office to get to his desk, ridiculed at every step by his colleagues for believing in this daft bat story. He is even mocked by the newspaper cartoonist 'Bob Kane' (Denis Lill), who gives him a hand-drawn picture of a bat in a thirties-era gangster suit with the caption, 'Have you seen this man?' Fun fact: that picture was indeed drawn by the real Bob Kane. When Knox reaches his desk, he sees a pair of lady's legs perched across it – and they are attached to a lady, they're not just a pair of severed legs. It's Vicki Vale (Kim Basinger). She's been reading his bat stories and thinks he's on to something. Knox knows her work – she's a photographer who's worked for *Vogue* and *Cosmo*, so obviously he mentions that she can take a picture of his penis but she'll need a big lens. She's just come back from the Corto Maltese revolution with some fine pictures of dead people. She wants to work with Knox and document his search for this 'bat man', and why don't they start at Bruce Wayne's charity fundraiser, as Commissioner Gordon will be there and, as luck would have it, Vicki has two tickets?

Carl Grissom is livid. True to his word, Harvey Dent has begun to crack down on his operations. He's closed all his American Candy shops in Piccadilly Circus and, if he makes a connection with his crew and Axis Chemicals, they could be in trouble. His lawyer says they need to move out of it immediately and maybe get into the PPE business if there's ever a pandemic (satire). Jack pipes up from his solo card game and suggests they break in, steal the records, trash the place and say it was industrial espionage. Grissom loves this idea and suggests Jack handle it personally, passionately telling him that he is his 'number one guy' in such a way that only Jack Palance can, with gritted jaw and frothing insanity.

Bruce Wayne's balls are always admired. More so than the charity ones he often holds for Gotham's socialites where they listen to the music of Prince and play roulette. Knox mingles and manages to get a few questions in to the top brass, but no one wants to talk. When Vicki and Knox wander into a room filled with suits of armour, they encounter Bruce Wayne (Michael Keaton).

It's here that we need to park in a superhero layby for a moment and talk about the reaction to Keaton's casting. The studio wanted square jaws, muscles and action stars, but Burton knew what he wanted. He could only think about why Bruce Wayne would need to dress as a bat if he was a man-mountain. As far as Burton was concerned, the man behind the mask should be a normal guy outside it. He wanted Keaton (and producer Jon Peters backed his choice) as he felt that he had a crazy look in his eye and would be someone who would need to create the look to make himself scarier. Fans were not happy when they found out Tim Burton would be directing *Batman*. They were even less happy when they heard Michael Keaton was playing Batman. Taken from the *Toronto Star* in 1988: 'The caped crusader may turn out to be a wimp. Batman's fans at first were thrilled by reports that Warner Bros. would spend $30 million to make a new Batman movie, for release next summer. They're no longer thrilled. Warner has cavalierly ignored their advice to cast a serious macho type – Sylvester Stallone or Clint Eastwood, say – in the spectacular. Instead, director Tim Burton has given the part to Michael Keaton. Michael Keaton is no Sylvester Stallone.

'Best known as a wacky prankster in Burton's 1988 comedy, *Beetlejuice*, Keaton has a receding hairline and a less-than-heroic chin. He stands an estimated 5 feet 10 inches tall, weighs in at 160 pounds or so, and "looks like a hundred guys you see on the street", says Beau Smith, a Batman fan in Ceredo, W. Va. "If you saw him in an alley wearing a bat suit, you would laugh, not run in fear. Batman should be 6'2', 235 pounds, your classically handsome guy with an imposing, scary image."'

Warner Brothers received over 50,000 letters of complaint (pre-internet, *handwritten* letters), which is akin to modern fans signing a petition to have *The Last Jedi* remade. To appease the fans, Bob Kane was brought in as creative consultant.

But back to the ball . . . Bruce is telling Knox and Vicki he's a fan of their work – though you get the distinct impression he's more into Vicki and is about to get into a much deeper conversation with her about his many leather-bound books – when he's interrupted by Alfred (Michael Gough), who tells him Commissioner Gordon has had to leave. When Bruce doesn't react, Alfred says it was '*rather unexpectedly*' with such force that he may as well say, 'And since you're fucking Batman, you should go and get changed right now and fucking check it out, you dopey prick.'

Axis Chemicals is a bust. The place is already cleaned out, and as Jack realises he's been set up, Eckhardt and the police arrive with orders to shoot to kill. This sequence was filmed at Acton Lane power station, which was the same location used for *Aliens*, and it really feels like not much set dressing was required. As Jack and his gang fan out in order to find an escape route, the police begin to open fire on them, that is until Commissioner Gordon arrives on the scene and demands that Napier be taken alive. Batman swoops in and begins to take some of Jack's men out while also silently tracking Jack's movements. Eventually, he has him on a high platform and picks him up by his lapels – undoubtedly hard work with a 1989 Jack Nicholson. A bullet deflects into Jack's face, causing him to tumble over the handrails and fall into a big vat of green sauce, where he will either turn into the Joker or die of cancer, we just don't know which.

Vicki sups her soup at the end of a dinner table. At the other end, Bruce asks if it's OK, in a way that suggests he's definitely dipped something in it. The table is at least thirteen miles long, with Vicki sitting in Sheffield and Bruce in Gotham. They eventually move into the small kitchen, where Alfred tells the most boring story about how Bruce once fell off a horse, but this seems enough for

Vicki, and they head upstairs to have sexual intercourse (Bruce, not Alfred). Say what you like about billionaire Bruce Wayne, but he commits to the Bat role. Vicki wakes up in the middle of the night to find him sleeping upside down, and I assume he also urinates in that weird bat way too.

In a basement office, under low lighting, a man is having a set of bandages removed by a stereotypical basement-dwelling doctor. He barks for a mirror and is handed one while the doctor hurriedly adds some caveats that he did the best he could, and although he's now the Joker, at least he doesn't have the cancer – oh, and, also, you can no longer dance in time during museum heists. The mystery patient is at once horrified and pleased with what he sees, laughing maniacally and uncontrollably as he stumble-exits up the stairs.

Grissom stalks around his cold, dark and empty grand office. He is robed in silk and slippers, ready for bed. He pours himself a whisky and, as the elevator bell rings, he asks if it's his 'sugar bumps', which we assume means Alicia, but he could well be talking to his own testicles. Sadly, it's Jack. He's silhouetted in darkness and brandishing a gun. 'You set me up over a woman,' he says, with steely anger in his voice. Grissom asks Jack if they can cut a deal, but he's immediately told that Jack is dead and he is now 'Joker' before he's pumped full of bullets.

In the morning, Vicki suggests she and Bruce meet up again, but Bruce says he's busy and that he has to go out of town for a few days, a lie that Alfred *immediately* exposes the moment he speaks with her on her way out. I would have fired him for that, to be honest. I don't care that you helped me when I fell off a horse or wiped my bum when I was a kid, you're cramping my player lifestyle, man. Never stand in the way of a man and his hunnies.

Gotham's gangsters are having a pow-wow, with Joker at the head of the table. He's donning make-up to make him look like a normal human being – sort of like Simon Cowell does – and is suggesting that they all team up for the forthcoming festival of Gotham to celebrate its 200th anniversary and run it into the ground. The assembled crooks are a strange-looking bunch, with everything from clichéd Italians to Albert Einstein (Albert Evansky – who also played the librarian in *Indiana Jones and the Last Crusade*, fact fans) in attendance. Rotelli (Edwin Craig), one of the most vocal of the bunch, asks what happens if they say no, so Joker answers him by burning him to death with a hand buzzer. As the shaken gangsters leave to think it over, Joker chats to the horrifically burnt skeleton, telling him he's glad he's dead and laughing as he wipes the make-up from his face. *Batman* was the very first UK film to receive the newly created 12 certificate, and it's scenes like this that explain why.

Burton is on record with how grateful he was to Jack Nicholson during the entire project: 'The casting of Jack as the Joker, I don't even think there was necessarily a conversation, he *is* the Joker. He was everybody's first choice. That was about as clear as it ever got. In fact, there was even a worry he was too perfect for it. You expect Jack to be the Joker, but for me he goes beyond that, he is so amazing that way. He was the godfather of this movie for me in the sense he was really supportive. Once he was in, it gave the project an energy that is hard to describe. It's the first time I met an actor like that – you see what someone like that does for the crew and me and for everybody, with the energy levels. You see people's pace get picked up – it's amazing to watch.'

Bruce walks out of Knebworth House, the lavish, grandiose Tudor mansion used as Wayne Manor. He slips into his car and sets out through the gates, unaware that Vicki is following close behind. He arrives in central Gotham, walks into an alleyway, places two red flowers in the middle of the pavement and takes a moment. Vicki watches on, confused. Just why would a man do that? The answer is obvious: he is clearly commemorating the life and work of Percy Thrower.

There's no time to dwell on this matter, though, as a gangster named Ricorso (John Dair from *Porridge*) is throwing a press conference, and it's not at a garden centre opposite a sex shop. He announces that Grissom has asked him to take care of his business interests until he returns from wherever he is. The assembled reporters begin to ask questions, but a lone voice from the back confirms it's true. Joker says he saw Grissom sign it with his own hand, then throws a quill into Ricorso's neck, killing him instantly. As he vacates the area in a hail of gunfire, a lone man follows: Bruce Wayne. He's seen this man before, either in *One Flew Over the Cuckoo's Nest* or from that time he dropped him into the cancer pool.

Bruce races home, mind all a whirl, so Alfred takes this moment to tell him that Vicki Vale's the best girlfriend he's had in ages, and he should know, he's had to drive enough home. He thinks it might be worth telling her that he's Batman. Alfred should wind his neck in, especially as he nearly scuppered everything by being a big mouth. Bruce tells him to forget about all that shit: Jack Napier is still alive, he's running Grissom's men, and he's forced them all to dress like clowns, which must have been a fun team-building day at Mob HQ.

'Jack's in charge now.'

'Oh, great. I like him. I'm sure his stern leadership and evil nature will get us back on top.'

'About that . . . he wants us to call him Joker now.'

'What?'

'Yeah. He's going for a sort of clown look.'

'Clown look?'

'Yeah. He's a clown now.'

'OK . . .'

'And we also have to dress like clowns and wear bomber jackets.'

'I didn't sign up for this. This is ridiculous.'

'You also need to listen to this Prince album.'

Joker's operation is starting to fly into action. He's made a chemical compound called 'Smilex' that he is putting into cosmetic products – the horrible side effects of which leave the poor victim with an awful rictus grin, sort of like Renée Zellweger after a round of Lambruscos. A TV news reader even succumbs to the Joker's evil mixture live on air, collapsing in laughter in front of a watching audience of terrified viewers. It's lucky it didn't happen on GB News, otherwise only three or four people would be aware.

Alfred checks the phone messages. There's one from Vicki telling Bruce that she'll be a bit late for their dinner at the museum, which is news to Bruce as he's not arranged to meet her. Will Alfred call her back and tell her Bruce might also be late as he is Batman, or will he just carry on doing his job and stop being a fucking buzzkill? We shall soon find out.

Vicki waits alone in the impressive Flugelheim Museum. Waiters buzz around the tables as the well-to-do of Gotham enjoy their meals. All in all, the museum restaurant feels like a Nando's. Production designer Anton Furst described this set as his most successful, speaking about it in the 1989 *Official Book of the Movie*: 'I wanted the museum to be a surprise, a new, radical edifice which concealed an older building underneath. The radical broad stroke of the exterior conceals a style which borrows from Otto Wagner as well as brownstone housing. The locomotive look of the outside is intentionally balanced by a roof light on top, through which Batman jumps in to save Vicki Vale. Having soft light inside was quite deliberate. I wanted to reverse the notion of a conventional building where you are normally happy to walk back outside into the light. Here it's just the opposite.'

As the restaurant becomes engulfed in poisoned gas, Vicki puts on the mask a mystery person had delivered to her table. Waiters fall, chefs collapse, and an old man wilts into his soup. The smoke clears, the door bursts open, and Joker lets out the infamous line, 'Gentlemen, let's broaden our minds. Lawrence?' As Prince Rogers Nelson sings with the usual dripping sexuality about a man who likes to party, we're forced to witness a dozen middle-aged white men staggering around the building daubing paintings in neon colours and looking out of breath while they do it. It's enough to make you want to throw up into your raspberry beret.

Joker looks through Vicki's portfolio, judging it all as crap until he reaches the pictures of death, guts and revolution, which are much more his style, and if this Joker gig doesn't work out, there's a place for him at TMZ. He wants Vicki to document his work and join him in the 'avant-garde of the new aesthetic'. Naturally, she's reluctant, what with him being an actual, all-singing all-dancing psychopath, but then she must remember that even the Tories have photographers. It's not long before Joker oversteps the mark, and as he's about to spray acid in her face, the glass ceiling smashes and Batman drops to the ground. He races Vicki out of the door, and they jump into the waiting Batmobile.

This Batmobile is one for the ages. Immediately iconic and usually at the forefront of people's minds when they hear the word, it was designed by Julian Caldow, who took inspiration from old salt-flat racers and thirties sports cars. It also has jet-engine parts thrust into the front for good measure, along with bat wings and the obligatory rocket booster at the back.

As they make their escape to the Batcave, Danny Elfman's 'Descent Into Mystery', a beautiful baroque nightmare of church organs, manic rolling strings and demonic choirs, whisks them into the heart of the night. As the vehicle reaches its destination, it's immediately clear that this Batcave is in dire need of a health and safety inspection. It's a nightmare in there, and with all those bats, you'd need a tetanus jab just to walk in.

Vicki is worried that he's brought her there for nefarious purposes, like maybe he'll whip out his E-meter and measure her for Thetans, but in actual fact, old Batman has cracked the Smilex code: when the tampered cosmetic products are mixed together, they activate and turn everyone into Danniella Westbrook at 5 a.m. Armed with this information, Vicki gets the story to Knox so the paper can run with it.

Pressured by Alfred, who seems to think Vicki is the best woman in the world (he's *definitely* got a peephole installed somewhere), Bruce pays her a visit. His intention is to tell her that he is actually Batman and that he didn't touch her the night before, but he's not so sure about Alfred. However, his visit is interrupted by a visit from the Joker. He has a package for Vicki and tells her that he hadn't finished talking to her the night before, but before he can get into it, Bruce reappears and tells Joker the story of a man called Jack who was a total psychotic loser who got sloppy. He then goes full crazy, with Keaton showing just why he was not only the perfect man to play the part, but also the perfect foil for Nicholson, as both have the capacity to go from zero to insane in milliseconds.

Joker responds to Bruce's angry theatrics by pulling his gun out and asking him a simple question – a question that holds more weight than he could possibly realise: 'You ever dance with the devil in the pale moonlight?' This stops Bruce in his tracks; not because it's deep or something out of a cracker (though it could be), but because he's heard it before. A shot rings out, and Bruce slides down the wall to the floor, with Joker leaving Vicki with a parting message: 'My smile is just skin deep. If you could see inside, I'm really crying. You might join me for a weep,' before pretend-farting his way down the hall. When Vicki turns to check on Bruce, he's gone, leaving behind a silver tray with a bullet jammed in it. Either he made a run for it, or he's now a silver tray.

Back in the cave, Bruce is poring over documents – old files detailing the death of his parents. This is the reason why he goes to that alleyway every year. His parents were murdered on that very spot, and he witnessed it all as a child. Little does Bruce know that we'll see this event repeated ad infinitum, to the point that it seems that a Batman film is simply a series of flashbacks of the death of Thomas and Martha Wayne, and that the Batman bit is all just side salad. We see a young Bruce face the man who fired the two shots, Jack Napier (played by Hugo Blick), who leans into the light and utters those same ominous words to the young boy, 'You ever dance with the devil in the pale moonlight?'

As the realisation sinks in that the man who murdered his parents is currently having the very worst midlife crisis possible (making Matt Hancock's seem like a walk in the park), Bruce's thoughts are interrupted by the appearance of Vicki, with a knowing Alfred walking away, clearly having shown her into Batman's most secret place, the rat. Vicki mainly wants to know why he chooses to dress up like a big flying rat and smash people over the head, and Bruce tries to take it in a more cerebral direction by telling her it's not a perfect world, and this sort of feels like a very highbrow version of the 'we'll just tell Mom we ate the pie' bit from *American Pie*. He tells her that the Joker is out there right now causing trouble and he has to go to work, so he leaves her to dwell on the thought that her new boyfriend is a weird cosplay dude who thumps burglars.

Bruce suits up and looks into the bright light, showing his bat symbol, which for this film is slightly different to the standard bat one. (The licence for Warner Bros. to use it hadn't cleared when shooting began, which seems insane.) Though a fun fact about the Batsuit is that the boots were supplied by Nike, and you can see this at times, if you look hard enough.

Joker is holding his own carnival, complete with balloons that are quite obviously designed by Tim Burton, with a crying baby and various crazed clowns. As the Joker floats round the corner of central Gotham, a Prince song begins to play ('Trust'), and we are again treated to the sight of the Joker and his men jiggling around, but with the added bonus of them distributing money to the good people of the city. However, the Joker soon announces that he has to kill them with giant poison-releasing dirigibles – and if that ain't just capitalism in a nutshell.

As the people run in panic to find cover from the gas, a distant rumble is heard in the sky, a faraway bellow that gains in volume and speed, becoming more of an ominous, whistling sound as it becomes visible in the night sky. It's a giant black plane, shaped like a bat. It flies in with one swoop and removes all the poisoned balloons, taking them high beyond the clouds and releasing them into the atmosphere. Because Bruce is an extra cool motherfucker, he then maximises the opportunity of a full moon to rise up in the plane and make a bat symbol, which looks awesome as shit.

He returns to the streets, guns and rockets aimed towards Joker, who, to his credit, stands without fear, beckoning this howling machine of death towards him, positively loving the fact that it opens fire on him but misses every time. He flicks open his jacket and pulls from his trousers a pistol so big that a psychoanalyst would be demanding he lie down on a couch and tell him about his mother at once. With one shot from his trouser cannon (not like that), Joker achieves a direct hit, sending the Batplane careering towards the street in a wrestle of smoke and fire (with some lovely Derek Meddings miniature work), eventually coming to rest on the steps of the vast Gotham cathedral.

In the 1989 making-of book, Anton Furst referred to it as the 'establishing part of the city . . . The problem here was to create a cathedral which was taller than the tallest skyscraper and still make it credible. It had to be over 1,000 feet (330 metres) high. I then remembered that some of the 1930s skyscrapers in New York produced a cathedral effect at the top by means of interesting gothic detail. I began to solve the puzzle.' Furst was primarily influenced by Gaudi, the Spanish architect who is best known for his cone-shaped cathedral in Barcelona, the Sagrada Família. 'I basically stretched Gaudi into a skyscraper and added a castle feel which was especially influenced by the look of a Japanese fortress.'

Vicki races to the crash site to see if Bruce is OK but is immediately intercepted by Joker, who has a helicopter coming to pick him up from the top of the cathedral in order to make his escape, though fuck knows how he thinks he'll get away with nearly murdering an entire city or where he'll go to hide, unless he's heading to Bin Laden's compound, and even that wasn't good enough in the end. As they make their way up the rickety, wooden stairs, Batman stirs from within the wreckage and follows them. On reaching the top, he's faced with some of the worst henchmen in recorded history, who, one can only assume, have been hiding up there the whole time. They either get beaten up easily, smashed in the nuts or fall down a hole. Not exactly elite.

As Vicki distracts Joker by pretending to give him a blow job, which would be quite the heel-turn, Batman appears beside him to ask if he's ever danced with the devil in the pale moonlight, before punching him right in the mouth. At last. The two titans of Gotham come face to face. What battle, what rumpus will break out? How long will it take? Who will be left standing after this long-awaited confrontation? So, the Joker gets the shit beaten out of him and plummets to his death. Oh.

As his body lies on the broken cement, his box of laughs peals through the dead air, and it's actually quite a haunting image that I am sure lived at the back of the minds of most kids who saw it. For those kids like me, who read the official comic before seeing the film, there's a scene missing from the ending, one where the press corps rush to a felled bat cape crumpled on the floor of the cathedral, only to find Knox under there smiling, which, let's be honest, was a bit lame, so it's a good thing it was never filmed.

Instead, we're left with a beautiful sequence of model shots, leading to the top of a skyscraper, from where Batman is keeping watch over the city. The newly installed Bat-Signal shines in the night sky, and Elfman's theme reaches a delicate and warm crescendo, ringing out tubular bells of joy to punctuate the steady triumph of the previous two hours and six minutes.

Batman was back. Warner Bros. had more merchandise than they could ever dream about, and without Burton's vision the rusted wheels of superhero films would never have got going again and Batman would only have been remembered as a man in a Spandex suit making puns while walking up a wall to surf guitar. Each and every superhero film that followed attempted to recreate the magic but never quite achieved the same trick. *Dick Tracy* the following year attempted to walk the same line (including the evocative logo poster), but it went too far in one direction and fell over its own feet.

This was lightning in a bottle – something that was incredible to witness coming to pass.

THIRTEEN

THE TRIAL OF THE INCREDIBLE HULK

1989

SUPERHEROES HULK AND DAREDEVIL JOIN FORCES IN AN EXPLOSIVE NEW ADVENTURE!

Every child has a story about something that sent them behind the sofa or out of the room altogether. It's often some sweaty *Doctor Who* creature or a scene from a horror film they shouldn't have witnessed so young. Something races into the psyche, peels open a scar and lurks there. Mine was very much the opening titles of *The Incredible Hulk*. If there was ever anything to ensure that I raced out of the room, apart from my father's gas, it was Banner opening those gamma-infused eyes.

By the mid-1970s, Universal Television (home of the mighty *Columbo*) had acquired a few characters from Marvel and were keen to make something out of them. Producer/writer Kenneth Johnson (*The Six Million Dollar Man*, *Bionic Woman*, *V*) was handed the job of picking one and running with it, so he chose the Hulk. He was reading *Les Misérables* at the time and saw some parallels, though I don't remember the bit in the musical where Hugh Jackman throws a bear across a pond. Johnson made some minor alterations from the comic-book source, changing the name from Bruce Banner to David as he felt it sounded silly (and executives thought it sounded 'gay') and not having the Hulk say the word 'Hulk' all the time (for example, 'Hulk threw bear across pond'). He certainly had a point there – and Stan Lee agreed with him. The finished show was essentially a man-on-the-run travelogue with Banner, having faked his own death, looking for a way to cure his terrible affliction while also helping those in need along the way (sort of like a radioactive *Kung Fu*, if you think about it), all the time accompanied by that iconic, sad theme as he wanders the winding highways of America. It was highly successful and ran from 1977 until 1982, but there was more to come.

The Trial of the Incredible Hulk was the second of three TV movies that were made to serve the function of 'back-door pilots' for other Marvel characters. In the previous outing (*The Incredible Hulk Returns* – also directed by Bill Bixby), it was Thor, and here we are introduced to the exciting Daredevil. Suffice to say, neither of them was picked up, and Hulk would go back into mothballs for the next ten years or so, angry but quiet.

'In each of us, there lives a kind of beast made of rage. Years ago, I used science to study this beast, to bring him out of me. I used gamma radiation to release him, but I used too much. Far too much. Now the beast is out of my control, emerging whenever anger strikes,' Banner informs us of his progress via an opening narration, with some clips from the TV show playing as we hear these solemn words.

Dr David Banner (Bill Bixby) digs ditches now. He's sporting a rough beard, weathered face and checked shirt. A hefty comedown for a once proud physician and scientist. He works hard, but there's no respect from the bigger men who dig with him – they push him to one side and throw him into the thick mud and dirty water, obviously unaware that he could quickly change and shove their heads up each other's arses. But they're in luck. This Banner has learned to suppress his anger. He simply turns the other cheek and leaves the site for the city, just in case he relapses and feeds a train up someone's penis. With his bag on his back, he takes a long walk towards another place, his sombre theme leaving pools of sadness in his wake. Upon his arrival in the city, he secures himself the shittiest room possible at a local flophouse.

An alarm wakes up a young, handsome, happening guy in his luxury apartment. He looks out of the window, soaks in the morning rays, dresses in his finest suit and heads downstairs. As he pulls his coat on, he reaches out to feel the air for his briefcase and his walking stick. This man is blind. This man is Matt Murdock (Rex Smith from *Street Hawk*): top lawyer, snappy dresser and man without fear. At work, a colleague asks why he spends so much time looking out of the window, seeing as he's blind and all. Murdock tells her it's so he can feel the sun on his face, and then asks if she slows down for car crashes. He wants to rid the city of Wilson Fisk (John Rhys-Davies) and his criminal empire, particularity the monstrous carbuncle of a skyscraper he's built in town.

Talking of which, Wilson Fisk is currently in his office giving precise orders via a microphone to two bank robbers. He knows every inch of the layout and walks them through the safety deposit boxes, where they score many a batch of diamonds. With the job well done, he leans back in his chair and exhales a satisfied sigh, the light glinting off his slicked-back, blackened hair and the sunglasses that he clearly stole off a dead cricketer. This is not the Wilson Fisk we've come to expect over the years. Gone is the well-groomed, oversized goon with a cueball head and gruff New York brogue. Instead, he's a Pavarotti impersonator, who's more at home on stage at the National Theatre booming about Kenneth Arrow than smashing Spider-Man in the face in a car park.

The bank robbers have disposed of the booty and entered the underground train network. Exuberant about pulling off the perfect heist, they decide to sexually assault a woman in broad daylight with everyone watching. David Banner is one of those onlookers, and he steps in to assist the poor woman but is thrown into a heap at the back of the train. Bad move. His eyes turn full gamma, and as he rises to his feet the whole train is shocked in unison. Not only is he now the size of three brick shithouses, not only does he now roar like a bear and not only is he now only wearing little shorts, but his grizzled grey beard has now completely fallen off. He makes short work of the criminals, throwing them to the east and west winds, before running into the tunnels and changing back into Banner. When the police arrive, they find him confused and in ripped trousers, as if he's just come from an acid-fuelled Morris dancing practice. The beard has also returned, which is nice.

Richard Kiel was originally cast as the Hulk, and a few of his shots remain in the very first episode of the TV show. However, it was felt that although he was very tall (7' 2"), he lacked the pure muscle required, so they decided to recast the role. Arnold Schwarzenegger was rumoured to have been turned down for being too small, before they settled on Lou Ferrigno, the other star of *Pumping Iron*, who relished playing the part. 'I loved the character,' he said in an interview with *Body Building* magazine in 2019. 'I love how he separates good from evil and how much he protects people and how he reacts to all of the adversity against him, especially the fact that he is not really a monster.'

'I'm Matt Murdock. I'm an attorney,' says the man behind the table, extending a hand to David Banner as he's brought into the interrogation room. Murdock explains that the men he beat up on the train work as thieves and killers for Wilson Fisk, and he wants to bring him down. Banner isn't interested, but Murdock reminds him that the men got away, a woman has concussion, and an elderly man was shot in the chaos and died. He thinks Banner's hiding something, particularly as people talked about a giant tree man going apeshit, and either Banner's connected to this or the Jolly Green Giant has fucked up this year's crop and gone on a rampage. There are no records of Banner anywhere, no fingerprints, no next of kin, nada. It's as if he never existed, like Jeremy Spake. Banner says that he wishes to live under the radar, off the grid and away from civilisation. Maybe a cage is the best place for him.

Wilson Fisk doesn't like loose ends, or loose women. He wants his men to kill the woman who survived the subway attack. If she talks, she could identify his men, which would lead back to the robbery, and that spells trouble for him and his awesome shades. So, a nurse at the hospital is ordered to do the job, and while Ellie Mendez (Marta DuBois) is sleeping, the killer nurse attends to her on her rounds, producing a giant needle, ready to plunge it in Ellie's neck. Suddenly, from out of the darkness, the nurse is grabbed by a man in black. Although his eyes are completely covered, he has the speed and agility of a mountain goat, and he proceeds to kill her in the most bizarre fashion imaginable: they struggle, she breaks free, he kneels and produces a stick, then she runs over it, trips and falls onto a machine that electrocutes her to death. Well directed, Bill Bixby. A male nurse walks in, and Ellie tells him a man helped her and jumped away into the night. 'Daredevil,' the man says, in awe. He's the only man who can trip people over with a stick.

'I want the Mendez woman taken alive,' Fisk orders his right-hand man, Edgar (Nicholas Hormann). This will lure out Daredevil, and he can finally have him killed. He also wants it captured on video, obviously so he can then sell the footage to *You've Been Framed* or *Faces of Death*, depending on how good it is. This will then lead to a big get-together with all the other crime gangs, and by showing them a video of a blind man being murdered, it will lead to them all joining forces to become one big cosy empire, like when McFly joined up with Busted. This all sounds wonderful were it not for a further fly in the ointment: Banner, or 'David Belson' as he's called himself. Fisk wants him killed too, as there must be no one left who can identify his men, though judging by his behaviour thus far, his mind could change on the flip of a coin.

In a courtroom dock, Banner sits and wallows in stress. The prosecution counsel shouts in his face. The judge joins in, and Murdock is on his feet, pleading for this harassment of his client to cease, but it's no good. Banner grips the stand with extreme force and begins the harrowing process of transformation as jury foreman Stan Lee watches on, looking positively juvenile. The beast rises and begins throwing shelves, chairs, pens and even people across the room, all the while flexing and roaring at the top of his lungs. Luckily, it's all a dream, and he wakes in his prison cell. He washes his face in the sink to regain his composure, but, sadly, this triggers a real-life transformation, leading to him bursting through his cell bars and racing out of the prison.

'David Belson? Don't be afraid, Matt Murdock sent me for you,' Daredevil says, standing in a now clean-shaven Banner's doorway. Banner is suspicious. It's not every day a man dressed like Zorro appears at your door and asks if you want to come with him to see something. Why should he trust this stranger? Why should he go with him? How does he know he isn't just another gangster sent to kill him? He gets his answer. The mask is pulled down, and Banner sees for himself: Matt Murdock is Daredevil, the man who can trip people over with sticks.

Back at Murdock's apartment, Banner reflects on how shit life must be if you're blind: the bare walls, no mirrors, the bland paint job and only one picture on the wall. I know you have your own demons, David, but there's really no need to rub shit in a blind man's face. Murdock explains the picture of the boxer. It's his father, his now dead father, who was killed for standing up for what he believed in. This picture is all he has left – a reminder that he needs to protect people who need protection, despite the fact that he can't see it. He's a lawyer, yes, but the law has become so corrupted, so hamstrung, in this city that he needs to go further and be there for those who need it most. After giving a potted history of his origin story, he asks for Banner's help to take down Fisk and save the kidnapped Ellie. Banner agrees to help him track down the two robbers, but that's all he can do. He can't control what happens if he goes further than that, much like Bill Cosby at a wine mixer.

Acting on a tip-off, Murdock races to an old movie studio to rescue Ellie and is greeted with the inevitable ambush. Fisk isn't stupid, and he didn't get where he is today without knowing how to murder blind people, even when they dress like a sous chef. He steps out of the shadows wearing a massive gaming headset, sunglasses and a huge overcoat, is tickled by how easy this all was. He laughs in Murdock's face when Murdock tells him to let the woman go and sends some ninjas out of the dark to deal with him. No problem, right? This is Daredevil. Wrong. Fisk also turns on confusing sounds and bright lights, taking away Daredevil's vast advantages. A camera is turned on to record the demise of the brave hero, and as he is kicked around the floor, things look exceedingly bleak. That is until Hulk bursts through the door and into the room, with Fisk giving off very strong 'What the fuck is that?!' energy. He wipes the floor with the ninjas, smashes up the room and carries Murdock away into the night, completely missing the chance to rescue Ellie, who is recaptured and taken away by Fisk.

Murdock is miserable. He's in bed, covered in bruises and has had to phone in sick, pretending he fell down some stairs. Banner, though, can see a lot of himself in Murdock (not like that) and admires the way he uses his curse to his own advantage while still holding down a decent job. Maybe one day he could do the same? Though I suppose you'd get sacked if you threw an Asda customer over a pond when they shouted at you for not having that awful Prime energy drink. Banner tells him he can cure his broken confidence and get him ship-shape again.

'Are you comfortable?' Edgar asks Ellie as she sits on a deluxe bed in her locked room, probably wishing by now that she'd taken the fucking bus that day. It's clear that Edgar is sympathetic to her plight and has come to realise just how monstrous and craven Fisk can be. He asks her, if all this crazy stuff hadn't happened and she was in a restaurant and he sent her some champagne, would she want to join him for a drink. She admits that, in those circumstances, she'd probably want the company of a nice man, but he isn't that: he's a killer. Edgar hopes to prove her wrong, and before leaving he tells her sometimes he saves lives too.

'Gentlemen, welcome,' Fisk booms as he enters a room filled with the darkest and worst the city has to offer. He raises a toast, but only with glasses full of ice – a special kind of ice of the diamond variety. He wants to celebrate the coming together of this vast criminal empire. The others enquire about his little problem (not his body odour), and he's so pleased to have been asked. He dims the lights and begins rolling his latest project: *Daredevil Gets the Shit Kicked Out of Him By Ninjas: The Movie.*

Edgar's weakness is on full display as he wanders into Ellie's room to tell her they can make their escape. What he doesn't realise is that the robber who molested her on the train is standing behind the door. 'This woman was supposed to be erased days ago,' he says, after thumping Edgar in the face. He hands Edgar a pillow as he lays Ellie down on the bed and tells him to suffocate her while he watches. Edgar looks down at her face, probably imagining that champagne rendezvous – the glasses clinking as they propose a toast to one another, the candlelight twinkling in their eyes, soft music in their ears, and, as they draw close for a kiss, his inevitable jizzing his pants. For the first time in his life, Edgar takes a stand. He throws the pillow to one side. He now faces an inescapable death, but it will be an honourable one. Luckily, Banner comes in and holds down the robber while Edgar knocks him out with a vase.

'Intermission!' Daredevil proclaims with misplaced confidence as he bursts through the screen showing the film of him being beaten up. He's cleared the building of Fisk's loyal criminals and watches in sonar as Fisk shits himself and runs away. 'Your power is finished in this city, Fisk,' he tells him as he blindly watches the villain awkwardly take off in a giant child's toy of a spaceship and escape. As exits go, it's up there with the shark exploding at the end of *Jaws: The Revenge* in terms of embarrassment, but at least this was made for TV.

'Do you think Fisk will be back?' Banner asks Murdock as he packs to leave. 'He'll try,' he answers before asking if Banner will stay to help, as he was particularly useful during this adventure, especially when he turned into a giant monster – that could have been very handy during the bit when he had to fight off loads of people. But Banner has decided it's time to be a doctor again (hopefully not Shipman) and to use his skills to find a way to cure himself. He's tired of running, tired of getting pushed into ditches by taller men, and really bored of turning into Hench Shrek. He thanks Murdock for making him realise this was all possible and, after shaking his hand, once again shoulders his backpack and, accompanied by his tragic music, makes his way back into the network of American highways. But this time he has a smile on his face. Still taking one day at a time, inevitably dogging of an evening and avoiding getting angry by curtailing his weekly watch of *Question Time*.

Ratings were very high for this film, although most audiences were annoyed that Hulk is barely in it and only went to trial in a dream sequence – obviously not thinking about how shit it would be if the Hulk actually was on trial with Johnnie Cochran front and centre saying, 'If the purple pants don't fit, you must acquit.' Daredevil wasn't as exciting as they'd hoped and had to wait to get his own show, and Hulk only had one more TV movie in him – and that spelled the end of this whole adventure. One can only hope that if anything came out of this, it's the knowledge that Edgar is still probably out there somewhere, sipping champagne in a kimono, knowing he did a good deed and, hopefully, reliving the memories of his highly erotic night with Ellie Mendez.

FOURTEEN

CAPTAIN AMERICA

1990

THE SENTINEL OF LIBERTY!
THE STAR-SPANGLED AVENGER!
THE MARVEL LEGEND!
CAPTAIN AMERICA SWINGS INTO ACTION WITH HIS MIGHTY SHIELD TO LAY THE STARS AND STRIPES ON THE FORCES OF EVIL!

In 1984, Cannon Films made a deal with Marvel to take over the rights to Spider-Man and Captain America for a mere $250,000. Obviously, the Marvel of today would sell you a pen for that, but in those days Stan Lee and the boys were effectively holding yard sales to keep the company afloat, and there was no film company that loved owning shiny things more than Cannon. Menahem Golan and Yoram Globus were great ideas men and had an eye for fantastic IP, but they were often hampered by the fact that they were pretty shit with money and all too frequently acted under the misguided impression that, once you sell a movie based on a poster, your work is done.

At Cannon, both *Spider-Man* and *Captain America* rolled around in development hell like old plimsolls in a tumble dryer for most of the eighties, with *Captain America* at one point being held in the sweaty palms of Michael Winner; thankfully, that version never got to see the light of day (although a couple of elements did). When Golan left Cannon, he took the *Captain America* project and rights with him as part of his exit deal and soon set about getting it made, as cheaply as possible, on his own. There was one problem, though – he was very close to losing the rights and had very little money to get it made. Enter the late, great Albert Pyun. He'd just made the Jean-Claude Van Damme film *Cyborg* for Cannon, which itself was a salvage operation, utilising the sets and costumes made for *Masters of the Universe II* (a film that was cancelled due to other financial woes). Pyun turned lemons into lemonade by writing *Cyborg* in one weekend and shooting it in a month, so he was clearly a man who could work under pressure and with a small budget. There was also the fact that he was a Captain America fan and had pitched a way to get the film made on a budget that would suit. What could possibly go wrong?

Porto Venere, Italy, 1936. Child genius Tadzio de Santis is wowing his family with his virtuoso piano skills. There is no doubt that this boy will go far. He could well grow up to be Bobby Crush or Richard Clayderman, but we'll never know if he could do a season at Blackpool, or seduce and destroy with his ivory tickling, as the room is suddenly invaded by fascists who, forever the art critics, murder his family and whisk poor Tadzio into the night. They want him for their top-secret super-soldier plan and, in a dark lab in the Loreno fortress, they show the results of their experiments to some Nazis: a big, red hench rat 'transformed by a secret process'. Now twice as strong and intelligent, which for a rat seems like it wouldn't be that impressive, it looks like a ruptured arse.

As with all Nazi plans in films, there's always one who has moral fibre, and in this case it's Dr Maria Vaselli (Carla Cassola), who was seemingly fine with turning rats into red lumps of meat but objects vociferously when it comes to using the same methods (of her own design) on little Tadzio. As the horrifying procedure to turn him into a baboon's arsehole begins, she makes her escape.

A caption then reads 'Seven years later', then a moment later, another arrives informing us that it's '1943', just in case you can't add up or have forgotten the first caption already, in which case just do one caption, guys. The President of the United States is being briefed about a new top-secret programme named 'Project Rebirth', which, he is informed, has been developed by Dr Vaselli, 'a scientist who escaped from Italy' – some lovely awkward exposition there, in case we've forgotten what literally just happened. The Rebirth project can make the weakest boy as strong as an athlete, one who will kick sand in the world's puny face. The President also mentions that Italy has managed to produce one such super-soldier and he goes by the name 'Red Skull' – and probably looks like a weird bollock. The US have a volunteer ready to go. He's in California and he's called Steve Rogers, and, after all this exposition, the President probably needs a lie down.

Steve Rogers, played by Matt Salinger (and yes, I know what you're thinking, he is indeed the guy from *Revenge of the Nerds*), is saying his last goodbyes to his mum (Melinda Dillon), who gifts him his late father's medal, before he sets off for the secret lab to become the world's finest.

'This isn't Mussolini's Italy,' Dr Vaselli tells him. 'You are free to change your mind at any time.' But Steve isn't interested, he wants to be a super-soldier. He's weak, thin, and has a marked limp – and this experiment will change everything. At the very least he'll be able to impress Bernie (Kim Gillingham), his beloved girl back home. With a steely look in his eye, he tells the doctor to carry on. She takes a moment to thank Steve for making it possible for her to 'make a wrong thing right' – obviously still feeling guilty about robbing the world of a *Bobby Crush Singalong at the Seaside Special* in the future. Though she should probably also apologise to Steve, as he may well be about to turn into a prolapsed anus.

As the procedure begins, the room falls into darkness. The crack of electrical activity permeates the silence, lights flicker on and off, and Steve's arms and legs begin to fill with muscle like bread rising in an oven – though no information on knob size. Although it looks painful, and although you have to wonder if it's all very stupid, it's a success, and he didn't turn into a prolapsed anus. Steve is now ready and looks twice the man he was. Army personnel crowd around Dr Vaselli and thank her for her amazing work. A particular admirer is an observer who has tagged along for the day. He's about to shake her hand when he instead produces a gun and shouts, '*Heil Hitler!*', which was shocking in 1943 but in 2023 is basically Southern America. Vaselli falls to the ground, and Steve breaks out of his experiment chair and kills the deadly assailant with one punch. 'God bless you, my boy,' she says, cradled in Steve's arms. 'Stop them. Never give up.' It's not clear if these are requests or Bon Jovi song titles, but Steve promises her he will as he watches her slip away to Valhalla.

There's trouble. United States intelligence have been informed that the Nazis are going to fire an experimental rocket at them that will be sure to suck the paint off American houses and give their families a permanent orange afro. They have five days. Only one man can help, and although he was only born yesterday and has had no actual military training, he's ready for tomorrow. They've dressed him in a bright blue suit, and before you ask why – surely some form of camouflage gear would be more beneficial for a covert mission? – it's explained that it's fireproof, and Vaselli loved the red, white and blue, which is great and all that, but maybe khaki would be sensible further down the line.

The important fact is that he's on that plane, bright red shield in hand, and that determined look has been replaced with one of pure confusion. Lieutenant Colonel Louis (Michael Nouri) asks if he'll be OK with such a bulky weapon as a shield, and Steve jokes that he could use some more practice. He asks if there are any plans for giving him a squad of some sort and, amazingly, is told that Dr

Vaselli had every single detail of this plan in her head yet wrote nothing down. They don't even know what his suit and shield are made of. Apparently, she thought it was safer that way. This seems problematic. Before Steve can digest this information, he's thrown out of the plane and wished good luck.

Somehow, through pure luck and brute strength, he manages to bulldoze his way through most of the Nazi army, finally arriving in a main launch hangar with a single rocket pointing at the sky, surrounded by Nazi flags, Nazi troops and a lone villain dressed in black. He turns to face Steve and reveals his dark red face with piercing blue eyes. It's the Red Skull (Scott Paulin) – although it could be David Dickinson, if you squint. Steve doesn't ask any questions. He just launches his shield as hard as he can at the man in black, but instead of it chopping him in half, Red Skull simply catches it in one hand, as if it's a frisbee, and fires it back towards Steve, where it slices into the concrete. Red Skull slowly walks towards Steve, mumbling the words (in broken Italian), 'Oooh, an Amerreecann, just when I am needing help of my Eeengleesh lesssons.' Steve gets his arse kicked and wakes up strapped to the very rocket he had been sent to stop. I mean, in some ways that's a win, right?

Red Skull mocks him (quite rightly) and informs him that this rocket is headed to the White House in order to kill the President. He then playfully asks Steve if he thinks he could be President one day? Steve doesn't answer as he's pathetically attempting to get out of the strap, but I can tell you, no. No, you can't. You're Italian.

As the countdown approaches zero, Steve has one trick up his sleeve, and that's to grab hold of Mr Skull's hand while he's delivering yet another cocky sentence and tell him he's coming with him. It's too late to abandon the rocket, and, in an act of sheer panic, he pulls out a knife and chops his hand off. The rocket begins to pull up into the air, and Red Skull is left cradling his severed limb, cursing the fact that this was the hand he used when he wanted it to feel like someone else was doing it. It has to be said that the make up for the Red Skull is actually very good, and Paulin's eyes pierce the darkness. Shame we don't see it again from this point. Screenwriter Stephen Tolkin said in an interview with *Cinefantastique*, 'I didn't think people wanted to keep looking at this horrible skull face forever.' He was wrong.

In Washington, D.C., young Tom Kimball is on a visit with his father, who has important government business to attend to. It's the middle of the night, and he wants to see the President, for some reason. So, camera in hand, he sneaks to the White House to take a snap of the Commander-in-Chief – who is probably crooning 'Tomorrow' with Annie and Daddy Warbucks inside – but catches sight of something altogether different: a man in red, white and blue, strapped to a rocket, kicking at the wing to take it off course. Which is exactly what happens, and, as the rocket flies by the building, missing it entirely, Tom takes a snap and is wowed by what he sees: a flying idiot.

A caption reads 'Somewhere in Alaska' – seriously, who is at the wheel, caption people? The rocket descends with force and speed, hitting the ground and, for unknown reasons, not exploding. Instead, it skates along the surface, eventually burying itself in piles of loose snow. If I was Red Skull and his mad Nazi lads, I would be livid that I sacrificed my best wanking hand for a giant fucking dud rocket.

Springfield, Ohio. Tom tells his best friend Sam (played by Thomas Beatty, son of Ned) what he saw and produces a very hazy picture to prove it. Sam, it turns out, is a plucky young reporter in the making, who has many questions about what Tom saw. It will make a great story for the school paper, headline: YOUNG LOCAL BOY SEES BASICALLY NOTHING – NO PROOF SHOCKER.

It's the nineties, and Tom (Ronny Cox) is now President of the United States. He's pro-environmental and is addressing the nation about how they will need to find ways of replacing all toxic materials in order to be green. 'If we don't take this medicine now, we'll all die,' he says, causing a *War of the Worlds*-style panic in those who only caught the last bit and doubtless causing many a conspiracy theory to pop up claiming that he's a lizard and the world is run by Jewish vampires.

One man isn't a fan of this airy-fairy, hippie mandate, and that's General Fleming (Darren McGavin). He thinks it's all mumbo-jumbo, practically impossible to achieve in this modern world. He attends a secret meeting of the Stonecutters – a table of the very worst and evil men (I guess all the women were busy) – and asks them all how they can kill the President, as his plans will set them back thirty years. A scarred man leans forward and tells the General they don't need to kill him; assassinations are basically a pain in the arse in terms of admin. It took him years to find Sirhan Sirhan (the very man Cilla Black sang about) and Lee Harvey Oswald, and the end result is always martyrdom. He suggests that, instead of killing the President, they should simply control him via a brain implant that he has invented. The scarred man is (drum roll) Red Skull, who now has hair and a tanned face, so he will really need to change that name, and my suggestion would be 'Nigel Havers'.

Meanwhile in Alaska an expedition makes a startling discovery in the ice: a red glove. They salvage the shape and cut it out of the ice, whereupon it thaws and, through a process of intense paranoia and body horror, wipes out their camp, or rather it sits up to reveal a figure in red, white and blue. A scientist manages to grab a quick snap, but before you can say, 'How are you alive?', he runs out of the tent and into the cold outside world.

President Tom is aghast. He can't believe what he is seeing. The scientist's mysterious photograph is on the front page of the newspaper, and it's a face he hasn't seen for fifty years. He takes out his wallet and checks the vague photo he took as a boy. It's a match. Captain America is back. He calls his friend Sam (Ned Beatty), now a working reporter, to tell him the news: a man he saw on a rocket in 1943 has been found alive and well in the ice in Alaska some fifty years later. Sam asks if it's 'some kind of hoax', only for Tom, the actual President of the United States, to say that it must be him, and he can actually talk to him. And I think I've just found out why the world is so unilaterally fucked. Sam is excited: this man, who has been in ice for over fifty years, may have met Red Skull and can give them information, so off he goes to find out more.

Northern Canada. Helicopters scour the forests, motorbikes patrol the dense woodland, and Captain America tries to avoid both, clearly still thankful that camouflage wasn't a consideration. He makes a break for it but is set upon by Valentina de Santis (Francesca Neri), who manages to graze his shoulder with a bullet. Thankfully, help is at hand, and as Cap rolls in the grass, a white truck pulls up, Sam at the wheel, and drives him away from danger.

Sam places a Dictaphone on the dash and begins to fire questions at Cap as they make their escape. He wants information about Red Skull. Then he tells Cap that Red Skull is using the name he had before the war, has had extensive plastic surgery, is a kingpin in a powerful international cartel, is responsible for all the misery on this planet and probably killed JFK. Steve looks incredibly confused; after all, why the fuck do you need information on someone when you clearly know more about them than someone who's been asleep since 1943? Steve mentions he once saw a movie where an English spy was fed false information to make him think things were not what they seemed. He also can't help looking at the Dictaphone, which reads 'MADE IN JAPAN' in big writing, and the truck's interior. It's a Volkswagen, made in West Germany. He's seen enough. He needs to take action. He asks Sam to pull over so he can throw up.

Steve heroically runs to the side of the road and leans forward as if to be sick. Sam kindly walks to his side to see if he's OK. It's then that the stout-hearted Captain America leaps into action, fearlessly running back to the truck, jumping in and driving away, abandoning Sam on his own in the middle of nowhere. Makes you proud to be American.

'You know this guy?' Sharon Carter asks her mother about the man she found lingering outside the house dressed in a big coat. 'Yes, I do,' an elderly Bernie says, with a wide, beaming, albeit wrinkled, smile. She embraces him, and they catch up over the kitchen table (not like that). She knew in her heart he was alive, she kept the house knowing that one day he'd come back, she stayed in the area knowing that one day she'd see his face, but she also got married and had kids all the same, just to make sure that, when he did come back, he'd be a massive cuckoo.

As Steve catches up at Sharon's house by watching videos of everything that has happened in history since 1943 (hopefully including *Debbie Does Dallas*), Sam knocks on Bernie's door. He tells her he's caught up on everything and knows all about Project Rebirth, but before he can ask any further questions, Valentina and her men show up and shoot everyone. Lovely Sam and old Bernie die just as Steve and Sharon arrive at the scene, but Sharon's dad survives, and you can bet no one was more gutted about that than Steve.

While they tend to Bernie's widowed husband as he sleeps in a hospital bed, a news flash comes on the television. President Tom has been abducted from his hotel in Rome by twenty armed men. Steve tells Sharon that it must be the same men who killed her mother, obviously not one for logistics. General Fleming appears on the news, feigning sadness at the kidnapping, pleading for world calm and predicting that everyone will be fine by the next day, which seems normal.

Steve leads Sharon to the secret lab where he was created. Amazingly, it's still there, in the basement of a functioning café, behind a secret wall. Everything looks exactly the same, save for a swathe of cobwebs, almost as if a set dresser has chucked them around for a couple of minutes beforehand. Steve runs his now strong hands over the very chair that made him, a symbol of his power, and contemplates for a moment just what happened in this room: the room that gave him the ability to steal a fat man's truck.

Suddenly, a commotion is heard upstairs. Valentina and her armed men are here, having followed the pair here. Steve races to a desk, opens it and pulls out a book. 'Vaselli's diary. Got it,' he says with a warm confidence. You mean it was in a fucking drawer this whole time? For fifty years? No one thought to look in a drawer in her lab? OK. The diary tells them that, although Dr Vaselli never knew Red Skull's name, she did know where he came from, so it's there they'll travel next.

President Tom is having a lousy time being tortured by Red Skull. He's being injected with chemicals that take twenty-four hours to allow the brain implant to be installed. He also finds out that the transmitter located in his tooth was removed while he was unconscious, so no one can save him now. Red Skull tells him that, once this all takes effect, he'll get to be the President and therefore control the world. As they take Tom away, he's able to pocket a capsule of acid that was lying around for some reason.

Steve and Sharon arrive in Rome, and as he checks the map, Sharon drives them around, confidently predicting that they'll be there by lunchtime, which all seems exciting. Steve looks up from his map and asks her to pull over as he thinks he's going to be sick. Surely, he won't pull this shit again? Not in the middle of Rome? Yes. Yes, he does. He jumps back in the car and tells Sharon he can't take her into danger, even though he's brought her to Rome, and then drives away, ironically leaving her in danger by herself in a strange city. WHAT A HERO. Gives me goosebumps.

Steve arrives at the childhood home of Red Skull and attempts to ask the occupants some questions, but as he doesn't speak Italian he flounders. Luckily, Sharon arrives, speaking perfect Italian, and gains them access. The owners of the house produce a box of old things, and inside they find a tape recording taken the night Tadzio de Santis was taken. They all sit around and listen to the carnage.

Sharon and Steve take a drink outside a beautiful Roman restaurant. They're having a brainstorm about how to locate Red Skull and save the President. Steve suggests looking him up in the phone book, and I am close to being done with this bellend. Sharon mocks him, quite rightly, but then notices Valentina at the table behind, slowly pulling a gun from her handbag. Our duo manage to escape, and in the chaos Sharon nabs Valentina's handbag, which just happens to have Red Skull's details in it. They have the location of the President, but Red Skull's men are still tracking them, so Sharon, far and away the brains of the operation, pulls a switch and abandons Captain America in the middle of nowhere, telling him he'll do better on his own. But after driving away, she is captured and put in Red Skull's dungeon.

'I'm not going to blow it this time,' Steve says to himself as he takes in the view of Red Skull's estate and retrieves his costume from his duffel bag. Armed with his shield, he begins to scale the rocks and enter the compound, all the while looking like he's lost on a stag do.

President Tom has just twenty minutes before the chemicals finally take effect, so he uses the acid to weaken his cell door, and escapes while the guards aren't looking, like a *Scooby-Doo* cartoon. He runs as fast as he can up to the roof but is met by Red Skull and his guards. 'Please come back, Mr President,' he says, with the deepest of sarcasm. 'It's over.' Tom takes stock of the situation and realises the plan is scuppered, so he throws himself off the roof, much to Red Skull's horror. As his body plummets down the face of the castle, a red hand reaches out and grabs him, saving his life. 'We've met,' Tom says in an excited voice to Captain America, showing him the picture from his wallet, which really looks like he sneaked it while the Cap was on the toilet, it's that blurred. Luckily, Cap remembers him, out there on the lawn near the White House all those years ago. As they dodge bullets and take cover, Tom tells him Sam said there'd be days like this, and Cap basically says, 'Oh yeah, your mate's dead, sorry about that.' I mean, it's hardly the time or the place. They split up, with the President instructed how to get out while Cap goes to save Sharon, knocking out bad guys on his way.

'I don't know how it is that you are here,' Red Skull says to Cap as he reaches his courtyard, 'or how you remain unchanged, but it doesn't matter, my brother. Today you will die.' They fight once again, with Cap once again getting his arse kicked but performing a Hulk Hogan-esque resurgence in the second half. With the chips down, and the fight lost, Red Skull produces a detonator from his bag and tells them all that if he must lose, he will take them all with him. But Steve has a secret weapon: the recording of Red Skull playing piano as a child, followed by the encore of his family being murdered, a tape even Werner Herzog would have told them all to destroy.

Red Skull wanders listlessly through his memories as the recording plays, and as he activates the detonator, he tells Steve that they are both tragedies and now he can send their tortured souls to rest, so Steve chucks his shield at him, sending Red Skull flying off the castle and down to a watery grave.

As a haunting photo of Captain America turns into a nice painting, we hear from a newscaster that in Rome the world agreed to President Tom's new environmental treaty and he used his speech to leave this odd, final statement: 'To Captain America, wherever he is, we're all back in the fight.'

As Ivan Neville's horrifying American opus 'Home Of The Brave' rings out, we're left to reflect on what we just saw. Was it an epic action adventure, with tales of derring-do that trotted the globe? Or the story of one man from the past who pretended to feel sick so he could steal cars? We may never truly know.

FIFTEEN

BATMAN RETURNS

1992

THE BAT
THE CAT
THE PENGUIN

After the raging juggernaut of merchandise that was 1989's *Batman*, there was no doubt that Tim Burton's gothic reinvention had changed the public perception of Batman for ever. The film had been a major success story on so many fronts. Coming out on top in a summer in which it was competing against James Bond (*Licence to Kill*) and Indiana Jones (*The Last Crusade*) and eventually grossing almost $412 million through the box office was a major coup.

Warner Bros. wanted to get going as soon as possible on a sequel. They spent $250,000 on storing all the sets from *Batman* and scheduled the sequel for 1990. Tim Burton said in 1989 that he would only return for a sequel if it offered 'something new and exciting'. He then went off and directed *Edward Scissorhands*.

Sam Hamm (writer of *Batman*) delivered two scripts for a possible sequel. The main contender (entitled simply *Batman II*) told the story of Penguin and Catwoman looking for secret statues and introduced the idea of copycat vigilantes that Christopher Nolan toyed with in *The Dark Knight*. When Burton returned, he threw out the Sam Hamm script and brought in Daniel Waters (*Heathers*), who introduced the idea of the sequel being a semi-social satire in which the Penguin could run for mayor.

Michael Keaton returned (with a nice $10 million fee), and Annette Bening was cast as Catwoman. Bening then learned that she was pregnant and couldn't take the part, so the hunt was now on for her replacement. Sean Young was an interested party. She was originally cast as Vicki Vale in *Batman*, however, while rehearsing for a horse-riding scene (which was later omitted from the script altogether) she fell off and broke her arm. Feeling that the role was rightly hers, legend has it that Young arrived at Tim Burton's office in a homemade Catwoman outfit and demanded the part. In the end Burton cast Michelle Pfeiffer after just one meeting. Pfeiffer attacked the part with real tenacity. She underwent extensive kickboxing training and learned how to use a bullwhip. She also took Jack Nicholson's lead from the previous film and negotiated a nice cut of the box office as part of her deal.

Given the massive wave of acclaim and hype that Burton was riding, it was inevitable that the studio would give him full creative control on the sequel, and this was arguably their first mistake. Burton chose not to return to Pinewood, instead shooting the film in Hollywood at Warner Bros. and Universal. With previous production designer Anton Furst having tragically committed suicide in 1991, Burton brought in his usual production designer Bo Welch. Welch blended 'fascist architecture with World's Fair architecture' for Gotham City. As a consequence, Gotham became smaller and much more like a soundstage set, a far cry from the massive, forbidding city that had been established in 1989.

Mr and Mrs Cobblepot (Paul Reubens and Diane Salinger) are scuttling through the tiny, snowy streets of Gotham with a baby carriage that looks like it once housed Eric Pickles. There's a sense of foreboding as they weave along the pathways toward their destination. When they come to a narrow bridge over a small river they check to see if anyone is looking. The coast seems clear.

Mrs Cobblepot recently gave birth, and it was to be a proud day for the wealthy Gothamites, but instead of a healthy, bouncing baby boy, they received an unhealthy-looking flipper baby that eats cats.

They tip the carriage, and a basket bound by straps drops and splashes into the icy water, rolling along with the current and eventually dropping down into the ominous darkness of the sewer.

The opening titles prepare the viewer for the film that is about to follow: claustrophobic, dark, dirty and, ultimately, underwhelming. Gone is Elfman's bombastic score that had florid echoes of Mussorgsky, and in its place is a smaller, less intense offering with a choral accompaniment, which would feel more at home in the hallways of Edward Scissorhands' cold mansion than the crime-ridden streets of Gotham City.

The basket meets its final destination, coming to rest at the feet of a group of penguins, and the mind races, thinking just how are these penguins, who have no hands, meant to rescue the squealing baby within? I guess they p-p-p-pick him up somehow (joke for the kids, there).

Thirty-three years later. Christmas. Gotham City's square hustles and bustles with a handful of extras, and it all looks more like a small municipal car park than a metropolitan city. The snow falls in sprinkles. A vast tree dwarfs them all. The Ice Princess (Cristi Conaway) turns on the lights so that festivities can begin, and at the top of a tower stands Max Shreck (Christopher Walken), a business mogul who looks like Angela Lansbury by way of a Dick Tracy villain (and with a name lifted from the actor who played Nosferatu in the 1922 original). He has a proposal for the mayor: a new power plant that will keep the lights on for decades to come. The model of the plant sits behind him, and it's candy-striped Americana – so quaint, so kitsch, that it could be Tim Burton's barber shop. The Mayor (Michael Murphy) points out that they're OK for power, thanks, so Shreck begins painting a picture of what will happen the day Gotham runs out of power – and it's a stark tale of low juice. Shreck's secretary, Selina Kyle (Michelle Pfeiffer), goes from guest to guest at the table, topping up coffee, but feels she has to say something, interrupting Shreck with subservient apologies. Needless to say, the room doesn't listen and laughs her off as a dizzy broad.

Shreck goes downstairs to address the waiting Gotham citizens from behind a podium. He's painting himself as a hero of the working man but, as always with these guys, he's just a regular piece of shit. He gives an impromptu speech about how he wishes he could give more back but is interrupted by an attack from the Red Triangle Gang, and they're not a Channel 4 content-warning gang; they're a gang of circus performers who have turned to crime, potentially after realising that bill posters just don't cut it these days. The performers race around the city square committing low-level ASBO-style crime that nowadays would end up on YouTube, like smashing windows, kicking over bins and setting fire to cuddly toys. Commissioner Gordon watches on in terror and cowers in his car when a sledge is thrown at the windscreen. Rather than calling in further armed units, or indeed a SWAT team, he whimpers into his handset that someone should call the Batman. What the fuck is wrong with this police force?

The signal is thrown up into the sky, and a corresponding one beams into the upper floors of Wayne Manor, shining directly onto Bruce Wayne (Michael Keaton), who sits alone in the dark doing nothing. The question has to be asked: what would happen if he was with someone who had no idea he was Batman? What if he's having a relaxing poo? It's a system that needs looking at, Bruce. Soaked in the light, he stands heroically before gearing up, driving into town and murdering at least three people. The Mayor and Gordon thank him for his wanton violence and for, once again, embarrassing the entire police force. He wanders off in near silence, presumably to head home and go back to doing some top-level jack shit and waiting for the next Bat-Signal to give him a sense of worth again.

Max Shreck awakes to find himself at the head of a table filled with unemployed circus performers (aka the Red Triangle Gang) throwing vacant stares back at him, which essentially describes every episode of *The Apprentice*. 'Hi,' says a large, hunched, bird-like figure in a dressing gown. He's feeding fish to some wild penguins and has a grin laced with black drool. His name is Oswald Cobblepot but round these parts he's known as the Penguin (Danny DeVito). He brings warnings of what Shreck's anti-green profiteering policies are doing to his beautiful sewers. There's toxic waste, pollution, harmful gasses, turds and piss. He has a deal for Shreck: stage-manage a way for him to enter society as a respected citizen or he'll tell the press about all the bad things he's done and all the people he's murdered. Shreck doesn't even think about it. He tells the Penguin he can orchestrate a little welcome-home scenario for him, like when Harold in *Neighbours* came back as a postie with amnesia, but better.

Selina returns home to her empty flat. It's pink and looks like it's spilled out of a 1954 edition of *Good Housekeeping* via a colander bought at Camden Market. She's at possibly her lowest ebb. She was humiliated at work, attacked during the Red Triangle chaos and now hears from her answering machine that her on/off boyfriend has dumped her on the advice of his shrink. All she has is her cats, and, let's face it, they'll end up eating her if she dies. She's just about to settle down for the night when she hears her message from work reminding her to do something that she's forgotten about, so it's shoes back on, lights out and off to work again.

Top tip for anyone who works for a nefarious, scheming, evil businessman: don't look in their protected files. Don't snoop around and uncover illegal shit. Also, don't tell them to their face late at night at work *when you're alone* that you've done so. Sadly, Selina observes none of these rules, and when Shreck hears what she's discovered, he of course takes a moment to consider his next action before throwing her out of the window, sending her falling from a great height and hitting the ground with a vengeance. As clever as Shreck is, there's no way he could have possibly known what would happen next, though. Usually when you push someone through a very high window, they die, and I am sure that as he made his merry way home that night, he wouldn't have suspected for one single moment that Selina's motionless, limp, possibly very broken, body would be brought back to life by some cats nipping and licking at her, but that's what happens.

Selina stumbles through the open door of her pastel-goth flat. Lucky to be alive. Lucky that the cats didn't eat her and the overwhelming smell of cat piss didn't finish her off. She limps through to the kitchen and downs a pint of milk before finally coming out of shock and deciding to trash her own apartment: spray-painting a doll's house black, putting cuddly toys in a garbage disposal and setting about making her own PVC cat suit. Not really sure why, but never mind.

The Mayor stands before another big Gotham crowd. This time, he's there to swear to the crowd that he's going to put a stop to the 'urban chaos' of the Red Triangle Gang, which is like Sadiq Khan calling a press conference to say that he's going to do everything in his power to rid the streets of people who draw pictures of cocks on white vans. As the Mayor talks about how it's the season when this sort of thing shouldn't happen, sod's law kicks in, and a Red Triangle Gang member springs out of a manhole and steals the Mayor's baby. Typical. However, as luck would have it, Oswald Cobblepot rises from the very same manhole, literally holding the baby, with the world clapping eyes on a new hero: a Penguin man, who probably stinks of shite, certainly looks like shite, and almost certainly has his knob out.

Gotham embraces Oswald as a tragic misunderstood hero, a man with obvious, terrible physical deformities who's just trying to fit in with society and is simply asking for a break to enable him to trace his parentage and find a slice of happiness that has, until now, felt horribly out of reach. Billionaire Bruce Wayne, who's never had to struggle for anything in his life and is in the peak physical fitness of his life, decides it's time this prick is taken down a peg or two.

'I'm pushing this power plant now, because it will cost more later,' Shreck tells Bruce, who sits across the table from him, deeply confused by Shreck's logic and unimpressed by his plan. Bruce tells him that the city has a power surplus and wants to know what Shreck's angle is, aside from generating more money so he can dress like a *Great Gatsby* porn parody. He also has the backing of the Mayor, which should be the end of things, but Shreck drops a chilling political comment that mayors come and go, and then makes himself sound like a proper dickhead when he says, 'Do you think you could go fifteen rounds with Muhammad Shreck?' They're about to get into a heated argument about how Cobblepot may or may not be a criminal when the tension is broken by the arrival of the alive-and-well Selina Kyle. Shreck plays off Selina hurting herself skiing while Bruce gazes at her like she's the most beautiful woman who's ever lived (because she possibly is), then bumbles his way out of the door with Selina's help, like he's suddenly contracted dementia. Shreck isn't worried. He tells his son Chip (Andrew Bryniarski) that if she even thinks about talking, he'll throw her out of a higher window.

Shreck has 'better fish to fry', and to prove it he brings one for Cobblepot to eat. The Penguin is seated at a gold desk in his loft, wearing his monocle and writing something with his quill in the dark – which is how I imagine David Walliams works. Shreck has news for him and asks if he fancies running for Mayor of Gotham. To be honest, it would be a bit awkward if he said no, as there's already a massive team of people downstairs running his campaign. Cobblepot agrees and, to celebrate, bites a chunk out of a smarmy campaign man's nose, sending a long streak of blood gushing across the screen. Fun fact: McDonald's released *Batman Returns* Happy Meals, and I do hope there was a ketchup dispenser tie-in. The film was given a 12 certificate, a fairly new BBFC rating at the time, and, like *Batman*, it does sail fairly close to the wind with a lot of the imagery. Penguin is enthused by his new political direction and turns to the team to make the short announcement of 'BURN, BABY, BURN!'

A bedraggled Bichon Frise, played by a dog named Darla (who also appeared in *Pee-wee's Big Adventure* and *Silence of the Lambs*) trots swiftly along the sidewalk of Gotham's main street. In her mouth is a hand grenade and in her mind is carnage, as she nips into a restaurant and runs back out as it explodes. The Red Triangle Gang are back, and this time they're blowing up empty shops and hassling shopkeepers as they spill out onto the street. Two dastardly men race after an escaped poor soul but are stopped in their tracks by Batman, who straps a bomb to one of the gang and pushes him down a hole, causing him to explode and die.

Catwoman decides that the best revenge is one served hot. She breaks into Shreck's department store, backflips around the room (though she's not showing off), whips the heads off mannequins (which Pfeiffer really did) and sends two horny guards scampering for the toilets. Fans of continuity will really enjoy her switching between heels and flat shoes here with abandon. It's that real attention to detail that makes this film really stand out. She uncouples some gas mains, loads a microwave full of aerosol cans and sets the timer.

'Admiring your handiwork?' says Batman to Penguin, like a bit of a messy bitch who has stopped by to check out the mess, insinuating that this is exactly the sort of thing mayors do. Batman takes a step and throws, 'You're not the Mayor,' back at him, with real 'You're not my real dad' energy. Oswald is happy to remind him that things can easily change – five minutes ago he was dwelling in the sewers with penguins and stinking of shit; now he's living above ground and stinking of shit and fish. Their thrilling conversation is interrupted by the sound of multiple backflips and the arrival of Catwoman, who offers a simple 'meow' before an explosion rips through Shreck's department store. Batman races to a rooftop to confront her, and they share an intimate moment where it looks like she's going to touch his penis but ends up stabbing him in the abdomen with a sharp nail. She is sent tumbling down into a passing truck filled with kitty litter, and Bats is sent home to nurse his wounds, though it sort of feels like he's into it.

Fun fact: Marlon Wayans was due to appear in this film as Robin. During an interview with *Gizmodo* in 2009, Wayans revealed the details behind the ill-fated situation: 'I was actually supposed to play Robin, in *Batman Returns*, but there were too many characters. I was cast, I was paid and everything. I still get residual checks. Tim Burton didn't wind up doing three, Joel Schumacher did it and he had a different vision for who Robin was. So, he hired Chris O'Donnell.'

'Just the pussy I've been looking for,' Oswald says with the gusto of a thousand sex offenders. He's high as a kite after wooing the press of Gotham at his mayoral launch, and now he's walked upstairs to find Catwoman waiting for him on his bed. He's overcome with sexual emotions and begins winding himself around the bed area, wheezing and grumbling. She has a deal for him to mull over: they combine forces and rid the city of Batman. But for the moment, Oswald is mainly interested in sniffing her shoes and producing sex ointments. He tells her he already has a plan to stop Batman: he intends to reconfigure the Batmobile and make it an 'H-bomb on wheels', but Catwoman reminds him that as a martyr he'd be even more powerful, so it would be better to turn the people of Gotham against him by making him what he hates the most: someone like them. The game is set, and to celebrate, Catwoman decides to start licking herself, taking this whole 'cat' thing a bit too literally. Oswald lies back and watches, and you can bet your house on the fact that those arms don't stay at his side for long.

Selina and Bruce sit on his vast pretentious red sofa, the fireplace roaring in front of them and Alfred tending to their every need. He met her again on the street and bumbled his way into asking her over for dinner. There's a mutual attraction there, as well as shared interests, but they're both clearly in need of extensive therapy. They talk of relationships, and he explains that he had a girlfriend once but she couldn't handle the truth about him and had difficulty with the nature of his duality, which all feels like a speech he should literally write on a red flag. He tries to reassure her that he's not Norman Bates, or even Ted Bundy (with Ted Bundy being the lost Batman villain), and then says that he'd like to kiss her – and you honestly have to admire the fact that despite sounding incredibly unhinged, he has the charm to pull it off. She contemplates for a moment and then dives onto his face like a tramp on chips. Their passion is interrupted when the TV bursts into life with a newsflash: the Ice Princess has been kidnapped as she was about to turn on the Christmas lights *again*, and one of Batman's weapons was found at the scene. So, they both make their excuses and break it off (not like that).

Bruce strides majestically into the Batcave and into the walk-in wardrobe that houses nine Batsuits. He hilariously pulls three to one side, before settling on the fourth one, and as the music swells, he strides out fully suited and poses for no one.

The Mayor is holding yet another public gathering, behind the same set of mics and in front of the same Christmas tree, and you really start to think this fucker has to go. It's only one or two gatherings away from being held at Four Seasons Total Landscaping. He tells the assembled masses that while he understands they're all a bit fed up right now with the constant circus-related crime, he wants to assure them that their elected officials and the police force have everything well in hand. Whenever something happens, they simply send a big signal into the sky and one man shows up and kills them. That, my friends, is a perfect system.

The Ice Princess is dead. She fell from a roof and landed on the very button she was to press to turn the Christmas lights on – right next to the Mayor, who must really fucking dread public speaking now. The people of Gotham look up to see Batman standing on the roof and swarms of bats streaming out of the tree and flying into their beleaguered faces. Obviously, Batman was not responsible, but it sure as shit looks that way. Police race to the roof and shoot him, sending him falling down a level and onto the floor in a heap. Catwoman joins him on the floor and tells him he's like catnip to her, that despite what side they're on and what crazy things are going on in this insane world, she feels something for him. Batman robs the moment of all sexual tension by telling her that 'mistletoe can be deadly if you eat it'. Jesus Christ, mate, no wonder you don't have a girlfriend. I imagine your postcoital banter is really on fleek:

'How was that for you, Bruce?'

'The dot on top of the letters "i" and "j" is known as a tittle.'

Penguin suggests a toast to Catwoman. With their new partnership starting off so well, he suggests a more intimate union. How about becoming his wife when he becomes Mayor? She, of course, has literally no interest in marrying this smelly, little pervert, and the thought of him in the nude, and the state of his undercarriage, is probably foremost on her mind. She rejects him, so he rejects her, sending her falling from a great height, for the third time in two days.

Batman escapes the insanity of the city square, with its potential murder charge and extreme bat problem, to the sanctity of his trusty Batmobile. However, his problems are only just beginning. Penguin has made good on his earlier boast and has taken control of the vehicle. Luckily, Oswald is a boaster, and as he takes the car on a rather chaotic joyride, he begins confessing to many a crime, and even leaves soundbites that Batman is able to record for future use.

Another day, and it's another press conference in Gotham, but this time it's Oswald's go. Although he seems nervous, the people seem to actually love him, and Shreck is 110% behind him, which means he can backtrack 10% and still be 100% behind him. He talks of their 'visionary alliance' and a celebration that very evening at his 'Max-querade Ball' to seal the deal. So, Oswald, with all the dignity he can muster, takes the stage and begins his speech about how useless the last Mayor was, what with him putting all the city's hopes of salvation behind a mentally ill man who runs around the streets in a black suit – and you sort of have to admit that he has a point. Over at the Batcave, though, Alfred and Bruce have heard enough; they decide to start playing a CD containing excerpts from Oswald's tirade the previous evening, the ones where he mentions that he'll take care of the 'squealing, wretched pinhead of Gotham', as well as playing 'this stinking city like a harp from hell'. The crowd begin to turn, probably more so when they hear Bruce somehow 'scratch' the sample via a CD, like he's Jam Master Jay. Seeing his mayoral ambitions go down the shitter, and Shreck making his excuses and leaving, Oswald races away, popping out the occasional machine-gun blast from his umbrella. The game is up, and he drops himself over the same bridge his parents utilised thirty-three years previously and follows that same current back into the sewer, back to anonymity – an act all politicians should be forced to carry out once they are sent from office in disgrace.

Back among his real underground friends, Oswald hatches a new plan. Gone is the charm offensive, gone is the spin. In is a plan to steal all the children of Gotham, kill them and dump them in the water. An honest politician can sometimes be refreshing.

It's Max Shreck's Max-querade Ball. A grand, *Eyes Wide Shut*-type affair, with bowls undoubtedly stacked with keys and elaborate masks on full display. Bruce wanders down the staircase and is immediately out of place. While he's dressed to the nines and looking every inch the billionaire, he's the only person not wearing a mask. Is that because Bruce Wayne is his real mask? Or did he leave his in Alfred's car?

Shreck tries to goad Bruce about his lack of a costume while wearing a giant turban with mystical symbols hanging in gold. Bruce fires back about how he nearly made a monster Mayor, but he hadn't considered that, in Max Shreck, he has met his match as one of the great orators of our time. On the one hand, Shreck is able to deliver a disquieting statement about how he is the 'mean and twisted soul' of Gotham, poured out with a guttural growl. On the other hand, he is able to throw out a quick 'yawn' in a camp New York accent as he exits from Bruce's self-importance.

Selina descends the staircase, and Bruce's face lights up with lascivious interest. She looks beautiful and has also arrived *sans* mask. They embrace in a slow dance to Siouxsie and the Banshees' sensuous song 'Face To Face', released to coincide with the film. The band were hand-picked by Danny Elfman, as he explained to *Entertainment Weekly*: 'I've always been a fan – Siouxsie is one of very few women who can create a realistic primal cat sound.'

Bruce tells Selina he came explicitly to see her and tries to build on their fledgling relationship, hoping to walk hand-in-hand through the mess of the city and find happiness in his big castle away from everyone. Selina tells him she came to shoot Max in the face with a gun. It's not perfect, but it's at least a mild foundation for a relationship. Selina spots some mistletoe hanging above them and decides to tell Bruce something she heard about how eating it can be deadly, which leads him to tell her that 'a kiss can be deadlier if you mean it', which is exactly what Catwoman told him that night. They look at one another in shock, embrace and realise what just happened, and it's honestly a shock that Bruce doesn't cut the tension by telling her that a single teaspoon of honey represents the life work of twelve bees.

An explosion rips through the floor of the ballroom, and from the smoke and mortar rises a giant duck vehicle being driven by an angry-looking Penguin man. He wastes no time in informing all assembled party guests that, as he speaks, their children are being kidnapped – and as a side note, I've always enjoyed that the current Mayor watches it all happen while wearing a costume that is a suit with a knife sticking out of the back. Oswald takes Shreck and heads back into the sewer, with the promise of submerging him in raw sewage up to his eyeballs, and in any other film, the collection of said children would be a harrowing spectacle, with armed men battering down doors and ripping innocents from their neatly tucked beds, but as this is a Tim Burton joint, it's all done with a nineteenth-century steam-driven car/train pootling along, trailing circus cars behind it to store the stolen kids. So, it's remarkably easy for Batman to intercept them and foil Penguin's plan immediately. Oswald shifts to plan B, which is to send an army of penguins with rockets strapped to their backs out into the city to blow it up, a plan that Batman also foils by sending the rockets back into the Penguin's lair. It's at this point that you have to ask whether Batman has ever truly been challenged at all.

'Shut up, you're going to jail,' Batman says to Shreck, shoving him to one side to get to Selina. She doesn't want him to be arrested, though; she wants his blood, and rightly mentions that the law doesn't apply to people like Max, and that even if he did go to jail, it would be rich-guy jail where you get to play tennis with Leonardo DiCaprio. Batman disagrees. He thinks the law should be followed. Plus, he probably knows some guys who could pull some strings and put him in Shawshank. He tells her they can send Shreck to jail, then go home, get some snacks in, maybe neck a pint of bitter and watch *Clash of the Titans*. To show that he means what he says, he pulls off his mask. Fans of continuity will love this moment, and it's bothered me for over thirty years now: as he goes to pull the mask off, the black make-up around his eyes disappears, leaving the eyeholes pink and fleshy, and you do wonder why it was chosen to be performed in one shot, when a quick cut could have fixed it.

Selina is not impressed. She pushes Bruce away and tells him she needs to make sure Shreck dies, so she kills him and herself in a vast explosion of electrical lightning. Bruce inspects the scene when it's over, finding only Shreck and his hilarious skeleton.

'I'll murder you momentarily,' Penguins gurgles with green liquid flowing from his disgusting mouth as he rises from the toxic waters of his own hideout. 'But first I need a cool drink of ice water.' He then collapses, and as his dead body flops to the stained concrete floor, his beloved penguins arrive and carry his corpse back into the very water where they found him all those years ago – presumably to eat him for sustenance and never think of him again.

'Alfred, stop the car,' Bruce says, on glimpsing a shadow of a cat slinking up an alleyway. He races out of the car but finds only a lone black feline sitting in the snow. He picks it up, stroking its dark fur as he looks around in the darkness, checking to see if it wasn't just his imagination. Nothing. He returns to his warm car with his new friend, and as he and Alfred wish each other a Merry Christmas, a Bat-Signal shines in the night sky and the back of the head of Catwoman rises to watch it shimmer. That was an afterthought, filmed when Michelle Pfeiffer was unavailable, so it's a body double. Apparently, that shot alone cost $250,000.

Presumably, Bruce will have to throw the cat out of the window and race back home to make sure no one can see the extra signal that's currently illuminating his empty library full of battered porn magazines.

The film was a hit, but not as big a hit as Warner Bros. were expecting. The end result meant that any plans Burton had for a third film were put to one side and he was told he would not be allowed to direct another, presumably because McDonald's couldn't really get behind a dying Penguin spewing green liquid.

At the end of the film, you are left to question whether Batman actually returned at all, seeing as he barely features in it and takes a distant and dark back seat on the bus of Tim Burton's continuing journey around the gothic jungles of whimsy.

SIXTEEN

THE SHADOW

1994

WHO KNOWS WHAT EVIL LURKS IN THE HEARTS OF MEN?

Yes, who knows? The Shadow knows. Who knows what will be popular at the 1994 box office? The Shadow doesn't know. Summer blockbusters can sometimes be a total crapshoot. You either have a surefire winner like a *Jurassic Park*, or a film that on the surface seems to have every key component to get people through the door and yet just falls down the stairs into a heap inside the bin of failure.

The Shadow began life as a radio-show narrator in the early thirties, with a booming, mysterious, maniacal voice promising knowledge of where the bodies were buried in the maps of the human heart, graduated to its own novel, comic books and radio show (in which the character was voiced by Orson Welles) and eventually became a series of films. That's a very impressive stack of adaptations, but if you asked anyone in 1994 about any of this, I'm sure they wouldn't know much, and that's just where the problems began. It was up to screenwriter David Koepp (*Jurassic Park*) to try to transport this passion project (he listened to the radio show as a child) that was sixty years old to modern audiences who had mostly never heard of it.

Tibet. An isolated fortress sits on top of a hill circled by poppy fields and mountains beneath a bright blue sky. Inside is a den of inequity: a haven of slow opium, fast women and mid-tempo lighting. On a throne in the darkest spot is Lamont Cranston (Alec Baldwin), only visible when he inhales his cigarette. His hair is long and his nails longer. His face is loaded with troubles, but they're hidden beneath a grin of knowing evil. A man is brought before him (James Hong of everything from *Blade Runner* to *Wayne's World 2*) for murdering some of his men. He makes threats to Cranston, who is going by the name Yingo Ko, but it's to no avail. Cranston has him shot, all the while yawning at the sheer tedium of it all. I'm sure being a kingpin is exciting for the most part, but there can be no doubt that it must have its slow moments. After stepping over the corpse, Cranston retires for the evening, to sleep under a pile of women in a giant bed – where did it all go wrong, eh? In the middle of the night, he's troubled by a vision and gets up to investigate, only to be floored by an intruder with a punch.

He's thrust into a golden temple, still only in his trousers, and brought before the Tulku, who describes himself as his new teacher. He is a man young in appearance but wise beyond his years, who is able to manipulate early nineties CGI to transport him around the room at will. He not only knows Cranston's real name but also that within him beats a black heart of wickedness, and he will help him harness this powerful malevolence to fight the evils of the world. As wise as he is, the Tulku makes no comment on Cranston's terrible wig, awful nails and chest so fluffy that it resembles a bear's gooch.

But Cranston's not interested in redemption or helping people in need, so he rejects his new teacher immediately and instead makes a grab for the nearest dagger, which immediately turns out to be an error, as this is no normal dagger. This is the Phurba, a mystical flying dagger that spins in his hands like a dervish and careers around the room like James Corden when 'Uptown Funk' comes on. The dagger has a mind of its own and treats Cranston to a game of cat and mouse, biting him and then finally pinning him to a wall and roaring in his face (the look of the Phurba's face was based on Billy Idol). 'Am I in hell?' Cranston asks. 'Not yet,' is the ominous answer. I wonder what will happen. Will we see Cranston being trained by the mystical wise man? Will we witness his mind being moulded into that of a valiant superhero?

No idea.

In a move some would describe as 'ballsy', others as 'taking the piss', the film then brings us a detailed crawl explaining what happens next, rather than showing us. We are told that Cranston has been 'taught how to cloud men's minds and to fog their vision through the force of concentration, leaving visible the only thing he can never hide – His Shadow' (not Hank Marvin). Seventy years later, and armed with these new powers, he returns home to New York City to stop injustice, help the needy and go flip the bird at Trump Tower.

A gang of hoodlums stop their car on a large suspension bridge. Dr Roy Tam (Sab Shimono) is pulled from the car sporting a nice pair of concrete shoes. It seems he's seen something he shouldn't have down an alley and will be taking a trip to sleep with the fishes. But before they can dump him, a mischievous laugh begins to ripple in the dark. The laugh becomes louder, more maniacal, and if I were one of these gangsters, I'd be seriously worried that Michael McIntyre was nearby.

'The weed of crime bears bitter fruit,' the disembodied voice booms from the darkness. It seems these guys murdered a policeman, and poor Dr Tam saw it happen. Duke, the gang leader, takes it all in good humour, shooting into the darkness before grabbing a machine gun from his car and firing indiscriminately at nothing. 'Did you think I wouldn't notice?' the voice says, once again following up with a blood-curdling laugh. Duke is worried now, especially when the voice takes the form of shadowy clouds and begins laying the odd sucker punch in his direction. He commands Duke to surrender himself to the police, threatening him that if he doesn't, he'll be around every corner and in every room, so he could very well be Michael McIntyre.

As Duke agrees to do what he's told, the voice exposes himself (not like that) to the rest of the gangsters. He's a tall, slim man decked in a heavy cloak-like coat, with a wide brimmed hat perched on top, looking every bit like Dracula's chocolatier. His face is obscured by a red handkerchief, and above that reasonably-sized hooter burn eyes of white fire. While it's a good disguise for Cranston, he looks exactly like Alec Baldwin's brother, William Baldwin, which may lead to trouble later. He frees Dr Tam from his concrete footwear and bundles him into a just-arrived taxi driven by Moe Shrevnitz (Peter Boyle).

'I saved your life, Dr Roy Tam. It now belongs to me,' the Shadow says from behind his crimson mask. He wants Tam to join his army of agents – the people he has rescued who now work for him delivering assistance when required. From now on, whenever Tam hears someone say, 'The sun is shining,' he must respond with, 'But the ice is slippery,' which is surely going to get awkward, but whatever. Tam asks how exactly does he know everything about him being a top scientist and that he was in danger. A normal person would just explain at this point, but the Shadow laughs again for about three minutes before replying, 'The Shadow knows,' in a very mysterious way – in a way that sort of suggests he's been watching Dr Tam a bit too much, and if I were him, I'd make sure my curtains were always drawn. Tam is given a special red ring that he's told to never remove, and then they drive away into the night, with Mr Shadow laughing excessively at a way too loud volume and with a bit too much reverb, and frankly I'd wish I was back in the concrete and under water.

The Cobalt Club. A beautiful art deco landscape of geometric wonder, with pools of ornate decadence oozing down the walls as diners and drinkers swim in the opulence and a singer (songwriter Diane Warren) stands in front of a swing band and peals out 'Some Kind Of Mystery'. Lamont Cranston walks through the door in his sumptuous tuxedo and slicked-back hair; he's as smooth as a pint of velvet, with an extra head of suave for good measure. He's there to meet his uncle Wainwright Barth (Jonathan Winters), who also happens to be the police commissioner. Barth is upset that he's made him wait an hour, and to make matters worse, he's sick of this 'Shadow' fellow (not Bruce Welch) always meddling in police affairs. He says he'll put a task force on his ass and bring him in. Cranston considers this for a moment before leaning back in his seat and suddenly becoming awash with darkness. He mind-tricks his uncle into not only dropping the task force idea, but also convincing him that the Shadow doesn't actually exist. He should have also got him to eat an onion like an apple or pretend he was a chicken, but I guess that's more of an 'at home' thing. With his uncle's mind altered, Cranston moves back into the light and carries on as if nothing's happened, which must have been a hell of a sight for the next table.

A moment please for Jerry Goldsmith and his sumptuous soundtrack, filled with creeping strings and snaking horns. It marries perfectly with the feel of the film and serves as a wondrous companion, wrapping the visuals in an immaculate suit of mystery. It's quintessential Goldsmith – and that's always a good thing.

As Barth comes back to his senses, he's deeply confused, and you get the impression this isn't the first time it's happened and will not be the last. It's a certainty at this point that he'll get Shadow-induced dementia within a few years. He asks what he was just talking about, and Cranston says he was about to tell him who the dame (not Judi Dench) is who just walked in bathed in a warm light. It's Margo Lane (Penelope Ann Miller). Her father is a scientist working for the War Department, and he tells Cranston that she 'hears voices', and that he should stay away from her. But it's no good: the Shadow knows he wants to have sex with her.

Cranston orders from the Chinese menu like a native, and Lane is impressed. They'd each had the strangest desire to ditch the club and head for a restaurant for some Peking duck, whereupon his Mandarin flows like Shaoxing yellow wine. She thanks him for complimenting her dress, which is strange as he didn't say a word but was only thinking it. It turns out she can read minds, which slightly perturbs Cranston, as he obviously has a huge secret, and he's also the Shadow. He decides that it's much too dangerous to see her again and ditches her in a cab.

Over at the Museum of Natural History, a room full of men scratch their heads. The dad from *ALF* (Max Wright) is troubled by the arrival of a massive sarcophagus from Tibet and tells the museum curator (Joseph Maher) all about it. Apparently, Tibetan sarcophagi are usually made of stone, but this one is very much of the solid silver variety. They unpack it from the wooden crate, and it becomes immediately clear that this is no ordinary Tibetan sarcophagus. It is the silver coffin of Temujin – a man who nearly conquered the globe eight centuries ago. While everyone in attendance wants to share the excitement at the mention of this name, they're all very much 'who the fuck is Temujin?', to which the curator answers in a dramatic voice that Temujin was the birth name of Genghis Khan, and you have to wonder why he didn't just lead with that, unless of course he's a hipster who has all of Khan's albums. While the eggheads go off to figure out how this arrived at their museum, Shiwan Khan (John Lone) bursts out of the sarcophagus and makes his escape into the night.

While wacky scientist Reinhardt Lane (Ian McKellen) is hard at work over at the War Department, Farley Claymore (Tim Curry) is sleazing up the joint, bubbling around the lab chatting about his various experiments, much to Lane's annoyance. His insalubrious behaviour shifts into an even higher gear when Margo arrives to see her father. He wants to show her his beryllium sphere, and if she's lucky, he'll get both out, along with his boiling tube. She has no interest in his spheres, though, and as his eyes keep dropping to her chest, she swats him aside on the way past his drooling cartoon face.

She wants to ask her father, who is a scientist after all, if telepathy is real, and he tells her it very much isn't but then goes on to stop listening to her, because he is wacky, with hilarious consequences.

Via his agents in the field the Shadow is informed of the events at the museum and a highly intricate pneumatic tube system that spans the entire city, a secret set-up that must never be found out, as it is prime for abuse. Hate the Shadow? Do a wee or poo in one of these babies, and Burbank (Andre Gregory), his poor message reader, will find out.

It's during this sequence that Joseph Nemec's production design particularly stands out. A wonderful blend of 'Streamline Moderne', capturing the feel of the period, with Mesopotamian influences, quasi-Egyptian themes and fantastical technology (Cranston's video call monitor in particular) really sets the feel of this film apart from its contemporaries. Combine this with some beautiful, living matte paintings intermingled with restored stock footage, and it very much feels like a living, breathing alternate New York.

'I know who you really are,' Khan says to Cranston, having invaded his secret hideout. 'Not this temporary version of yourself, Ying Ko.' This raises an eyebrow, as Cranston is both confused as to how he got in here and how he knows his identity. Khan tells him he's the last descendant of Genghis Khan, and after telling him he loves his work under his old name (which Cat Stevens must get all the time), he proposes a deal for him: world domination by finishing the work his famous relative started. Cranston says no, and refuses to be called Ying Ko, as it will probably get him cancelled, so Khan vanishes, leaving a message that he'll finish the job in three days – and a mysterious coin.

It's breakfast time. Dr Roy Tam gets up and answers his door to be greeted by Cranston standing in shadow. 'The sun is shining,' he booms, and Tam instantly replies with the obligatory, 'But the ice is melting,' which brings a smile to our hero's face. I'm so pleased I wasn't ever rescued by the Shadow, as there's no way I'd remember this. I'd be too easily distracted by the Finley Quaye song and tell him, 'The weather is sweet.' He wants Tam to analyse the coin, and it's a good thing he did, as it's made of bronzium, a substance that the ancient Chinese believed formed the universe. If this stuff got into the wrong hands, it could easily become an 'implosive-explosive submitecular device' or 'an atomic bomb', Cranston offers, with Tam commending him on his branding skills. But it would have to have a beryllium sphere to work, and fortunately such a device does not exist, so there's nothing to worry about. Uh-oh.

Reinhardt Lane has stopped receiving callers at the War Department, even his own daughter. Margo pleads with Barth to have the police look into it, but there's nothing he can do. She mentions that he's working on a harmless implosive device for energy research purposes and the last time she spoke with him on the phone, he was distant, confused and speaking in Chinese. This may well be nothing to worry about; after all, there have been many cases of people who receive head injuries and wake up speaking in a Jamaican patois. He may well have just slipped on a petri dish and now sounds like Ken Hom. Cranston has heard enough and leaves with purpose. Margo tries to stop him, and in doing so reads his mind and hears the words 'Ying Ko', which is bad. He steps into the darkness and, with eyes of black, begins to unleash his supreme gaslighting powers, telling her she has to forget everything she knows about him and to give him no further thought, while also remembering that he has a huge penis and to actively say out loud, 'Hey, there's that guy with the huge penis.' Sadly, none of these mind tricks work on Margo. Her powers are too great, so he jumps in his usual cab and changes into William Baldwin, the Shadow.

He arrives at the Federal Building to see what Lane is up to, and it's immediately clear that Khan has taken over his mind and is controlling his every move. The Shadow is accosted by a small army of Khan's men, all dressed in armour and with flailing swords. The Shadow is in his element, zipping along in the dark, thumping anyone who looks his way and sending men wheeling around the room with vim and vigour. Then he basically runs away.

Margo enters the baroque study. In one hand, a long pistol. Fully loaded. She sees Cranston in a chair, tending to the wounds he picked up in the fight. She aims and fires, but it's merely Cranston's reflection in a mirror. She's bewitched. Hypnotised by Khan to take a life, and she hasn't even eaten an onion like an apple. She has no idea how she got there or what happened or why she's walking like a chicken, only that she was sent to kill the Shadow, which, seeing as she's in Cranston's room and he's the only one there, is a bit awkward. It should be noted at this point that Baldwin as Lamont Cranston is the spitting image of Bruce Wayne from the animated Batman TV series.

Cranston races out to Chinatown to face Khan and boast that he knows his grand plan about blowing up the city, but he'll never succeed as he doesn't have a beryllium sphere. Khan is deeply unimpressed by this smug discovery and has some boasting of his own to do: just before he murdered Tulku, he stole the Phurba, and now he produces it as a threat, with the main threat being that we have to look at CGI from 1994, which has an almost quaint-pathetic quality, more rubber than metal, and has dated like fine warm milk. Cranston wants revenge, but once again is unable to tame the annoying dagger, still frustrated by the Billy Idol-looking thing – much like most of Generation X when he left for California. While Khan monologues, Cranston's face once again leans into the darkness, and he fixes his eyes on a guard who throws a gun his way. Cranston chases Khan through the streets but loses him at a mysterious, empty lot.

Russell Mulcahy (director of *Highlander* and many stylised music videos of the eighties) and director of photography Stephen H. Burum (*Apocalypse Now*, *Outsiders*, *The Untouchables*) have such a pure visual flair and a confident approach with this film. These 'hypnotising' sequences really stand out as sublime paint strokes of almost silent movie-era quality, with the darkness and light being so perfectly balanced.

'Farley Claymore!' Margo proclaims as they take a walk along the grey streets of New York. He was working on a beryllium sphere and wanted to show it to her. This is just the news Cranston needs right now: not only is a warlord running around the city, making taxi drivers blow themselves up and sailors throw themselves off ships, but now he hears that a rubber-faced pervert with obvious body odour issues is about to help blow up the city/world. He asks Margo to scope out that empty lot while he dons his Shadow gear to pay Claymore a little visit.

Claymore's facility is a giant bumhole of metal splayed out in the shadow of Brooklyn Bridge. When Claymore enters he is instantly aurally accosted by the Shadow asking him where his sphere is, but instead of dropping his trousers to show him, Claymore tells the Shadow he's too late, the sphere has been loaded on a truck. The Shadow laughs again and tells him he's an idiot and being manipulated, but Claymore disagrees. There's a new world order coming, and he's going to be king of the castle, so he pumps the test facility full of cold water before pulling a gun on the Shadow, who once again laughs, saying the famous last words: 'Who are you going to shoot with that, Claymore?!' While standing in two feet of water and exposing his body shape. Two shots are fired, and as blood trickles into the running water, the door is locked and a bar placed along the mechanism. The Shadow is wounded, soaking, and will probably drown. Luckily, Margo picks up on his mental trauma and races to free him from his watery grave.

As Cranston recovers, she informs him the lot was bought by a Far East investor six years ago and there is no record of the Hotel Monolith, which occupied it, being pulled down. As they take another look, he discovers the secret: the whole city has been hypnotised by Khan into thinking that the lot is empty, but he can see that it's actually still the Hotel Monolith. And there hasn't been a case of mass psychosis like it, apart from when *Avatar* became the highest-grossing movie of all time fifteen years later.

Later that night, the Shadow seamlessly floats through the mirage, through the halls and up the staircases, but, once again, he can't help himself, giggling as he does so and alerting Khan to his presence, which considering Khan is literally sitting on an atomic bomb seems foolish. Talking of foolish, Khan dispatches middle-aged and tubby scientist Farley Claymore to deal with his uninvited guest, armed only with a Tommy gun and a torch. It ends exactly how you expect, with him spinning on the spot firing a machine gun at laughing sounds before jumping through a glass window to his death.

'You are losing your concentration,' Khan says, after watching Cranston lose yet another battle with that fucking dagger (which is voiced by Frank Welker). At least now he has lost his mask, that giant prosthetic nose can be seen in its full glory, before he once again morphs into his beautiful face, which makes you wonder why they needed the giant nose make-up when he's wearing a big red handkerchief anyway. Khan mocks him for still being unable to master the Phurba and stalks the room monologuing, muttering and mocking, paying no attention to the fact that, deep within the struggle, a writhing Cranston is actually making progress, opening his eyes to reveal that they're now bright silver and in tune with the dagger for the very first time, producing the most unlikely alliance since Lady Gaga and Kermit the Frog. The Phurba sinks deep into Khan's stomach, breaking all the spells, releasing the city from its mass hypnosis and revealing the giant building to its citizens. The world is saved. Khan enters a lunatic asylum, with the glass injury having robbed him of his extraordinary powers – much like getting older robbed Richard Gere of his. Cranston can once again slip into the night, into the darkest corner of the shadows, and, now with the help of Margo, search for the evil that lurks in the hearts of men. Reminds me of Banksy.

Sadly, *The Shadow* was not a success, as it had the unfortunate task of competing with *The Lion King* and, much like the man himself, slipped away into the jet-black recesses of the human mind, becoming more of a novelty than a must-see, which is a real shame as Cranston definitely had more than one adventure in him, and Alec Baldwin was such a perfect fit. File this alongside films like *The Rocketeer* that were wrapped in promise, drenched with emotion and lush production design, but the gamble for more felt too rich for the studio execs.

SEVENTEEN

BATMAN FOREVER

1995

COURAGE NOW,
TRUTH ALWAYS,
BATMAN FOREVER!

In *Batman Returns*, Gotham had become a teeny-tiny sound stage full of extras from *A Nightmare Before Christmas*. It had also not performed as well as Warner Bros. had (understandably) expected it would. It was time to take Batman back into the mainstream. They wanted a third movie and most of all they wanted more light. Burton was shifted to (title-only) producing duties and Joel Schumacher was brought in to take over directing duties. This was *Batman Forever*.

Schumacher originally intended the next instalment of Batman to be an adaptation of Frank Miller's *Batman: Year One*, however, the studio insisted they wanted a sequel and not a prequel. The work began with Schumacher bringing in his own design team, their remit being to bring Gotham out of the darkness. Make it grander, bigger and more over the top. Fill it with neon, Japanese symbols and multi-coloured spotlights. Essentially turn it into Liberace's idea of a utopian paradise.

The first stumbling block was Batman himself. Michael Keaton took one look at the script and the general concept and turned it down flat. He was offered $15 million to play Batman/Bruce Wayne again, but Keaton was smart and saw the train wreck coming. Schumacher had seen Val Kilmer in *Tombstone* and liked what he saw. You can understand why – Kilmer dominated every scene in which he appeared. Given that the cast was littered with eye-catching performers, that was no small feat. His portrayal of Doc Holliday is one of the most memorable acting turns of the decade. When Kilmer got the call from his agent, he was in an actual cave full of bats in Africa, so he accepted the Batman role without seeing a script, such was his desire to don the cape. Rene Russo was originally attached to play the love interest (Dr Chase Meridian) but was dropped once Kilmer was cast. It was felt that Kilmer should have a younger woman to play against, therefore Nicole Kidman was the final choice.

The villains of the piece were set to be the Riddler and Two-Face. Billy Dee Williams had played Harvey Dent in the original *Batman* and had signed with the agreement that he would play Two-Face when the time came. The filmmakers had other ideas and paid Williams a full fee for not appearing in the film. Instead, they cast Tommy Lee Jones to play the coin-flipping baddie. Schumacher wanted Jones from day one as he had enjoyed working with him on *The Client*. Robin Williams was interested in playing the Riddler, though Jim Carrey was so hot at the time that he was a shoo-in.

Schumacher was keen to sail under his own steam, so out went Danny Elfman's incredible original score, and in came Elliot Goldenthal. Goldenthal was told by Schumacher to ignore Elfman's style and come up with something new altogether, and the end result isn't all that bad, although it lacks the simmering menace and grandiose punch of its predecessor. In terms of tone, it fits perfectly with the visuals, brooding and bursting along with the opening credits, which now resemble a Windows screensaver, but with added fantastical sound effects as the names whoosh by like fluorescent speedboats in the night.

Bruce Wayne suits up in his Batcave: snapping on gauntlets, pulling up boots, fixing his belt and picking out gadgets. As he makes his way up a set of stairs to stand in a hero pose, the new Batmobile rises in unison, changed from the sleek, stealthy-looking Formula One car to a giant kids' toy with glowing bits and wobbly bat wings. While it's difficult to look at, it looks a lot better than the design H. R. Giger had in mind. The production sought the artist's input for the new version, and he submitted one that looked like an alien's cock, and, honestly, what did they expect?

Alfred (Michael Gough) asks if Bruce would like a sandwich prepared before he goes out into the night, but Bruce tells him he'll get drive-through, and it's this joke, and its rather stilted delivery, that truly sets the tone for the piece: well-intentioned humour attempting to counterbalance the weight of a supposedly serious piece of work.

Two-Face (Tommy Lee Jones) has taken over the Second Bank of Gotham. He's killed two guards and holds another for ransom. Tommy Lee Jones has made a choice here. He's decided that Two-Face should be insanely annoying from the get-go. He has two modes: running around like a circus seal that's inhaled a fat bag of cocaine or sprinting around like a fat bag of cocaine that's inhaled Medellín. There is no in-between and, frankly, it's a lot. The costume is half black suit, half DayGlo zebra, and the make-up (by Rick Baker) is wild – with his 'other face' a bomb crater of neon-coloured scarring, as if he was holding a bag of highlighters when they exploded.

Batman has been called by Commissioner Gordon (Pat Hingle), who's somehow remained in a job, and as he arrives on the scene, looking just a perfect fit for the suit, he's introduced to Dr Chase Meridian (Nicole Kidman). Gordon has asked that Dr Meridian come to Gotham to consult as she specialises in abnormal psychology and multiple personalities. Batman is well aware of her work and takes a moment to add that it is naïve, which is what you have to love about Batman – he's such a messy bitch. They all decide as a group that Two-Face may well kill if pushed, as a trauma powerful enough to create multiple personalities leaves the victim in a world where normal rules no longer apply. Chase puts the same logic to Batman, suggesting that there's a paper to be written about a man who dresses as a flying rodent. 'Bats are not rodents,' he corrects her, and she's at least honest enough to tell him she didn't know that, and this is thrilling flirting.

Upstairs, Two-Face smashes a demolition ball through the wall and uses the remaining guard as bait to lure Batman and finally kill him.

Batman arrives to a feast of Dutch camera angles (where the camera is tilted, a trick to make things seem wacky or uneasy) and is attacked by Two-Face's goons – their costumes consisting of wrestling masks and multiple piercings, which sort of gives off the vibes that old Two-Face runs a sex dungeon in his spare time. Batman makes short work of them and then jumps into an open safe to rescue a tied-up guard. It's only as his gag is removed that he lets Batman know it's a big trap, and the vault door is slammed shut. The vault itself is then attached to a helicopter and pulled through the hole in the wall made by the wrecking ball, dropping Miley Cyrus on the way. As Batman sets about freeing them, the guard becomes a one-man script note explaining what is happening at an annoying volume: 'Oh no! It's boiling acid on the floor!', 'That's my hearing aid!', 'My shoes are melting!', and, at this point, I'd cheerfully drown him and say Two-Face did it.

Batman escapes and manages to get up to the cockpit of the helicopter, only to watch Two-Face flee via the most garish parachute available, a black and pink yin and yang logo, like the *The Spy Who Loved Me* for arseholes.

Bruce paces the floor of Wayne Enterprises, carrying out an inspection of the electronics projects that are currently being worked on. Fred Stickley (Ed Begley Jr), the area manager, is his guide (with a young Jon Favreau walking along as an extra), pointing out the various areas of note and trying to keep him away from someone, but it's too late. That person is Edward Nygma (Jim Carrey), a man in love with the idea of Bruce Wayne and whose desk serves a dual purpose as a work station-cum-shrine. Edward runs to greet him and tells him he's his absolute idol, and that he's invented a machine that beams any TV signal directly into the human brain, making the person feel like they're inside the show they're watching. He hassles Bruce for an immediate answer on whether it can be made, and as Bruce has noticed the Bat-Signal, he gives him his answer immediately: no. Messing with brain waves and manipulating minds, it just raises too many questions, plus, imagine a billionaire wanting the power to hassle with people's minds? What next? Rockets that explode? Cars in space? Social media platforms that get ruined?

Edward is devastated. Bruce was the one person who was supposed to understand.

Batman races to the rooftop to see what the emergency is, but instead of Commissioner Gordon panicking in his underwear, he's met with Chase (not Chevy) in her smalls. She basically wants to get down and dirty with him on the spot, and he's forced to remind her that the Bat-Signal isn't a hook-up beeper. She then pretends it's work-related and tells him about Two-Face's coin, how it can be manipulated, which Batman obviously knows already. 'It's the car, right? Chicks love the car,' he says, just asking to get cancelled. Chase reflects on just why she always goes for the wrong kind of man while he reflects on the fact that he's never had much luck with women. She leans in for a kiss just as Commissioner Gordon emerges in his dressing gown and hat, to ask what's going on, and I'd like an answer as to where he's been sleeping. Batman tells him it was a false alarm and then leaps off the roof and into his waiting Batmobile. 'Women,' he mutters to himself before firing up his engine and speeding off – definitely to have a wank.

Back at Wayne Enterprises, Edward is tinkering with his Mind Machine when he's interrupted by Stickley, who wants to know what the hell he's doing there late at night shouting at a photo of Bruce Wayne. He threatens to get security, but Edward knocks him out with a coffee pot before strapping him into his machine to test it on a human subject. (Clearly no ethics committee at Wayne Enterprises.) As he fires up the machine he quickly realises that, while Stickley appears able to watch 3D fishing, he's absorbing his brain power. 'Riddle me this, Fred,' he shouts obnoxiously. 'What is everything to someone, and nothing to everyone else?' and he means his mind. To celebrate, he does an insufferable dance for far too long. It's hard to be annoyed with Jim Carrey here, as this is exactly the performance he was hired for, this is literally his schtick, and he's pulling out all the stops for everyone in the back row.

There's been an accident at Wayne Enterprises, Arthur informs Bruce. Poor Fred Stickley threw himself out of a window and there's CCTV to show the sad sorry scene. As Bruce tells his assistant to ensure that Fred's family get full benefits, he receives a letter in the mail. A greeting card containing a riddle: 'If you look at the numbers on my face, you won't find thirteen any place.' Bruce solves the riddle immediately – a clock – and the real riddle is who sent it and why it's so shit.

Edward comes home to his elaborate apartment. 'Bad Days' by The Flaming Lips is quietly strumming to underline his weirdness, as we're treated to a broad stroke of fairy lights, hanging art, gadgetry, too many TV screens and, in the corner, a baffling green-suited wish machine that, instead of dispensing wishes, giggles occasionally while pointing at a green lightbulb that contains a question mark. What is it for? Why is it there? What does it do? That's the real fucking riddle. Edward sets himself down at his work station and begins cutting out more letters from newspapers in order to create yet another riddle that is in no way taxing.

Bruce smashes down Chase's front door, but not like that; he's visiting her office and heard noises coming from inside that indicated she may be in trouble. However, she's simply utilising a punch bag, and so his excessive entrance was a bit over the top. He apologises and introduces himself, telling her he has an appointment. Kilmer's Wayne is a bit of a wet lettuce (not helped by the roll-neck jumper in this scene), lacking Keaton's charm and his boiling-under-the-surface psychopathic nature; however, his Batman shines just as brightly as his predecessor, if not more. He's visited Chase under the guise of showing her the riddles he's been sent and asking for her opinion (her insightful professional opinion is that the letter writer is a 'total wacko'), but really he wants to take her out to the circus and show her his big top.

It's the Gotham Charity Circus, live from the Gotham Hippodrome. Everyone who's everyone is there, including Gossip Gerty (Elizabeth Sanders, Bob Kane's wife), a gossip columnist who wants to know everything about Bruce's latest date. Considering the Gotham Hippodrome looked as big as Madison Square Garden from the outside, it's odd to see how small the actual circus is inside. First act: the Flying Graysons, a family of trapeze artists who seek to entertain Gotham's finest with their high-flying birds act, swinging in the air, linking arms and generally wowing the assembled punters with their defiance of gravity. Bruce uses this event to ask Chase if she fancies going rock climbing with him at the weekend. She tells him she can't as she's met someone. He dropped out of the air and it was love at first sight. Bruce pretends to be disappointed, but inside he knows he's hit the jackpot.

Sadly, the fun of the fair is ruined by the arrival of Two-Face and his irksome gang. He's dressed as a ringmaster, which of course has been designed to the hilt for this fucking egomaniac. He's brought with him a giant round bomb packed with TNT, and he's slowly hoisting it into the rafters. He wants Batman dead, immediately, or he'll set off the bomb in two minutes, which seems a bit too ambitious as a plan. What if Batman is more than two minutes away? What if he's having a strenuous poo? It's just a bad demand,

and any negotiator would tell him as much. For a former lawyer, this guy is a fucking simpleton.

As the bomb is raised to the rafters, the Graysons decide to shut that door and save the day. Young Richard (Chris O'Donnell) manages to get it onto the roof, pushing it down the dome of the Colosseum and dropping it harmlessly into the water. When he returns to the pandemonium, he finds his entire family dead on the floor, shot down by Two-Face, who has just escaped. He's had better nights.

Bruce saw the whole thing happen, so he suggests Richard, or 'Dick', stay with him in his big mansion for a while. For some reason Commissioner Gordon brings him, and I'm starting to worry about this man: sleeping rough by the Bat-Signal, personally overseeing a suicidal man's death and now taxiing orphans around the city. Has his wife kicked him out or something?

As the Commissioner leaves, Dick tells Bruce thanks but no thanks, he's off to find Two-Face and kill him. Bruce should get extra points for not laughing in his face; instead, he warns him against revenge, telling him it won't bring his parents back, and he should know he's lost a few, but the young, hot-headed Dick's mind is made up, and Bruce knows he can't change it – but he can try to tempt him to stay by showing him into the garage for some petrol for his motorcycle. He compliments Dick on his choice of wheels, and Dick asks him if he hangs around in biker bars, an accusation Bruce takes in his stride.

It turns out Bruce's garage is full of classic cars and motorcycles (I wasn't expecting a bag of charcoal and some dried cement) that could do with a steady hand to fix them all up. Alfred is apparently a pretty good mechanic (so he's the one who goes to biker bars), but some of these bikes need real work to get them running, and he tells Dick that he can keep one as a fee, if he's up for it.

'Is this a Robin?' Alfred asks Dick, spying the painting on his motorcycle helmet. Dick explains that it is, and that he once had to save his brother from falling during their act. Apparently, he was so swift in doing so that his dad commented that he 'flew in like a robin', and what a very bizarre choice of bird to pick. Eagle? No. Hawk? Swift? No. Robin? That's the one, yes, a robin, you know those tiny birds that swoop and dive. I've only really seen fat ones sitting on the handle of a shovel in Christmas scenes, but OK.

Dick mourns the fact that he could have done so much more to save his parents and is saddened that he didn't live up to his dad's observation that he was a fat bird with red tits. Alfred, though, gives him hope by telling him he's definitely a hero; he can tell as much. Dick, though, has lost all faith in himself and asks Alfred to throw his circus costume away as he won't be needing it any more. Alfred says kindly that 'broken wings mend in time', but he should have said, 'Well, no, you won't. The rest of your act is dead,' given that Robin is now very much the Syd Little of the circus world.

Two-Face is a man filled with frustration and rage at Batman's 'stubborn refusal to expire'. He stomps like a toddler around his hideout, which is of course decorated in two distinct ways, split right down the middle. One side looks like DFS, the other the aftermath of a fire at DFS. He's being soothed by his two girlfriends, Sugar (Drew Barrymore) and Spice (Debi Mazar), who light his two cigarettes and give him the news of their dinner plans. Sugar has champagne, poached salmon and lemon soufflé; Spice offers an elaborate, charred black boar spit-roast, served with a side of raw donkey meat – I mean, what the actual fuck? It's at this point that you have to ask how the hell he managed to woo these women and does he flip a coin come bedtime? It's all very Manson Family, mixed with Jim Jones and served with a side of burns ward.

'Hope you made extra,' a voice springs from the darkness, and as he steps forward he introduces himself formally – it's a bowler-hatted Edward, dressed from head to toe in green, covered in question marks. He announces himself as 'The Riddler – a friend'.

Carrey told a story on *Norm MacDonald Live* about meeting Tommy Lee Jones away from the *Batman* set: 'It was at a restaurant, and the maître d' said, "I hear you're working with Tommy Lee

Jones? He's over in the corner having dinner." So, I went over and I said, "Hey Tommy! How you doing?" And the blood just drained from his face, like he'd been thinking about me for twenty-four hours, and he started shaking. He must have been in mid-"kill me" fantasy. He went to hug me and he said, "I hate you. I really don't like you," and I said, "Gee, man, what's the problem?" And he said, "I cannot sanction your buffoonery."'

The Riddler has a plan to pitch to Two-Face: rather than kill Batman, they should humiliate him, expose his weaknesses and then crush him. To demonstrate what he has in mind, he activates his machine and tells Two-Face that if he helps him raise enough money to get the device on the market, he will help him solve the ultimate riddle: who is Batman? Sounds like a hell of a *Dragon's Den* pitch.

Alfred is ironing in the laundry room. He tells Dick to leave his washing, he'll attend to it shortly, but Dick has other ideas; he's too proud and macho to allow an old British guy to touch his smalls, and he's far too used to dealing with them himself. So, he decides to pointlessly 'karate' his clothes onto a washing line, in the most embarrassing way possible – a homage to the 1981 Hong Kong film *Dreadnaught*, in which the character Mousy (Yuen Biao) does the very same, but on a larger scale and with less absolute cringe.

As the wet items dangle precariously on the line and Dick mops up the water, he strides out of the room with a passing wink of self-assurance to Alfred, who does very well not to piss himself laughing on the spot.

Bruce watches the news of the crime spree currently being perpetrated by Two-Face and the Riddler on TV. In his hand is a further riddle for him to solve: 'The eight of us go forth not back, to protect our king from a foe's attack.' It's chess pawns. So, he and Alfred go to the Batcave to try to put all these riddles together and see if there's a connection, and they come up with nothing.

It's the launch of NygmaTech, which looks like a ride at Thorpe Park, and Edward is boasting that it will bring the joy of 3D entertainment to every home. Standing behind the many microphones, he presents 'The Box', which, as with every other prototype of his machine, is a food processor with polystyrene chunks inside. The Box of course becomes the hottest item on the market, and in a world where people were paying £100 for a bottle of Prime, a drink that is basically unmixed concentrated squash, this fails to surprise me. As the poor unfortunate people of Gotham sit gawping, hypnotised and bathed in warm green glow, Edward is ensconced in his private lair, inhaling all their brain power vapours.

The Batmobile screams around the dry-iced, spotlit, hyper-coloured streets of Gotham. The Offspring's cover of The Damned's 'Smash It Up' is blasting out of the speakers as it bumps and judders along at awkward speeds. Inside is Dick, who broke into the Batcave and stole it out of spite. As he cruises the sidewalk trying to pick up sex workers, who mock him and call him Batboy, he spots a street gang covered in bizarre face paint glowing in the dark, trying to hassle a young girl. While he holds his own with a few (using his laundry skills), he is soon outnumbered, and Batman arrives to save him, sending the gang running for the hills. Dick attacks him, pounding on Batman's chest and tearfully shouting that he should be dead, not his parents. Ungrateful child. A simple thank you would have sufficed.

Back at Wayne Manor, Bruce explains to Dick that if he kills Two-Face, the pain will still grow inside, and revenge will be his only path in life. He also mentions that he heard about the shenanigans in the laundry, and he's lucky there's no CCTV in that room, or he'd put it on the internet and he could be the next *Star Wars* kid. Dick tells him he could never possibly understand, as his family weren't killed by a maniac (LOL); he wants Bruce to train him and to be his partner, to which Bruce simply says no. Dick still has a choice with what to do with his life, plus he's really fucking annoying and an embarrassment to be seen with.

It's the NygmaTech gala unveiling of a new, improved Box. The Ritz Gotham is packed, the lights are bright, and Edward, Sugar on his arm, is loving being the centre of attention for the first time.

That is until Bruce Wayne arrives and steals all his admirers away, much to his chagrin. He approaches the great man and tries to rub his face in how well his company is doing, carrying major crypto energy as he does so, but Bruce isn't fazed at all, merely complimenting him on his success like the pass-agg bitch he is.

Edward launches the demonstration of fully interactive holographs that can introduce images into the mind, and Bruce spots a small snag with this plan: what's to stop him extracting images from someone's mind? A good question, and one that probably had reporters from *The News of the World* tugging at their collars in guilty discomfort. Edward laughs it off and wanders away, so Bruce pops into the machine for a sneak around, unaware that Sugar has begun the recording.

'Tell me your dreams. Tell me your fantasies. Tell me your secrets. Tell me your deepest, darkest fears,' the machine purrs over a digital image of a brain, with all the deepest hemispheres being explored via clunky animation. Bruce stands transfixed in the green shard of light, probably thinking about shagging on a giant tortoise while sitting an exam and trying to shoo away a bat that's nibbling on his tootsies. However, before he can get too enveloped in his erotic reverie, Two-Face decides to crash the party, shoot up the room and rob the guests. He explains to Edward that his plan was boring and going nowhere, and he's fed up waiting. He wants Batman dead, and nothing brings him to the party like murder and mayhem – and how right he is, as moments later Batman crashes through the skylight, snogs Chase, then chases Two-Face and his men down to a subterranean construction site.

A lone hand reaches into a pile of crushed scaffolding, dust and gravel, and pulls Batman from within. It's Dick, decked in his circus costume, dangling from the rafters, wearing a Zorro mask and a shit-eating grin.

Back at the Batcave, Bruce is livid that he saved his life, and isn't interested in his ideas for what name he should use – Batboy? Nightwing? – dryly suggesting 'Richard Grayson, college student'.

(Anything is better than Robin, FYI.) Dick tells Bruce that he's looking at his new partner and, wherever he goes, Dick will follow. As he storms off, Alfred reminds Bruce that young men with a mind for vengeance need guidance – or they could go to his room later while he's sleeping and Alfred could hold him while Bruce rains down hard punches to his throat. Bruce changes the subject and tells him he's in love with Chase, that he's never been in love before, which is demonstrably bullshit, but OK. Alfred tells him to go to her and tell her just that, and let her decide who she loves: Batman or Bruce Wayne.

Chase is awoken by a figure at her window looking in at her slumber. Carved out in the moonlight, Batman waits for her to open the door, and she does so immediately, gripping the bed linen to her body. They embrace and kiss in one swift motion, with passions high and breathing heavy. She stops, looks him in the eyes and admits that she's met someone else (and he's a billionaire, though what first attracted her is unclear). Batman considers the information, then tells her he understands before stepping into a close-up to serve the stupidest grin ever seen in cinema.

Armed with the new-found information that Chase fancies him, Bruce takes Dick on a tour of the Batcave, deactivating everything bit by bit and telling him that because he's got a new girlfriend, he can't be Batman any more. Dick begs him to reconsider, reminding him that there are innocent people he needs to protect, there are monsters out there, and Batman needs a partner to help him take down Two-Face, but Bruce has made his mind up. Chase is coming for dinner, and he's going to tell her everything, especially the laundry story. Dick packs up his things, grabs his bike and heads out into the real world.

After dinner, triggered by Chase knocking over a vase of two red roses, Chase and Bruce talk endlessly of secrets and buried memories. He tells her of his parents' death (yawn) and of his first encounter with a giant bat in a shadowy cave that changed his life. Chase asks him what he's trying to tell her, and he spells it out by kissing her. With his tongue being the same as Batman's, she recoils at first, realising what has just happened, but she comes back for more, knowing she's hit the fucking jackpot.

As the lovers fumble in the living room, Alfred answers the door to a couple of trick-or-treaters, who knock him unconscious and stuff him in a cloakroom. A house invasion begins, with Bruce fighting a horde of bad guys as Riddler invades the Batcave and acts like a proper tit, spouting words like 'joygasm' as he wanders around blowing everything up like some awful fucking TikToker. Upstairs, a bullet from Two-Face catches Bruce, sending him tumbling down some stairs and knocking him out cold. As the villains depart, Riddler places yet another pathetic riddle on Bruce's unconscious body.

On Bruce waking up, Alfred informs him that Dr Meridian has been taken, Dick's run away and the Batcave's been destroyed. Basically, everything's fucked. Oh, and there's *another* riddle.

'We're five little items of an everyday sort. You'll find us all on a tennis court.' The answer is vowels, but the real mystery is what do a clock, a match, chess pawns and vowels have in common, Alfred asks. Every riddle arrived with a number attached – 13, 1, 8 and 5 – and they obviously relate to letters of the alphabet, and if you put 1 and 8 together, that makes 18, which all spells: MR E, or 'Mystery'. Bruce then asks Alfred what another name for mystery is, and he immediately barks '*Enigma!*' Which is all very neat, and whoever wrote that deserves a biscuit or a small holiday. Bruce then pieces it all together. It's Edward Nygma who's behind it all, and therefore Stickley's suicide was obviously a computer-generated forgery, and he should cut all the widow's benefits at once.

Amid the rubble of the Batcave, only one Batsuit has survived, one that Alfred informs Bruce is a prototype with sonar modifications that he recently invented, so that will obviously do. Bruce plunges his body inside it, including a lingering shot of his tight arse, and as he emerges he asks Alfred if he should go by sea or by air, and Dick answers the question, emerging from his secret dressing room, decked in new threads: 'Why not both?' Bruce asks after the identity of his tailor, and Alfred takes the credit so should be fired immediately. Dick tells Bruce his name is now Robin, and Bruce agrees that they can be partners, as long as he walks five paces behind him at all times and never speaks to him when people are around.

As the Batplane soars through the sky, rushing through the Bat-Signal, Commissioner Gordon jumps up and down in glee, once again ecstatic that his police force can have another night off to play blackjack with strippers.

'Holy rusted metal, Batman,' Robin announces as they reach Riddler's island. 'Huh?' Batman offers, with the resignation of someone who wants to know what the fuck he's going on about. Robin explains that the ground is all metal, rusted and full of holes. This is a joke that is obviously supposed to make the audience titter and remember the days of Adam West and Burt Ward, whereas in actual fact it acts as a reminder of where this is all heading once again: exactly the landscape of pantomime that the film of 1989 was so keen to remove itself from.

The two heroes become separated, Robin battling with Two-Face on a rocky outcrop and Batman finding himself alone in Riddler's vast room of question marks, spotlights and spot projections. 'Riddle me this, riddle me that. Who's afraid of the big black bat?' Riddler shouts, perched on a gold throne and now dressed in sequins, with a spiky pink rinse. Batman tells him to hand over Chase, that his mind-reading scheme is over, but Riddler has another scheme up his sleeve. He knows who Batman really is and gives him the final riddle. Who will he save? In one glass tube he has Dr Chase Meridian, in the other, Robin. Below them is a well full of sharp rocks and a very long drop. Which one will he save? The love of Bruce's life or the annoying lad who does karate laundry and never shuts the fuck up. Before he can decide, Batman tells Riddler he has a riddle for him: 'I see without seeing, to me, darkness is clear as daylight. What am I?' The Riddler cackles at the ease of the puzzle and tells him the answer is 'as blind as a bat', which is music to Batman's ears, as he activates his sonar suit and throws a giant Bat-a-Rang up at the brain machine, causing it to smash, explode and suck back brainwaves from the Riddler's brain.

As Chase and Robin fall from their glass prisons, Batman jumps down and saves them both with a dual grappling gun, which perhaps was the answer to the earlier riddle all along. He then performs a wonderful encore: causing Two-Face to fall to his death by throwing coins at him as he goes to decide if they'll all live or die. Robin watches with wide eyes of passion as Two-Face explodes on the rocks, spilling blood, bone and viscera as the water laps at the wreckage. Justice has been served, and he should do a wee on it.

As Dr Chase Meridian exits Arkham Asylum, she reassures Bruce that Edward is definitely a wacko, that he's locked up in a very padded cell, and even if he did tell anyone about who Batman is, they wouldn't believe him. She'll also arrange for him to be visited by 'The Shagger' after lights out every night, just to make sure that the message gets through. Bruce tells her his mind is clearer now, that the dreams of his parents' death have stopped and he now has a new dream of happiness. He'll be Batman for ever, and he can't wait to see her later in her pants.

As the music raises to a military march, we're met with the immortal silhouettes of Batman and Robin racing towards the screen in front of a Bat-Signal, the wobbly bat ears flapping in slow motion – perhaps a portent of the horror that was to follow.

EIGHTEEN

JUDGE DREDD

1995

IN THE FUTURE, ONE MAN IS THE LAW

They say you should never meet your heroes, and while that is true, there's another maxim that always seems to come to pass: never make a film about something you love. It'll never go the way you want.

The tale of Danny Cannon is one that is in no way unique. It's a story that has certainly happened since and will definitely happen again, but it remains a tearjerker. Cannon was an exciting indie director riding high on the success of the stylish mid-nineties thriller *The Young Americans*. It was a film with so much buzz that Hollywood inevitably poked its nose in, and Cannon was offered his first big studio job, which just so happened to be the job of a lifetime: to direct *Judge Dredd*.

Cannon was a *2000 AD* nut, especially regarding *Judge Dredd*. He'd had artwork published in the comic in 1987, so this was to be his dream. As is the way of things, of course, it ended up as a living nightmare.

James Earl Jones reads an opening narration to inform us that the Earth of the third millennium (in Robbie Williams' singles or years?) is broken. It is a world of scorched lands and poisonous deserts, affectionately referred to as the 'Cursed Earth'. Mega-Cities popped up to house the populous, but they quickly became hotbeds of crime and savagery, where justice feared to tread. In response, a new order rose from the ashes: a police force that was judge, jury and executioner all in one – the Judges. It has to be said that an opening narration alone feels lazy, and hiring James Earl Jones to read it also feels particularly egregious.

Herman 'Fergee' Ferguson (Rob Schneider) has been released from his six-month prison sentence, presumably having served his time for being the world's most annoying arsehole, and is assigned his new living quarters: Y Block, Heavenly Haven. As he steps out onto the beautifully realised set (designed by Nigel Phelps, a concept artist on *Batman*), with its broken shards of dense architecture looming over neon signs, rusted pipes and dry ice, it's clear that there's no haven to be had, especially if you live next door to Rob Schneider. Sadly, Heavenly Haven is an example of sarcastic nomenclature, much like 'Ashby-de-la-Zouch' or 'visionary directors, the Russo Brothers'; it's a hellish war zone in reality, and there's a riot in progress. Fergee manages to navigate through the turmoil and reach his new apartment, only to find that it's currently being used by a gang of gun-wielding maniacs led by the Block Warlord (James Remar), who informs him that he can't leave as there's a block war, and one can only imagine Bob Holness dressed like Lord Humungus from *Mad Max 2*, playing his sax on top of a skip while the world burns to ashes.

The Block Warlord and his men begin to fire indiscriminately out of the window down to the streets below, and as the people die in a hail of bullets or flee from the scene, two Judges arrive on the corner of Abbot and Costello on giant motorcycles, or 'Lawmasters', if you will. Judge Hershey (Diane Lane) and a rookie are instantly caught in the crossfire and decide to wait for back-up.

They radio for help. But who will come to save them? Judge Dredd (Sylvester Stallone), that's who. He glides through the bullets, sails through the fire and steps off his Lawmaster, hands on hips, inviting us to admire his ridiculous uniform (that Stallone himself requested be made by Gianni Versace). It looks less like he'll stop a block war, and more like he's there to star in a Madonna video.

'I AM THE LAW!' he bellows via his helmet microphone before telling the whole block to drop their weapons. Suffice to say they don't listen to him, so he decides to walk upstairs and blow away all the Block Master's men. Block Master himself is executed for killing the stupid rookie, and just when you think the court is adjourned forever, Dredd's keen instincts detect that Fergee is hiding inside a food droid. He's about to give him six months in jail for tampering with a robot when he finds out that this isn't his first offence and he only just got out of jail, so he ups it to five years (this is also based on Dredd having seen *Deuce Bigalow: Male Gigolo*). He asks Fergee how he pleads, and he, naturally, says he's not guilty, to which Dredd brings out the 'I knew you'd say that' catchphrase that he hopes will be memorable and fun for the paying audience. Dredd points out that, instead of getting inside the robot to hide, he could have jumped out of the window to escape, which although would have been certain death, is at least legal.

Online trivia has it that Stallone personally called Schneider to offer him the role of Fergee, after his first choice, Joe Pesci, turned it down, and you cannot begin to imagine how happy Joe Pesci must be about that decision, even to this day – and he did *Moonwalker*.

'Mega-City 1, Cursed Earth, Texas City, Aspen, Mega-City II': these are the only points on a map on the screen at a meeting of the Judge Council. Judge Griffin (Jürgen Prochnow) is concerned that the block wars are becoming an epidemic; he thinks they should be dealt with immediately by updating the criminal code. Other council members agree and begin talking about how violent crime is rising and how their resources are inadequate. Chief Justice Fargo

(Max von Sydow) calls for calm. He points out that real growth and change takes time, and they should all chill out. Griffin, though, calls for executions for lesser crimes to try and bring the population down, and I have managed to get a hold of his list:

1. Using your mobile phone like it's a walkie-talkie instead of putting it to your ear: *Execution.*
2. Riding a bike without using the handlebars: *Execution.*
3. Talking at any time in the cinema: *Execution.*
4. Eating at any time in the cinema: *Execution.*
5. Shouting 'wooohhh!' when a barman drops a glass in a pub: *Execution.*
6. Wearing a backpack on a busy train/tube/bus: *Execution.*
7. Skimming a stone at the beach more than three times: *Knighthood.*

Fargo tells the room that he's been a Judge long enough to know that freedom is much more important than oppression, and the other Judges look soberly at him, knowing deep down that he is right. Yes, it would be awful if this new utopia you've built becomes oppressive – good thinking, it's perfect as is.

Reporter Vartis Hammond (Mitchell Ryan) has no time for the Judges. While he accepts in his news report that the violence has become endemic, what he cannot accept is that the Judges kill just as many in the course of their duty, and as he releases a diatribe against them, Dredd watches on a TV at the Council Chambers, hands once again on hips, and mouth very much looking like he's just licked piss off a nettle. He's there for a meeting with Fargo, and as the other Judges leave, he's told he can stand at ease, so he removes his helmet and shows us his Stallone face, replete with blue contact lenses.

This is the moment that loses everyone. Sure, the Mega-City set was very impressive: that did put some credit in the bank. The use of *2000 AD* slang is fun, a little credit there. But removing the helmet is just not what Judge Dredd does, ever, and that's perhaps the main issue: this isn't Judge Dredd, this is Sylvester Stallone, the man who was on the comeback trail. *Cliffhanger* had just given new wind to his sails, and there was absolutely no way he'd be obscuring his big face for a whole movie, especially as, according to most reports, he'd never even heard of *Judge Dredd* when he accepted the role. He was also keen to make this a comedy-action movie, rather than a dystopian tale of urban decay, and it's these factors woven together that end up creating a cold rice pudding of a final presentation that liquefies into a mess, pleasing absolutely no one and serving only to stand as a big middle finger to the fans of the source material.

Fargo asks him if the executions he carried out at Heavenly Haven were absolutely necessary. Dredd tells him they were unavoidable and that he'd understand more of what is necessary out on the streets if he spent less time at the academy training new recruits – and it would appear his training is pretty bad, as we just saw a rookie get killed. Fargo tells Dredd that he wants him at the academy two days a week to help out, teaching ethics, and Dredd looks as confused as we do. 'Ethics', as in the place outside London, yeah?

Aspen Penal Colony (which is what I call my pants), a snow-covered fortress in the middle of a white wasteland (see last comment), is a maximum-security jail housing the very worst people in the Cursed Earth, the worst of whom is former Judge Rico (Armand Assante). He is imprisoned within a forcefield, his crime having been that he killed innocent people, which seems to be what Judges do anyway, so it's all very woolly. He's visited by the warden (Maurice Roëves from *Rab C. Nesbitt*), who brings him a package from his 'mysterious benefactor'. Inside a small box he finds his old Judge badge and a picture of Vartis Hammond. The warden asks what the package is, and Rico converts the box into a gun, tells him the meaning of life is that 'it ends' and shoots him through the throat.

Dredd is showing the new recruits at the academy how the Lawgiver (the special big gun Judges use) works – basically, it's a gun with a built-in computer capable of controlling its operation. He then shows them the Lawmaster, the fancy motorcycle that can also fly. Unfortunately the display model they have is malfunctioning and is in for repair at the academy. He tells the green cadets that all these exciting gadgets will be theirs, *if* they graduate, and the only thing that counts is the law.

'We're closed for the night,' Geiger (Ian Dury), owner of the antique weapons store, says from behind a pair of magnified glasses. Rico tells him he has a package held for him, in the name of Lazarus. The box is retrieved, and it's a set of Judge equipment, with a Lawmaster that recognises his grip. Geiger knows his time is up and adds this to his list of reasons not to be cheerful, before he is murdered on the spot. At the back of the shop is a docile ABC Warrior from the old days of war (which sort of looks like a mechanical Bruce Campbell) – a giant machine based on the Hammerstein character from the comic, which he reactivates and commands to serve as his bodyguard.

Vartis Hammond is chilling at his house with his wife. He tells her that the 'cancer of oppression' goes far deeper than he imagined and he's going to go on air and tell the world about it. His wife tells him he'll never be allowed to say that, as it could bring down the Council, so he may have to save it for his 'too hot for TV' DVD at Christmas. He's not scared, though. He's determined to tell the truth. But before he can go on YouTube to interview some cranks, his door is broken down and Judge Dredd storms in, murdering them both with a few short gun bursts of justice.

The next day, while dealing with a bland traffic violation by blowing up the car (fucking ACAB, lads), Dredd is arrested for the murder of Vartis Hammond. He pleads his innocence to Fargo, who immediately takes his side and says that although the punishment is death and there is irrefutable evidence, all he had to do was look into Dredd's eyes to know he didn't do it, and I now have serious questions about how this whole system works. Dredd is found guilty at a tribunal, based on the video evidence and his DNA being on the bullets. Fargo tells the Council that if they spare Dredd's life and only send him to prison, he'll retire and take the 'long walk', venturing into the wasteland like Captain Tom did. The Council accepts this offer and orders Dredd to serve a life sentence in Aspen. One rule for the law, then.

As Dredd is sent away and Fargo is booted out into the dust, Griffin, who is now in charge of the Council, returns to his chamber to be met by a giant grumpy robot and Rico behind his desk, pulling on a piece of ham the size of Belgium and chewing it with the vigour of a starving man. Assante's performance is one for the ages, especially the twirling of the biggest moustache ever placed on a face – without even having had to grow one. Griffin castigates him on his choice of meeting place, and it becomes very clear that Rico's mysterious benefactor was actually Judge Griffin. He says that Hammond had to be killed as he'd found out about 'Project Janus', which one assumes is a comedy name generator they've been developing. Griffin tells him that now Dredd and Fargo are out of the picture, he wants chaos, fear running down every street, violence, murder, dogs and cats living together, the works. Then the Council will have no option but to turn to him and his exciting Janus thing.

As is always the way with solo air travel, Dredd has been put in the worst possible seat: next to Fergee, who is enjoying the irony of Dredd talking about a wrongful conviction, and if it were any other person, you'd enjoy his righteous indignation, were it not for the fact that he should always be sent to prison, no matter what. During his frenzied, high-pitched, annoying moaning, the rest of the prisoners on the airship can't help but overhear, and, led by Ted Hastings from AC-12, they immediately set upon Dredd to avenge his frankly wicked police practices.

Down in the Scorched Earth, the Angel Gang spy the transporter flying overhead. They decide to shoot it down with a rocket, which is good news for Dredd, as he was about to be stabbed in the throat.

'Am I dead?!' Fergee exclaims, waking up to find himself and Dredd hung by their hands in a cave. There's no time to answer, though, as the Angel Gang enter, giggling like *Space Deliverance*. They're made up of all the main 'hick' food groups: a religious patriarch, a toothless beardie-type, Spud from *Trainspotting* and a cyborg chap by the name of 'Mean Machine', who is more machine than man and is covered in burnt flesh and scratched metal. Pa Angel (Scott Wilson) proclaims them as sinners, presumably as he's recently watched *Stop or My Mom Will Shoot*. They're well aware of Dredd and are very excited to have 'the great man of the law himself' hanging in their living room. Fergee is over the moon when they tell him they're cutting him down until he finds out that they're cannibals. He he tries to sweet-talk his way out of being dinner by telling them he's got gonorrhoea, which is the only thing he's said that I actually believe.

Things look bad for our hero, with Mean Machine more than ready to rip him to pieces and tell him that although he was excited about *Rocky V* in the build-up, it was ultimately a deeply disappointing experience. Luckily, a rescue team sent by Griffin himself, arrives, but not to save Dredd: to destroy him and cover up his escape, though these poor fools forget that he is THE LAW, and he begins exterminating them. As the dust settles, a lone hooded figure appears from the darkness, having helped kill the last of the team: it's Fargo. 'Together again,' they say in soft unison, once again united in their solemn bond of justice, warmth, love and friendship. A moment mildly ruined by Mean Machine plunging a colossal knife through Fargo's back and out through his chest. What a pooper. Dredd and Machine fight briefly before the latter gets his robot hand stuck and Dredd asks him how he pleads before delivering the deadly blow. To give Machine his dues, he doesn't say either way, but rather makes a guttural roar, to which Dredd rolls out the carpet of his 'catchphrase', saying, 'I knew you'd say that,' before executing him.

On his death bed, Fargo tells Dredd all about the Janus project. They created the perfect Judge in a lab, who was to be the best of the best, and that experiment was Dredd. All the pictures he has of his family were fake, and he lied about them dying when he was very young, and it all feels very Jeremy Kyle. That's not all, though; another clone was created, and something went wrong. They accidentally created the perfect criminal, with the Council later releasing a statement saying, 'This is the one thing we didn't want to happen.' That man is Rico, which Dredd isn't very happy about, as he judged him, as most brothers do to one another. 'My whole life is a lie,' Dredd says, rather dramatically. He realises that Rico killed Hammond, and it's how the DNA matched. With his final words Fargo tells him that Griffin is behind it all, and even though Dredd asks him not to die, he dies. Is there no end to this man's duplicity?

The chaos Rico promised is delivered in Mega-City. Shops are blown up, bins pushed over, doorways sullied with piss and dumps, phone boxes smashed, and Judges assassinated. Griffin tells the Council there's only one thing they can do now, and that's activate Project Janus, which Mark Corrigan was working on before his brain condition took hold. The majority of the Council sadly agree to his proposal and begin the activation, which will create the perfect specimen of Judges, ready to bring peace and prosperity to the terrified citizens of Mega-City, within eight hours. A couple of the Council members, however, baulk at playing God and withdraw their support, so Rico walks in and murders them all. Luckily for him, Dredd and Fergee have sneaked into the building, so Griffin can pin the murders on them.

They make their escape, and it's this scene that contains one of the best bloopers in the making of this film, with poor Rob Schneider taking a tumble down some stairs and face-planting the floor. The footage is readily available on YouTube and is well worth watching on repeat. Luckily for our heroes, Chekhov's Lawmaster is still at the academy, and this time it works, leading our intrepid heroes on a very well-rendered flying bike chase around the city.

'We're dying out there,' Hershey tells Dredd when he reaches her trashed apartment. A hundred and eight Judges have been killed in the last forty-eight hours, and six stood on rakes. Dredd explains that he'll never let anyone hurt her, and they share a moment of unearned tenderness. It turns out that Hershey has been busy doing her own detective work and has figured out the full machinations of the Janus project. She asks him who Rico is. Dredd explains that although he's heavy, he's also his brother. He's known this fact for about an hour and he has to stop him at once.

Rico meanwhile speaks to the computer (voiced by Adrienne Barbeau) and tells it there's been a change of plan. He wants to swap the DNA sample on file for his own, and thankfully this is all done via a series of needles, and not a jazz mag and a cup. Janus scientist Dr Hayden (Joan Chen) tells him that this was never the plan and Griffin will never agree to it, but Rico laughs in her face and basically says he can do what he likes. Griffin, though, disagrees and wants to put a stop to it by killing him before the robot pulls his body to pieces and probably puts his leg where his knob was and his arms in his arse.

Dredd, Hershey and Fergee (who assures Dredd that he can crack the computer) arrive at the lab to put a stop to all this, only to be immediately captured by Rico and his robot and presented with the Janus clones, who all look like scrotums liberally doused in talcum powder.

'Your brothers and your sisters,' Rico proudly informs him, like he's a mother who remarried years ago and is now living in Stoke. He monologues and posits all sorts of scenarios where naked scrotum men help him rule his new dystopia, but he's really wasting his time. Dredd has no interest in letting any of this happen, so there's only one thing for it: fight! As some of the clones begin to wake up and presumably imprint on the first thing they see like a lizard, they tumble, roll and punch their way to a ledge. The lab begins to disintegrate around them as Dredd finally gets the better of Rico. Mumbling the words 'Court's adjourned', Rico is thrown out of a mock Statue of Liberty to his death, and the day is saved.

'Central broadcasted the Janus plan after Griffin's death. They all know the truth,' Dredd and Hershey are informed on the front steps of the Council chambers, and there is much celebration from the remaining Judges who didn't step on rakes. Dredd is therefore offered the position of Chief Justice, which he of course turns down. He tells them he's a Street Judge and he just loves murdering people, and you can't do that behind a desk. He puts his uniform back on and straddles his Lawmaster once again. Hershey questions if he's OK, as they've just experienced a war and maybe he'd want to have a little sit down, or at least some karaoke, but he simply tells her goodbye. Hershey grabs his helmet (not like that) and holds his face between her hands, giving him a lovely kiss, as Fergee is taken away, presumably to be put in some sort of bin.

'Feels good to be human, don't you think?' Hershey asks him with a smile.

'I knew you'd say that,' Dredd offers in return, and she really needs to tell him to stop.

He fires up the bike and drives to the highest point to keep a watchful eye over the now repaired city, leaving the citizens below in no doubt that if they park badly, he'll detonate their car and send them to prison. As the sun sets over the fractured landscape, there's a bright future ahead – if you do what you're told.

Danny Cannon was not allowed on set for the post-production reshoots and swore he'd never work again with such a 'self-absorbed actor', and with that, another familiar tale of a budding, hungry new director ends, and another dream dies.

NINETEEN

SPAWN

1997

BORN IN DARKNESS.
SWORN TO JUSTICE.

'The battle between Heaven and Hell has waged eternal, their armies fuelled by souls harvested on Earth. The devil, Malebolgia, has sent a lieutenant to Earth to recruit men who will turn the world into a place of death in exchange for wealth and power, a place that will provide enough souls to complete his army and allow Armageddon to begin. All the Dark Lord needs now is a great soldier, someone who can lead his hordes to the gates of Heaven and burn them down.'

Typically, if a film begins with not only a narration but also a hastily cobbled-together montage, it's not a good sign.

At a military air base in Hong Kong, CIA operative Al Simmons (Michael Jai White) has just assassinated a group of 'bad men'. He leaves the scene, using an explosion to cover his tracks. Nicholas Cogliostro (Nicol Williamson, also the overworked narrator) watched the whole thing happen from behind his trench coat and hat, and as the fire rages, there's another narration explaining that 'the war for Heaven and Hell depends on the choices we make' before the horrible-looking opening credits (worst font EVER) spill out from within a digital can of spaghetti, and we're dragged to Hell along with the dated dulcet tones of Orbital's 'Satan'.

Spawn was the brainchild of legendary comic-book artist Todd McFarlane, a character he'd had in his mind for decades, and one that since he left Marvel, where he'd become something of a rockstar, he was keen to commit to paper. Such was the interest in what he'd do next, *Spawn* was an immediate hit, selling over a million copies for the first issue, so it was only a matter of time before a film arrived. New Line pictures bought the rights, and in a move that echoed McFarlane's own, the film was to be made by some other people who'd just jumped ship from a titan – Mark A. Z. Dippé (who directed the film) and producers Clint Goldman and Steve 'Spaz' Williams – all formerly of Industrial Light and Magic and all visual effects wizards. This is the trio who conjured the water face in *The Abyss*, the liquid metal in *Terminator 2* and the dinosaurs of *Jurassic Park*. What could possibly go wrong?

After hearing on the TV that Simmons not only killed the intended targets, but also TWENTY-SIX unarmed civilians, thus leading to near-global anti-US sentiment, CIA Director Jason Wynn (Martin Sheen) turns in his chair and declares that 'Simmons is the best'. Sheen said that he did this film because he wanted to be in a comic-book film, and you get the feeling that he said yes during his notorious *Apocalypse Now* freakout.

His office is of the standard you'd expect to see for a CIA Director – flags, medals, books and so on – however, the walls are also decorated with pictures of various huge nuclear blasts, and you can't help but feel that Dena Roth, the set dresser, took the brief and slam-dunked it.

Simmons doesn't share the celebratory mood, though. He was told the airport would be cleared of civilians before he fired a massive rocket at it and he wants out. Wynn is unmoved, reminding him that it's his job to kill people and fire rockets into densely populated public spaces. He can't just quit the CIA, they're not the US Postal Service, though you could argue both carry the dangers of being shot at in the workplace. Wynn puts a full stop to that statement by hilariously putting out his cigarette in an ashtray that's nestled in a tiny tank of scorpions, which is exactly the sort of thing Andrew Tate would do. Wynn reminds him of his personnel file that has him down as a borderline psychopath, perfect for government service (no argument there) – no guilt, no fear. A proper killing machine, and what else could he possibly do? Work in a garage?

Watching on as the two men argue the toss is Jessica Priest (Melinda Clarke), another hard-edged CIA operative who laughs in the face of death and has a small gun strapped to her thigh. She's languishing on the office sofa, teasing a large tarantula over her hands and suggesting that maybe Simmons isn't the man Wynn thinks he is. Wynn finally accepts his ultimatum. He can leave, but only after he does one more job: take out a North Korean refinery that's secretly producing biological weapons.

However, like all good final jobs, there's a massive double cross waiting for him.

'Enjoy your retirement, old friend,' Wynn says as he stands over Simmons' bullet-ridden body. Unbeknownst to our hero, Priest tagged along on the factory mission and shot him from behind. As Wynn is lighting another cigarette, Priest douses Simmons in flammable liquid and laughs in his sad, confused face. 'Don't worry about Wanda, I'll take good care of her,' Wynn says with boner eyes. Wanda (Theresa Randle) is Al's wife, and even though she was in the film a matter of minutes ago, we are shown a flashback of her, just in case we don't know what's going on.

When the factory explodes, Simmons is sent hurtling through the same digital spaghetti can from the opening credits before landing on a cold, dark, rainy, abandoned church roof surrounded by rubble, decay and garbage. His face now resembles a burnt sausage, he probably has no knob, and he has no idea how he got there. He's greeted by Cogliostro, who informs him he's been gone a long time and shows him around an alleyway full of homeless holy people, burning barrels and makeshift bedding. He's told he's welcome to join them if he wants, to become holy, but Al basically tells him he's a mentalist and runs off to find Wanda. He will try and explain away his appearance to her, maybe blaming a chip-pan fire.

Another narration surfaces, telling us that although to Simmons, North Korea was mere moments ago, it was actually five whole years, and on Earth things have changed in ways that will feed his desire for revenge. Basically, Wanda has moved on and married Al's best friend Terry (D. B. Sweeney), a fellow CIA agent who now works for Wynn. Al has arrived on the day of his daughter's birthday party to give her actual nightmares for years to come by crawling out of the bushes and making disturbing noises. I can't help but feel he should perhaps have thought of a better entrance. Standing up, perhaps? Bringing a cuddly toy, maybe? Using words? Anything but this. I think last on that list would be crawling out of bushes and gurgling.

The Clown (John Leguizamo), a short, fat, monstrous man, with blue paint on his face (think Alan Brazil doing *Braveheart*), appears and whisks Al away to another alleyway, where he farts and then shows Al his skid-marked pants. The make-up on Leguizamo took up to eight hours to apply, and it is legitimately impressive, as is his performance. Clearly having lots of fun with the role, you can't help but feel that Jonah Hill's Donnie Azoff in *Wolf of Wall Street* has echoes of it.

He tells Al that the reason his skin is hurting so badly, apart from the obvious, is that his 'viral necroplasm' is going through its larval stage, which means his body will become a living weapon at some point and move the plot along. He also drops the bombshell that, as far as the world knows, he's dead, and he then takes Al on a flashback of what really happened.

After the explosion, Al woke up in actual Hell, well, a Hell that's been created via 1997 CGI, and it's a fucking *nightmare* on the eyes. It's like a Windows 98 screensaver dipped in a cheese toastie or a magic eye picture you'd find in a shop that sells crystals, but the shop is covered in thick piss, and the owner is a bucket of piss who is also blind and has a seeing-eye dog that is another bucket of piss, but the piss is like soup. Rising from the background of this horror is Malebolgia (Frank Welker), a CGI creation that looks like Anubis, but if he'd developed a full-blown crack addiction. A bit like a rubbish precursor to the *Donnie Darko* bunny, this CGI model just has a wide-open mouth, frizzy barnet and floppy ears, and there's no movement when it speaks. This, from the guys who revolutionised visual special effects in Hollywood, who put stop-motion animators out of business and changed the industry for all time. None of them could have been happy with any of this – the filmic equivalent to Stonehenge in *Spinal Tap*, except rather than little people and a prehistoric monument that was the wrong scale, we have a computer literally self-immolating before our very eyes. Malebolgia offers Al a deal: he can see Wanda again if he will lead his army of evil Hell soldiers on their quest to take over Heaven (not the night club). Al immediately agrees: he'll do anything for Wanda. So, he's told that he will need to avenge his own murder and kill Jason Wynn as a starting point. He is then dubbed 'Spawn – Leader of Hell's Armies', is given a suit of black and white, and hopefully gets gym access and dental.

Wynn and Priest are in the mood to celebrate. Their Heat-16 virus is ready for launch, and it will apparently make Ebola look like a skin rash (feels too early to think about new viruses, thank you). The North Korean biochemical operation really paid off. As it's a manufactured virus, they have the only vaccine, and now I realise what all the conspiracy YouTubers watched during lockdown. They're on the way to an important international reception, to greet world leaders and reassure them that everything is on schedule. When this is all over, they will be very rich, very powerful, and only Right Said Fred can stop them now.

As Wynn mingles with clichéd caricatures of world leaders, he's informed by Terry that there's been a breach at the armory by a mysterious figure and they should think about leaving, but before they can get their coats, the skylight shatters, and down plunges a giant, billowing blood-red cloak. Inside it is a man in black and white, and he's absolutely livid. He reveals to Wynn who he is and lets him know just how much trouble he's in, before grabbing Terry to bark in his face about how could he possibly marry Wanda after all they've been through together, which seems a bit unreasonable seeing as he was dead for five years. Terry and Wanda grew close in shared grief, and he was there to comfort her, to soothe her loss, plus he always liked the garden. Al utilises his living suit when the security team arrives, then murders Priest and makes his escape from the arriving police.

As Priest is loaded into an ambulance, Wynn meets with Clown, who is over the moon with how things are going. He's playing both sides off each other and tells Wynn that Simmons is necessary for their plan to work: if they hadn't got him on their side, the man upstairs would have, and they'd have had real problems. He says Wynn will have to have a small operation that links his heartbeat to the Heat-16 bomb, just as an insurance policy. 'That's a good idea, I like that,' Wynn says, contemplating putting himself under the knife in a very overly complicated medical procedure that could just possibly kill him. As Clown wanders off with two ladies of the night, Wynn tells no one in particular that when this is all over and he's king of the world, he'll make sure Clown is dead.

Simmons, meanwhile, has figured out that Clown was pulling Wynn's strings and asks him just what he has in mind. He explains that with his intelligence, Wynn's bomb and Simmons' killer instinct, they can blow up the world and make one final push in taking over Heaven. Simmons refuses to help, so Clown turns into his true form, the Violator – a giant spider-headed man on two very spindly legs that walks like he needs a shit, all brought to us via the magic of more execrable CGI. The battle among the homeless alley, tumbling walls and dropping debris – everything generally looks fake as shit. In the end, Spawn is defeated, and Clown tells him that it doesn't really matter if he wants in on this scheme or not. He either leads the army or is left to watch Wynn take Wanda before he destroys the world. As he walks away laughing, Al is left beaten, broken and stuck in a Christ pose on a metal fence.

Cogliostro steps out of the darkness, arriving, as always, when he isn't needed, to help Al down from the fence and offer boring advice: forget Wanda, leave his old life behind and lose his anger. He explains that the war between Heaven and Hell depends on the choices we make, like whether to use practical effects or the non-oven-ready CGI that was available at that time. Simmons accepts all this, but says he has to nail Wynn, and so Cogliostro agrees to help him utilise the power he now has. But guns are useless; only the suit can help him win, and he must first learn to control it. Which he does, quite easily, within moments.

Terry has had the feeling for a while that something isn't right with his boss. Yes, he's a smart dresser, has a lovely voice and the kind of beard that would get him on any right-wing show in America, but he still gets the very real feeling he's hiding something. He decides to delve deep into the secret files in his boss's work computer, and there he uncovers the truth: Wynn is going to unleash a biological weapon and has been using his CIA department to run some sort of criminal consortium (which D. B. Sweeney seems to pronounce as 'consorshium'). He immediately gets onto a video call with a contact at the news station and tells her he's going to email everything over for tonight's broadcast.

'You disappoint me, Terry,' Wynn says, machine gun in hand, standing over his computer as he watches the words 'upload in progress'. He fires at the screen, causing it to explode (though this wouldn't stop the email, Jason), and takes them all into another room at gunpoint. He knows Spawn is coming and he tells them he's ready for him. His plan is to chain Wanda up on a rack and then stab her to death when Spawn arrives, and he pulls it off. As Spawn cradles her dead head and screams her name, he must be left to wonder why he didn't use the flying chains he'd literally just been taught to use, instead of running slowly and throwing Wynn over a sofa. 'It's all your fault, Spawn,' Wynn says, rubbing salt into the wound a bit. He tells him that all he had to do was agree to lead the Hell Army, but oh no, he couldn't even do that.

Spawn holds him down and tells him that, with Wanda dead, he no longer cares what happens. He will gladly kill him and unleash the virus, and as he pulls his arm back and blades appear from his charred skin, he catches a vision of CGI Hell. Millions upon millions of soldiers waiting to join him and destroy Heaven (still not the nightclub) and send the world into eternal immortal darkness. He brings his arm back down and somehow uses his eyes to extract the device from Wynn's heart and destroy it, confirming once and for all that he's through with Hell's dirty work.

As Al looks into Wanda's dead face, she flickers to life, still with the knife in her chest, but now angry that he let her be killed. She kicks him across the room, and it's immediately clear that she was Clown all along (hopefully not for the entire marriage). He's not happy with Spawn, not one bit. He's been working very hard on this plan and was counting on Spawn killing Wynn as part of his complicated ploy. He then drops the lovely joke that all these events would 'kickstart apocalypse now' while looking directly at Martin Sheen, which is a nice touch. After slicing Spawn's throat, Clown jumps through the fireplace, back to Hell, and challenges him to join him for battle. Cogliostro arrives, again when the fighting is over (probably stopped for a haircut – didn't but should've), but this time he's dressed in full chain mail. He revives Spawn, telling him they need to go and finish this fight once and for all. As Cogliostro struggles with the Violator (God, that sounds like porn), Spawn faces up to the Malebolgia to reiterate that he will never lead his army, especially as they look so poorly rendered and shit. Can you imagine the embarrassment? Like leading a carnival float full of melted plasticine figures. So, he tells him where to get off, and after finding his true purpose is to finally kill the Violator, it's now up to the police to lead Wynn away and Terry to tell the truth about what he's been up to. Spawn has stepped out of the darkness, to save the light, or something.

We hear via *another* Cogliostro narration (is this fucker writing a book?) that Spawn is now the only thing standing in the way of Malebolgia and his maniacal plans to destroy Earth and plunder Heaven (still not the nightclub). As the music swells, Spawn poses on top of that one church set they have, with his ridiculously voluminous cape blowing in the wind and probably knocking passing birds out, watching out for more poorly rendered demons, ready to stop them whenever and wherever, hoping beyond hope that CGI will get better.

It's safe to say that *Spawn* isn't very good, in fact it's as true now as it was back then. It's much too visually offensive, badly edited, badly acted (John Leguizamo and Spaz the dog aside) and all over the place story-wise, though it did make more at the box office than it cost to make, so it wasn't quite the catastrophe history remembers.

'If anyone researches me speaking about *Spawn*, there's not one time I said it was a good movie. I have never, ever defended it as a good movie,' Michael Jai White said to *VladTV* in 2022. 'There was a bunch of special effects where I was like, what the fuck am I watching?'

Spawn was initially an R-rated film, but much as Cogliostro says in the film, a sacrifice was needed to ensure that it was seen by as many as possible. 'The problem is,' continued White, 'there was a version of that movie that was far better until it got edited and edited down.' The choice has been made, for now.

If you want to see Michael Jai White in a much better film, being amazing, do yourself a favour and watch the imperious *Black Dynamite* as soon as possible.

TWENTY

BATMAN AND ROBIN

1997

STRENGTH NOW.
COURAGE ALWAYS.
FAMILY, ABOVE ALL.
BATMAN AND ROBIN!

With the massive commercial success of *Batman Forever*, Joel Schumacher was tasked with repeating the same feat with the sequel; only this time he was told by Warner executives to make the next Batman film a bit more child-friendly, and the expression they invented to describe this task is enough to make you want to smash your own face repeatedly with a Bat hammer. Schumacher was told that the next film should be 'toyetic'. In other words, a hollow exercise of a toy commercial. One thing is for sure, Schumacher stuck to his brief very well.

The first obstacle was who would play Batman. It was during this period that Val Kilmer was carving himself a reputation of being a very difficult man to work with indeed. He and Schumacher didn't exactly see eye to eye, and at the end of *Forever* things had come to a head. 'He sort of quit, and we sort of fired him,' Schumacher later said. Kilmer instead poured all his amazing accent and disguise skills into *The Saint*, a film which presented Simon Templar as some sort of Dick Emery-type character who spent most of his time wearing false teeth and impersonating vicars.

George Clooney was setting hearts aflutter in the medical drama *ER*, and there was no doubt that he would make a charismatic Bruce Wayne and have the appropriate sense of authority in his voice to portray Batman. As a casting decision it was pretty sound. Sure, he's no Keaton, but with the right tone and in a not-rubbish Batman film he could have been great. Next up was the casting of the film's main villain: Mr Freeze. Patrick Stewart was initially considered. However, he was later dumped to accommodate the biggest movie star in the world at that point: Arnold Schwarzenegger. Arnie was paid a very handsome (more like fucking gorgeous) $25 million (that's one and a half hospitals) to play the villainous Freeze (as well as being given a private jet). I would like to think that to earn that money Arnie did some method preparation by putting his head in a fridge every now and then or working in an ice cream van every other Tuesday, but I'm pretty sure he didn't. More's the pity. Uma Thurman was next, cast as Poison Ivy. Thurman said she was attracted to the role because she liked the 'femme fatale' element of it. Demi Moore was briefly considered, and with hindsight one could suggest that, as a bullet dodge, it's up there with anything from *The Matrix*.

The Batcave. Once a dark, moody, dead space, with nothing but a black car, a community of bats and a bank of computer consoles, it now resembles a shiny new Toys 'R' Us. We watch as this once proud emo retreat now regurgitates gaudy vehicles like a child that's accidentally chewed on Lego. In this DayGlo madness, Robin (Chris O'Donnell) is compelled to run a quote from the previous film about how he wants a car because 'chicks dig the car', and rather than kneeing him in the bollocks or slapping his stupid face, Batman (George Clooney) says, with all the awkwardness he can muster, 'This is why Superman works alone,' and it's immediately clear that Clooney is to Batman what Joe Biden is to public speaking, and the further the film farts down the track, the more uncomfortable and embarrassed he seems, with even Clooney himself admitting to Graham Norton on his chat show in 2015 that he is forever apologising for *Batman and Robin*.

Bats jumps in his horrendous Batmobile, which looks like it was purchased from a cornershop from among the tiny plastic sheriff badges, guns and Transformers knock-offs, with the name 'Dr Bat's Car' written on it in broken English. It's an utter embarrassment.

The biggest problem with the film is the tone. While *Forever* was camp as hell and like being kicked in the nuts with a big hob-nailed boot with the words 'mugging for camera' written on it, it had its dark moments and some elements that still felt like a proper Batman film. *Batman and Robin* makes the sixties TV series look like Ken Loach. It's as camp as a row of pink tents at an Erasure festival, and the moments in *Forever* that made you wince (nipples on the Batsuit, neon, UV paint and so on) are all here with a degree of arrogance that would suggest that they were previously used successfully.

Gotham now resembles the worst dystopian nightmare of a coked-up interior designer circa 1987. Any building of significance seems to be resting on the back of a giant stone muscle man with nipples that could down a 747. It's a gaudy horror show of epic proportions. Production designer Barbara Ling admitted her influences for the Gotham City design came from 'neon-ridden Tokyo and the Machine Age. Gotham is like a World's Fair on ecstasy.' Yes, it may look very nice as a picture, but the logistics of Ling's Gotham are mind-boggling. Imagine working in the left tit of a giant man and looking out of his 'window nipple' at the building across the street, which is most probably a giant man's arse, while someone climbs a home-made gallows at the cock-shaped newsagents down the street. Terrifying. The suicide rate in Gotham must be sky-high.

Commissioner Gordon informs Batman that there's been a break-in at Gotham Museum by a new villain who is turning security guards into blocks of ice and calling himself 'Mr Freeze'. He doesn't mention why he isn't sending any police to deal with it; he just sits in his office, probably only dressed from the waist up, nipping to the kitchen to make banana bread while Batman and Robin solve his problems.

Mr Freeze (Arnold Schwarzenegger), a giant dad-joke wrapped in tin foil, marches around the museum, either icing guards with his freeze ray or throwing them in the air while dropping a million puns with such scant regard that you're left to think that, before his accident, he was a writer on *Gigglebiz*. He's there for a fist-sized diamond that he needs to power his suit and is accompanied by a group of henchmen on skates, dressed like Sherpas. He will stop at nothing to get it.

'Hi, Freeze, I'm Batman,' says Clooney in the flattest tone imaginable before surfing down a model brontosaurus's neck like Fred Flintstone as a leather daddy. 'You're not sending me to the cooler,' Freeze replies, as the two grapple over the freeze ray with basic pantomime blocking.

As these awful performances play out and the eyes dart around the set – a cacophony of museum props, basic dressings and ridiculous amounts of revolving spotlights depression sets in. You know that this is what it's going to be like for the next two hours. Worse than the last one, this is a new nadir of awful, with each scene sending the elevator in your stomach lower and lower to previously unfelt levels of despair and frustration until a point is reached when the eyes become mere blank receptacles, devoid of feeling and now refusing to process information, just staring into the darkness as *Batman and Robin* wriggles, grimaces and writhes on top until finally reaching fruition and leaving you alone, questioning everything and longing for the warm embrace of a bullet.

Leaving behind a perfect Looney Tunes-style hole depicting his symbol, Robin (Chris O'Donnell) bursts through the wall on his motorcycle to help but does anything but. As he and Batman struggle to deal with both the Mr Freeze henchmen and the icy conditions, they click their heels together and conjure ice skates from the bottom of their boots, tackling the 'hockey team from hell' with renewed vigour, using Freeze's diamond as a puck. Mr Freeze, meanwhile, has decided to grab the diamond and get back into his giant ice-car, which also somehow doubles as a rocket, and with booster rockets igniting, it takes off from the museum, with Batman inside and Robin holding on to the exterior for dear life, like he's the living embodiment of the lingering sense of affection for this franchise, clinging on as it rockets into a sky of shit.

'Cowabunga!' Robin exclaims as he and Batman surf down from the exploding rocket towards the inevitable duel with Mr Freeze at ground level, which sadly ends with Robin being frozen stiff during the chase, leaving Batman with the ultimate conundrum: stop the bad guy or save his partner from freezing. If it were me, I'd be digging Robin's shallow grave in the woods while Freeze was in jail asking for his first phone call.

Brazil. A *Scooby-Doo*-style laboratory sits in the midst of the Amazon rainforest. Bolts of lightning fire down around it, just to underline how evil and nefarious a lab this truly is. Dr Pamela Isley (Uma Thurman), bespectacled and dowdy (by Hollywood standards) is wrapped in a lab coat, headscarf and sweating brow. She's picking up the pieces after her experiment to mate an orchid with a rattlesnake has failed – her plan to give plants a better chance at defending themselves. She's sad about what could have been. This comes weeks after her other failed attempt to mate a daffodil with a chimpanzee, a daisy with John Cleese and a geranium with Peter Andre. She hasn't given up hope, though, and tells her Dictaphone as much. In another fucking mad room, Jason Woodrue (Jon Glover), a deranged, wide-eyed scientist, is demonstrating his latest 'supersoldier' formula to investors.

In terms of acting, both of these performances are very much right out of the Widow Twankey drawer, and as Glover would tell *Looper* in 2019, '[Joel Schumacher] would sit on a crane with a megaphone and yell before each take, "Remember, everyone, this is a cartoon!"'

A skinny runt of a man is manhandled into position on an operating table. He's a serial murderer serving life, and as he's chained to the table, Dr Woodrue explains that he's drilled three holes into the man's limbic system, and once he pumps his supersoldier serum (code-named: Venom) into the man's system, the scrawny pipsqueak will be transformed into the powerful Bane (wrestler Robert Swenson who died shortly after filming was completed), which is exactly what happens. He's now the size of Bermuda but is no longer fun at parties.

Pamela has watched this all happen, and Woodrue has just noticed, so he leads her away, explaining that the research is vital, even if he's using hers to create giant muscle men who won't live to see thirty-five. He asks her to join him in the avant-garde of the new aesthetic, but she's appalled: her work was meant to protect plant life, not populate the next series of *America's Strongest Man*. Woodrue says he respects her opinion but can't handle rejection, so she'll have to die. He pushes her over a table and tips a desktop of heavily toxic chemicals on her screaming body, laughing as her body, entwined with vegetation, sinks into the ground, a terrifying portent of the upcoming critical reviews.

Bruce has a show-and-tell for Alfred and Robin: a potted history of Victor Fries (Mr Freeze) via some CCTV taken from his lab. Apparently, he's a two-time Olympic decathlete and Nobel prize winner in the field of molecular biology. It doesn't mention if he knows how to build rocket ships, but I guess one science does all. After his wife contracted a rare disease, 'MacGregor's Syndrome', he hoped to freeze her in a cryogenic sleep until he found the cure, much as they did with Walt Disney when he fell ill, except Fries didn't put his wife down the well at the *Pirates of the Caribbean* ride.

During one such experiment, Fries was injured in an explosion and sent flying into a vat of liquid fifty degrees below, and although he survived, his body mutated. It now needs extreme cold to survive and a suit that requires diamonds to enable this. He has also become obsessed with puns about cold things.

As Bruce wanders around this vast buffet of exposition holding a metaphorical paper plate and topping it up with information, Alfred winces in the dark, pained and wounded, clearly not having a nice time. And, boy, do I feel you, brother. Bruce and Robin decide to set a trap to ensnare Freeze using the Wayne diamond collection.

As Alfred and Bruce walk the corridors of Wayne Manor, Bruce tells him he's having trouble relying on Robin: he's too eager and impulsive and very nearly got himself killed on the last outing. Alfred, ever the wise owl, tells him that they both follow the same star but get there on their own course, and trusting someone is the very nature of family. All right, Vin Diesel. Bruce tells him, with the smuggest face imaginable, 'I trust you, Alfred.' Alfred considers this, then reminds him in no uncertain terms that he won't be here for ever before retiring for bed, presumably to watch *Fast X*.

The laboratory shakes. The ground rumbles and shifts as if an earthquake is piercing the silent night air. Woodrue steps in to see what is happening, to be greeted by the sight of Pamela rising from the earth like Shirley Manson, on a sunflower, but now with tangled red hair, scant clothing and a quasi-English accent that sounds like she'll be manning a dirty phone line for the rest of the evening. She tells him that she's a new woman, with the toxins replacing her blood with aloe, her skin with chlorophyll and – after pulling him in for a kiss – her lips with poison. Woodrue collapses dead, and Pamela blathers on to an empty room about being Mother Nature's avenger. After noticing the lab belongs to Wayne Enterprises, she decides to fly to Gotham with Bane on her arm and plant-based revenge on her mind.

The bell rings. Robin pulls open the door to be greeted by a pair of legs. 'Please be looking for me,' he says, but she's not. She's there to see Alfred, and he hasn't even ordered her from Thailand. It's his niece Barbara (Alicia Silverstone), and she's come all the way from

England to see him, all the way from 'Oxbridge Academy', where she studies in the new computer sciences division, and she's hoping to get an A. Bruce and Dick meander awkwardly behind Alfred and Barbara as they walk the grounds catching up, but her attention is diverted by Dick's chopper – a competition racer project that he's been working on. Alfred is concerned about her being near such a machine, but she tells him not to worry as she's terrified of these things. Bruce offers her bed and board, but Alfred mentions that it can get 'busy' at the house, and it's unclear as to whether he means the Batman stuff or the sex parties. Either way, Bruce says it's fine; after all, she's family.

In the back of a limousine, Pamela opens a box and fits a wig on her head, tucking it neatly into place. (A disguise that seems utterly pointless. No one knows who this woman is, so why is she in disguise at all?) In the front seat, Bane, wearing a trench coat and hat, receives instructions to step on it to Gotham Observatory, and he acknowledges with a grunt. Yes, he was a serial killer, but that's no reason to steal a man's banter.

Bruce Wayne leads a tour of the newly restored observatory, where Wayne Enterprises is donating the world's most advanced telescope. As Gossip Gerty (Elizabeth Sanders) changes the subject from asking what the satellites can do for world hunger to ask Bruce if he's going to marry Julie Madison (Elle Macpherson), Pamela strides into the press conference to put a world-saving proposal under his nose. He gives it a cursory look and tells her that, with no diesel for heat or coolant for keeping food cold, millions would die, which she refutes as 'acceptable losses in the battle to save the planet'. Bruce hands back the paper and tells her that people come first, and she takes this with the grace and decorum you'd expect, announcing to the room that a day of reckoning is coming and they will all be killed by plants, causing them all to laugh heartily in her face.

It's the 'Save the Rainforest Costume Ball', an event designed to raise money for the trees and act as a trap for Mr Freeze. Batman and Robin are special guests, mingling on the stage with the assembled dignitaries as dance numbers flood the room as if Allan Carr has produced it. Commissioner Gordon takes to the stage, holding the precious diamonds on loan from Bruce Wayne, clearly bored witless and wondering what those years of police training were all about. He spent decades learning the skills, walking the beats, learning the ways of the streets, sharing the awful stories of the bad people and ugly events on this planet with his closest friends and loved ones, only to end up in the autumn years of his life sitting behind a desk, fat, stupid and relying on a rich arsehole dressed up as a bat to thump men decked out in robot suits.

An erotic beat begins, and the room turns as one to seek the source, hypnotised by a slow Arabian percussion with a fixed bayonet of slinky guitar, taking the room on a wander through exotic sensuality. Poison Ivy slowly strips from a gorilla costume and sashays onto the stage. She turns one way, then the other, blowing kisses that send out seductive clouds of pheromone dust, instantly hypnotising all the men into being so horny it hurts their stomachs and makes them fall in lust with her. As it happens, she interrupted a charity auction for an evening with a selected number of beautiful ladies, so she includes herself among their number and asks for the bidding to begin. Batman and Robin openly fight over who will pay the most to have sex with her first. While the old men in the crowd take their shots with bids in the thousands, the Caped Crusaders step it up into the millions, with Batman stumping his partner by producing a Bat-Credit Card (with an expiry date listed as 'FOREVER') and repeating the 'Don't leave home without it' line, thereby causing many a viewer to pick up the shotgun they'd been only caressing up to this point and tearfully place it in their mouths while screaming.

The ploy worked. Freeze is captured after stealing the diamonds and sent to Arkham Asylum, where he tries and fails to break the ice (sorry) with the unfriendly guards.

Robin is livid. During the exciting chase, Batman again failed to trust him and powered down his motorbike. Robin puts this down to the fact that Bruce was jealous that Ivy clearly fancied him more and he would do anything to make him look foolish. He tells him that back in his Flying Graysons days, they worked as a team and trusted each other. Batman reminds him that his rules keep them alive and they'd both be dead if they went with Robin's instincts. He then seeks another wise chat with Alfred, asking him if he thinks he's pig-headed. Alfred tells him that since his parents died, he's definitely had trust issues and has wanted to control death itself, but no one can do that. Bruce thanks him, and *still* doesn't get the hint that Alfred is trying to tell him he thinks he is dying.

'Master Bruce, my piss is green, and I've been coughing up lumps of black shite. It's agony, and I think I'm dying.'

'Thanks for the chat, Alfred. I feel so much better.'

Checking the garage CCTV, Dick watches with a smile as he sees Barbara run in and steal a motorcycle – the same motorcycle he's seen her steal before, only this time he's going to see where she's going. Sadly, she's only going to see Coolio, who seems to have assembled some sort of *Wacky Races*-style competition among the ruins of the city. There are teams of punks, goths, metalheads and Droogs in all manner of costumes, face paint, mullets and corsetry shouting at each other, perched on motorcycles, ready to enter into battle. One of the punks asks Barbara if she's the 'chick' who won the 'tunnel run' the other night, and she is guilty as charged. I guess Jarvis Cocker was right about those posh ladies. In a frantic race that takes in the fiery sights and sounds of the dark city, Barbara is in the lead – not bad for a 'chick' – until an unfortunate accident causes her to slide towards the end of an exposed bridge and a certain drop to death, only to be saved at the last by the welcome hand of a black-gloved saviour: Robin.

Back at the garage, Robin has a chat with her. She's been racing since her parents died; the speed and danger help her deal with the feelings and make the pain go away. However, street racing isn't an acceptable major at Oxbridge, and they kicked her out after she ran over and killed Inspector Morse. It turns out she's already raised enough money to do what she's always dreamed of: to free Alfred from his dismal life of servitude and take him away from it all, like he's fucking Dobby, and she also has a sock for him to put in his copy of *Fast X*. Robin thinks she's fucking insane and points out that Bruce and Alfred are like father and son, but the sort of father you pay to look after you, which is fine – ask any child star. She then drops the bombshell that Alfred is dying, and Bruce overhears. He mentions that he 'could tell'. Bruce, that is a barefaced lie. He's tried to tell you at least two fucking times and you've ignored him.

Freeze has escaped Arkham, with the help of Bane and Poison Ivy, and so Batman and Robin race to his secret hideout, which is a giant abandoned ice cream factory. Mrs Freeze is floating in a glass chamber of cold water, still alive, and his machine is working as a treatment for the early stages of MacGregor's Syndrome. As they observe the floating woman, a light crop-dusting of pheromone drifts past their noses, and a further sexually confusing time begins. Batman warns Robin not to kiss her as her lips are clearly her kill method, but Robin, all horned-up, takes this to be Batman's jealous feeling rising to the surface again, telling him he has real issues with women and couldn't take that she wanted to kiss him. Bruce throws him into a vat of mint ice cream, and Robin makes an undignified, drippy exit, saying he's going solo, and there can be no doubt about what he'll be up to when he gets home.

Freeze and Ivy have hatched a plan. They both have vengeance on their minds; especially Freeze when Ivy tells him that Batman has defrosted his wife, causing a single, badly rendered CGI tear to roll down his face. Ivy wants revenge on humanity for the destruction of the green planet and has perfected her mutant snake plants. Freeze announces he will cover Gotham in ice, and Ivy is right behind that plan. She's convinced that once everything is frozen, her very tropical-looking plants will take over the globe, and I'm equally convinced that that won't work in any conceivable way.

'It's stage one of MacGregor's Syndrome,' the doctor tells an anxious Dick and Barbara as he leaves; all they can do is keep him comfortable. Not the news they wanted to hear about Alfred, who's lying in the dark, asleep, attached to a machine that goes *ping*. Bruce tells Dick that Freeze has a cure for stage one, and no one else has even come close, so he'll go and get him and Ivy, alone. Dick's mind is still clouded by Poison Ivy's sex dust, though, and he tells Bruce that he's just jealous, and maybe it's time he stopped living in Bruce's shadow and maybe it's time there was a Robin-Signal and maybe it's time he did poos in the big-boy toilet. Alfred, meanwhile, hands Barbara a package and implores her to track down his brother Wilfred and give it to him, as there are various secret duties to fulfil. It's a private, encrypted CD, so obviously Barbara takes it up to her computer and immediately tries to crack the code, eventually doing so and learning all about the secrets of the Batcave.

Freeze's plan is to fire a giant ray into Gotham's most powerful telescope, sending it to various satellites all around the world and freezing it immediately, and as he sets these plans in motion, Poison Ivy blows Commissioner Gordon (not like that). He succumbs to her love dust and hands over the keys to the Bat-Signal on the roof. Ivy commandeers the Bat-Signal and turns it into a Robin shape, just as he wanted. As he strides out of the Cave all suited up, Bruce offers a word of caution: it's clearly a trap. But smitten Dick still thinks it's jealousy talking, even though it demonstrably isn't. Bruce plays a final, weighty card, telling him that they're not partners, they're brothers, they're family, and family trust one another, causing Dick to wilt.

'I expected you might find your way down here, child,' an Alfred Headroom computer image splutters as Barbara races into the Batcave alone. He anticipated she'd want to help Batman and Robin, and so took the liberty of making a costume in her size, a vehicle she can ride, and turned himself into a living computer algorithm that's able to anticipate every question, and also raps: 'I'm Alfred P, and I'm here to say, Batgirl is here to save the day.'

The Robin-Signal is coming from Ivy's secret hideout, a former bathhouse now serving as a flourishing garden, with vines cascading under purple lighting. Life blossoms in every corner, and pads of green lie over the pool of water that runs down the middle. Ivy reveals herself, seated in the very mouth of a giant orchid, washed in pink lighting, beckoning for Robin to come to her and water her bloomers. He approaches tentatively, and she brings him in for the kiss, but first he wants trust. He asks her what Freeze is up to, and, figuring that he'll be dead in a minute, she spills her buds, then plants a smacker on his lips. But he has a secret for her: his lips are coated in rubber and therefore immune. So, she pushes him into the pond, and it's here we find that a film that costs $160 million has the kind of editing you'd expect to find in a high-school student film, as a shot of Robin struggling to save himself from drowning is reversed to show him submerging again, and once seen can never be unseen.

'You're about to become compost,' Barbara says, after crashing through the glass ceiling in her new Batsuit to stop Ivy. Tip for bad guys in Gotham: don't have glass ceilings. It's always asking for trouble. A 'girl fight' begins, but this one will never be watched by weird men. Ivy tells her that it was she who pulled the plug on Mrs Freeze and has no regrets about it as, with the wife out of the way, she'll take Freeze for her husband and have a good look at his icicle. Barbara kicks her across the garden and into her own giant flower, which, despite nurturing her just minutes ago, has now decided to smother her in a horrible Venus flytrap way. Batman asks Barbara what her name is, and she tells him 'Batgirl', to which he replies: is that PC enough? Would she not prefer 'Batperson'? It's like he's a *Guardian* journalist or something, but she's happy with the monicker she has, thanks very much.

Freeze has started covering Gotham in arcing jets of cold white fury, turning people into popsicles, dogs into cold dogs, and roads into ice rinks, cackling to himself as he does so. Luckily, Batman, Robin and Batgirl arrive on the streets with their own ice vehicles (sold separately), battling underlings in a race to get to the observatory and try to begin the thawing process. Their plan? To redirect sunlight via the satellites from the other, hotter side of the world and thaw the entire city in one swift movement. Trouble is that Bane and Mr Freeze arrive to stop them, but they're defeated fairly easily, with Freeze being dropped off a high platform and Bane's brain pump being removed, thus causing acres of yellow liquid to spew from his head, reverting him back into a living pipe cleaner that's also a murderer.

The city thaws. People who were frozen in hilarious poses return to their business, dogs that were frozen peeing on a hydrant come back to life, and Walt Disney staggers out of Disneyland with his head under his arm asking who the president is.

'Kill me too, just as you killed my wife,' Freeze begs as he lies supine under the rubble of the exploded observatory. Batman shows him a video of Ivy admitting to pulling the plug on his wife and tells him that, rather than killing her, he saved her, restored her, and she's back in her tube, frozen but alive, waiting for him to find a cure for the advanced stages of MacGregor's Syndrome. In exchange, Batman asks if he can help him save another life, that of a dear friend who has a terrible disease, a man who's always been there for him, nurtured him and has seen the entire *Fast and Furious* franchise. Freeze reaches into a compartment of his suit and hands Batman two glowing blue tubes – cures for stage one MacGregor's Syndrome. These are the very things that could save Alfred's life, that could bring an end to this nightmare – or turn him silver and become a living pun machine.

Alfred emerges from his room to declare that he is quite well again. He's had plenty of rest, plenty of time to think and, thanks to the teachings of Dominic Toretto, he's ready to be part of a family again and wipe all their arses once more. The room erupts in jubilant celebration, and so Barbara hijacks this deeply emotional and triumphant time to tell Dick and Bruce that she's now part of the team, whether they like it or not, and, as it turns out, surprisingly, they do, although it's probably due to pure fatigue.

As they all join hands and declare a partnership, Alfred announces that they're going to need a bigger cave and waits for a laugh that never comes, before remembering he needs to go and change all the beds, do the ironing and take the bins out.

As the new trio run towards the camera in silhouette, Bat-Signal behind them, the score rises to strident heights, to burn them into the mind of the viewer and tease that there will be another adventure, before the Smashing Pumpkins' godawful 'The End Is The Beginning Is The End' whines tinnily into our sad ears. One can't help but think of the words of Joel Schumacher tucked away within the making-of documentary on the 2010 Blu-ray release: 'If there's anybody watching this that, let's say, loved *Batman Forever*, and went into *Batman and Robin* with great anticipation, if I disappointed them in any way, then I really want to apologise, because it wasn't my intention, my intention was to just entertain them.' That same year, *Batman and Robin* was number one in *Empire* magazine's list of the top fifty worst movies ever made.

A sequel to *Batman and Robin* was planned but swiftly cancelled. It was to be called *Batman Triumphant* and feature the Scarecrow, Harley Quinn and Joker's ghost. However, *Batman and Robin* was so badly mauled by the critics ('You sit there feeling brain-damaged and praying for the mayhem to cease' Anthony Lane, *The New Yorker*) and left such a sour taste that the whole sorry affair was put in a sack with rocks and thrown into the canal, leaving everyone to wonder if Batman would ever come back from this. Little did everyone know that, over twenty years later, he'd be back every other year, over and over again, showing us endless reconstructions of his parents' death, like some sort of mourning relative with old holiday snaps.

EPILOGUE

'OUR DESTRUCTION COULD HAVE BEEN AVOIDED HAD IT NOT BEEN FOR THE VANITY OF SOME WHO CONSIDERED US INDESTRUCTIBLE' – JOR-EL

Despite the putrid stench of death and humiliation, *Batman and Robin* wasn't quite the end-of-the-genre event everyone remembers it as. The only thing damaged was Batman himself. No longer the dark, haunted stalker of the night, he was now right back where Tim Burton found him in 1989: leaping around in nauseating comic-book colours, high-fiving a shit Robin, socking pantomime goons and handing out Bat-Credit cards like Alan Whicker.

I remember coming out of the cinema after seeing it, feeling that rather than checking in with the Dark Knight, I'd just watched a vivisectionists' training film in all-too-vibrant 4D. There was no charm, no wit, no delicate touch, and certainly no fucks given. It filled a hole, it sold a lot of toys, and that, at the end of the day, was all that mattered.

But elsewhere there was life. Green shoots of recovery. Flickering vital signs. The highly underrated *Blade* was released the following year, *X-Men* followed two years later, and then *Spider-Man* swung into cinemas, kicking off the next run that would define another generation of fans and ultimately birth the MCU behemoth.

Batman's corpse would be back too. In fact, only eight years later, he began again, raised from the grave, comforted in familiar darkness and in the hands of someone who knew what he was doing.

Over time the superficially offensive gaffes of the past ceased to be insulting; rather, they became giggles up sleeves, shared cringe memes, cult amusement fodder for the YouTube generation to point at and wonder how the hell they ever got made. Packed-out ironic screenings in laughter-filled rooms. Grist for the culture mill. Shipwrecks serving as beacons to steer the studios in different directions, for a bit anyway.

The reality is that as long as certain people refuse to grow up (which doesn't look like changing any time soon) and as long as the world is a thoroughly grim hellscape where people yearn for escapism (which doesn't look like changing any time soon), there will always be superhero films. It's a genre that's bullet-proof, iron-clad and phoenix-like, continuously flying from the ashes ready to dazzle with all-new feathers for the next generation and then, predictably, inevitably and embarrassingly, burning itself out in the funniest way possible, only to repeat/reboot/remodel the cycle over and over and over again.

Be bored by it, be not arsed about it, hate it by all means, but I suspect that as sure as eggs is eggs, it will always be here, for better or for worse, for ever and ever.

John Rain
2023

ALSO AVAILABLE

'Beautifully observed and a laugh-out-loud joy'
KATHY BURKE

'An affectionately droll Bond-by-Bond stroll through the films we know and love, whether we like them or not'
AL MURRAY

'A book full of Bond love and occasional bewilderment'
SAMIRA AHMED

'Nobody does it better. John Rain delivers his love letter to Bond with a raised eyebrow that would do Roger Moore proud'
JOEL MORRIS

ALSO AVAILABLE

'A hilarious, gripping and muscular flex through every bulge and bruise of 80s action cinema . . . I LOVE this book'
SÉAMAS O'REILLY

'Funny, hilarious, comic and very well-informed, *Explodobook* is the ultimate guide to every apocalypse movie ever made'
DAVID QUANTICK

'A laugh-out-loud, impeccably detailed nostalgia trip through the golden era of action movies . . . I loved it'
JIM HOWICK

'Pulse-pumping, hilarious and deeply affectionate, I fell in love with these films all over again.'
ALISTAIR PETRIE